How Not to Go Broke at 102!

How Not to Go Broke at 102!
Achieving Everlasting Wealth

Adriane G. Berg

WILEY

John Wiley & Sons, Inc.

Published by John Wiley & Sons, Inc., Hoboken, New Jersey.
Published simultaneously in Canada.

No part of this publication may be reproduced, stored in a retrieval system, or
transmitted in any form or by any means, electronic, mechanical, photocopying,
recording, scanning, or otherwise, except as permitted under Section 107 or 108 of the
1976 United States Copyright Act, without either the prior written permission of the
Publisher, or authorization through payment of the appropriate per-copy fee to the
Copyright Clearance Center, Inc., 222 Rosewood Drive, Danvers, MA 01923,
978-750-8400, fax 978-646-8600, or on the web at www.copyright.com. Requests to
the Publisher for permission should be addressed to the Permissions Department,
John Wiley & Sons, Inc., 111 River Street, Hoboken, NJ 07030, 201-748-6011,
fax 201-748-6008.

Limit of Liability/Disclaimer of Warranty: While the publisher and author have used
their best efforts in preparing this book, they make no representations or warranties
with respect to the accuracy or completeness of the contents of this book and
specifically disclaim any implied warranties of merchantability or fitness for a
particular purpose. No warranty may be created or extended by sales representatives or
written sales materials. The advice and strategies contained herein may not be suitable
for your situation. You should consult with a professional where appropriate. Neither
the publisher nor author shall be liable for any loss of profit or any other commercial
damages, including but not limited to special, incidental, consequential, or other
damages.

For general information on our other products and services, or technical support,
please contact our Customer Care Department within the United States at 800-762-
2974, outside the United States at 317-572-3993 or fax 317-572-4002.

Designations used by companies to distinguish their products are often claimed by
trademarks. In all instances where the author or publisher is aware of a claim, the
product names appear in Initial Capital letters. Readers, however, should contact the
appropriate companies for more complete information regarding trademarks and
registration.

Wiley also publishes its books in a variety of electronic formats. Some content that
appears in print may not be available in electronic books.

For more information about Wiley products, visit our web site at www.wiley.com.

Library of Congress Cataloging-in-Publication Data:
Berg, Adriane G.
   How not to go broke at 102! : achieving everlasting wealth / Adriane G. Berg.
      p. cm.
   Includes bibliographical references and index.
   ISBN 0-471-46727-8 (CLOTH)
      1. Aged—Finance., Personal. 2. Retirement income—United
States—Planning. 3. Retirement—United States—Planning. 4. Saving
and investment—United States. 5. Social security—United States. 6.
Medicare. I. Title.
   HG179.B435 2004
   332.024'01'0846—dc22   2003016316

Printed in the United States of America.

10 9 8 7 6 5 4 3 2 1

To my mother,
Gertrude Horowitz Berg,
who is as beautiful at 86 as she was at 16;
maybe more so.

And to Dorte Schreiber,
my friend,
who proves that wisdom and grace are ageless.

Acknowledgments

I would like to thank and acknowledge some very special people who have meant so much to my life, my way of thinking, and consequently to the contents of this book.

To my husband and the wind beneath my wings, Stuart Bochner, who encouraged me to write as I think and speak, and never fear revealing too much of myself.

To my daughter, Rose Phoebe Bochner, who saw mostly my back as I bent over the computer for months on end, but who never lost her good temper or the song and dance of her spirit.

To my son Arthur Ross Bochner, a brilliant young writer whose good judgment steered me right many times.

To my close friends Sharon Streicher and Dr. Stanley Streicher, Judy Block and Dr. Fred Block, Nancy Jacobi Akbari and Ahmad Akbari, Risa Olinsky and Mark Olinsky, and Lorri Grief, and to my life coach Daniel Chayefsky, all of whom will understand every joke and reference in this book.

To one of the great pioneers in the field of aging and longevity, Dr. Robert Butler, Pulitzer Prize winner for his *Why Survive? Being Old in America* and founder of the International Longevity Center in New York.

To Dr. Ken Dychtwald, author of *Age Wave* and *Age Power* and prolific speaker who has raised our consciousness about aging and longevity.

To Dr. Rose Dobrof, whose lifework is synonymous with elder studies and advocacy and welcomed me into the world of social work and aging without hesitation.

To Dr. Janet Sainer and Commissioner Elinor Guggenheimer, who started me thinking about aging and the law in the days when I was Assistant General Counsel of the Community Service Society.

To my brave editor Jeanne Glasser, who had the temerity to ask me if I wanted to write another book, and then supported me every step of the way.

And a very special thanks to:

Mr. Milton Gralla, my co-author of *How Good Guys Grow Rich*, who keeps me plugging away when everything seems bleak, and who is an inspiration to me because he so genuinely believes that the world needs to hear what I have to say even when I'm not so sure. He has enhanced many lives, and together with his wife Shirley Gralla will enhance thousands more. His platform is simple: Life will shower you with wealth if you live on the give and not on the take.

Mr. Robert Danzig, whose morning coffee mentoring sessions kept me focused and engaged in my task, even when the end was unclear. He is an inspirational speaker and the founder of the Confidence Academy and There's Only One You, which empowers foster children and adults everywhere.

Top elder law attorneys Peter J. Strauss, Daniel Fish, Robert Freedman, and Howard Krooks, for their constant refresher courses.

Mr. Pat Gilberto, of Brookdale Center for the Aging of Hunter College, for his many introductions to the Who's Who of Gerontology.

Special thanks to Darin M. Myman, CEO of DealNerd.com, and Peter J. DeAngelis, CFA, author of *The Individual's Guide to Winning on Wall Street* and the executive director of DealNerd.com, for the superb www.wealth102.com web site they have designed.

And to the following organizations that provide the research that made this book possible:

AARP

American Society of Actuaries

American Society on Aging

James N. Jarvie Commonweal Service

MetLife Mature Market Institute

National American Homebuilders Association

National Council on Aging

Society of Actuaries

And to my new friends, Karen Prudente, executive secretary for International Ministries, Women's Division, and Susanne Paul, president of Global Action on Aging, who are propelling my thinking into the world of global longevity.

And to my partners and strategic associates:

Commissioner Anita Kramer, who proves again and again that true friendship is the real everlasting wealth.

Kenneth Greenblatt, CFP, and Brad Spitz, attorney and planner, who always encourage my wildest ideas and bring stature and credit to our professions.

Michael Checkan, Glenn Kirsh, and Richard Checkan of Asset Strategies International, who prove that friendship is better than gold, and that gold is better than anything else.

Television producer Richard Hall, who plans to chronicle it all and with whom it is a joy to work.

Contents

Foreword

Eight years ago, when I was 48 years old, I learned that I had Multiple Sclerosis. I had some early warning signals. Still, a definitive diagnosis is, well, so very definitive. The doctor said I had a relatively mild form of the disease, and along with my general excellent health I could expect to live a very long life. But, I knew better! Right then and there I resolved to plan for the doomsday that was my future. Little did I know that this event would be the defining moment of my life. Little did I know that one year later the then New York City Mayor Rudolph W. Giuliani would appoint me a commissioner at the New York City Department for the Aging. Or that, now, at age 56, I would just discover the defining mission of my life.

What I did know was that I had to share my diagnosis with my then 79-year-old mother. Though Mom had endured a few defining moments herself, like the Depression, World War II and widowhood, a child of any age telling her mother that she has an incurable disease is, at the very least, painful for both.

Mom, always the optimist, while upset, assured me that I would always have her unconditional love and be her beautiful, brilliant, fun, and resourceful daughter who faces every challenge with courage and a plan! With that kind of support, from an almost octogenarian, I decided to try to believe my doctor and prepare for anything, including, a long life.

My most logical next step had to be the preparation of a financial plan, a task I had been putting off for years. However, the defining moment that my illness presented or *crucible* as Warren G. Bennis and Robert J. Thomas also call it in their wonderful book *Geeks and Geezers How Era, Values, and Defining Moments Shape Leaders* (Harvard Business School Press, 2002) propelled me to consider tackling what would become a life plan. Of course, not knowing where or how to start, I procrastinated until the day I turned on the radio and serendipity struck.

As I was flipping through the radio dial in search of my favorite Sinatra program, I heard a vaguely familiar voice that identified itself as Adriane Berg. I was struck dumb, recovered, and continued to listen. I soon realized that this Adriane Berg was the same Adriane Berg who was my friend and classmate in both junior high and high school! Here she was 35 years later, a radio talk show host on one of the biggest stations in the New York City metropolitan area, an elder law attorney, a popular speaker, and a consultant to nonprofit and for-profit organizations on the financial challenges of longevity. It seemed that her help could kick start my plan, so long as I believed in my own longevity.

By then I was deeply involved with my work with seniors. Thinking back, I was well suited for the job. A certified social worker since 1982, I had received training at the prestigious Brookdale Center on Aging at Hunter College, and had worked in the field for years. Now, as assistant commissioner, I made policy that directly affected the lives of tens of thousands of seniors residing in the five boroughs. In addition, I had direct responsibility for six programs, including work training for seniors, and intergenerational initiatives, and a budget of over $20 million. My diagnosis gave me a special additional credential. I knew that peace of mind, money, and fulfillment could not be separated.

It seemed obvious that serendipity had become fate and some greater force was telling me to call Adriane—I did.

After a hiatus of more than three decades, Adriane and I were not at a loss for words. We discovered that while our family, lifestyle, and work situations were different, our attitude about the world was very similar. We are both generally optimists who take obstacles in stride and try to deal with life's challenges with a sense of humor and a plan. Quickly, our conversation turned to our personal and professional interest in the area of aging and its "kissin' cousin" longevity.

As members of the baby boom generation (those born between the years 1946 and 1964) a cohort I called Generation B, and as professionals in fields dealing with human potential, Adriane and I both meet and talk to tens of thousands of seniors and boomers. My world, basically that of people over the age of 65, while filled with much too many isolated and frail elderly who must not be forgotten, also includes many older people who greet each day with a purpose and a plan, even if the plan is to meet friends for lunch or a card game. These people keep active and upbeat. Their respective stories are a life lesson.

Adriane's audience is much larger than mine. As one of the first observers and analysts of the worldwide megatrend called *longevity*, Adriane's world includes everybody. And, as a lawyer, talk show host, lecturer, and author, it seems as if she has had a conversation with everybody!

She, too, has observed that those people, young or old, who use life's turns or crucibles (Bennis and Thomas) as defining events from which to extract life's enhancing meaning, are also those who, as they age, become *neotenic* (Bennis and Thomas). A neotenic is "someone whose vigor and openness to new experiences marks him or her as the antithesis of stereotypical old age . . . these people are still full of energy, full of curiosity, full of confidence that the world is a place of wonders spread before them like an endless feast."

In this powerful book Adriane, in her warm, caring style filled with a profound understanding of the human condition, presents us with a road map to not only this state of renewal, but also the ability to pay for it!

In our age of longevity where all stages of life will be so much longer, we will have time to create dreams, realize them, and then make new ones. We will be able, if we choose, to not only think but do what once seemed impossible.

Through a series of profiles, vignettes, and anecdotes, Adriane's always witty and insightful commentary provides us with a show and tell of how people of all ages can and are looking at the passage of time as an opportunity.

But, many people do not think this way. Not yet. In my experience as an assistant commissioner, and as someone who now uses a cane, it is painfully clear that if a person does not look perfect, that is, robust, stylish, young, he/she is written off in at least two similar ways. If you are old, you cannot be physically attractive, mentally agile, healthy, and definitely not fun. In the same way, if one is handicapped she/he is seen at best as imperfect and at worst, the visible handicap, whose origin is not known, is presumed to be hiding some hideous incurable disease. Both the handicapped and the elderly are to be pitied if not shunned.

The truth is that with any luck we are all going to get old and many of us will suffer some sort of visible incapacity during our lives. We are all in the same boat and it is time that, as both a society and as individuals, we realize that to write off people for no reason, but for life's natural progression, is to write off ourselves!

And so I have embarked on my defining mission, to produce videos and other information on *How May I Help You?*, a guide to deal with the infirmity of others. I used my crucible to leave a legacy I could never have imagined. And Adriane's courage and advice has made it possible.

I highly recommend this book to neotenics and neotenic wannabes of all ages!

Oh yes, Adriane helped me put together a financial plan that will keep me solvent to at least 102, my health is excellent, and my now 87-year-old mother is goin' strong!

So, how are you doing?

Anita Kramer

A Day in the Life of a Megatrend

It was 5:45 A.M. and already Jeannie was out jogging. She could feel her ponytail moving back and forth like a metronome. Maybe it was the Biotin that her dermatologist gave her. Her hair felt thicker lately. Jeannie thought she looked great for 55, but wondered for how long she would keep up her routine. All those creams were expensive and the Botox needles hurt, no matter what they said. Besides, she was beginning to wonder if it wouldn't be just as wonderful to grow old with a few laugh lines showing.

Jeannie passed the part of the park with the baby swings. Her son Larry, now 23, would be coming home that evening. He planned to live with her and her husband Harold for a while. He had definitely decided to live home and save his money and go to graduate school. Why didn't they anticipate this? She and Harold had been careful to plan for Larry's college and even that was tough. But graduate school! Larry would be nearly 30 before he really launched his career.

At that moment, Harold was not thinking about Larry's future. He was thinking about his own. It was 7:00 A.M., and Jeannie was back from her jog and had completed her morning weight-lifting routine. Harold admired how trim she was after 30 years of marriage. But it was also annoying. She was always after him to exercise more, or to get a colonoscopy, or to eat more tomatoes for his prostate. He knew she was right, but all he really wanted was a beer and a ballgame.

This morning he was worried about his job. There were rumors of a downsizing, an accepted euphemism for getting fired. Part of him wished it would happen. When the stock market was so great last year he thought about early retirement. He and Jeannie could move to Utah and have a horse. He dreamed of a fat severance package. He even pictured himself talking to their accountant Bernie, or that financial planning guy about whether to take a lump sum or annuitize, or maybe refinance the house and buy a place to rent out until Jeannie was ready to retire. He wanted to buy early and avoid the baby boom rush. He wondered if their house would go down in value as boomers downscaled in droves. He wished he had the cash to buy now.

But then, Larry was coming back to live with them, and Lizzy was still a little girl. Besides, it would be hard to keep an eye on Jeannie's mom or visit his own mother. He blessed Jeannie's job as a teacher. He never expected that her pension would outstrip his investments.

By now, it was 10 A.M. and Grandma Peanut had woken up late. This was very unusual for her. These days, she found herself needing less and less sleep and rising at the crack of dawn. (Grandma Peanut, a nickname to distinguish her from Harold's mother who coincidentally was also named Helen, counted out the 10 nuts she ate every morning.) She took out her pillbox which was almost a foot long. It had big writing with a compartment for each day of the week. She counted out her pills, Zocor, Plavex, Tenorman, and that new one her doctor gave her for indigestion. Sometimes she took seven pills in one day, not counting the vitamins she bought from the radio infomercial. Rosemary, her geriatric care manager, would be happy to see that she was on top of things. Rosemary came every month just to look at her fingernails and toes, to make sure she was not dehydrated, and to check on the oxygen concentrator and minitank supply that kept Grandma Peanut going on her own two feet. She wished she had long-term care insurance. She knew that she was spending her grandchildren's inheritance with all the extra home care, but what could she do? She considered transferring what money she had to the kids and filing for the Medicaid program like her friend Lucy. But she didn't want to be restricted in who would care for her. Besides, she'd have to spend a lot before her eligibility kicked in anyway. By then, well, at 91, who knows.

It was already noon and Elizabeth could not believe that her mother gave her yogurt for lunch again. At 10 A.M. it didn't mean much to Lizzy that her chances of living past 100 were excellent or that fatty foods might cause plaque. But, it didn't matter, either. It was a good day: soccer practice, then violin, and a drive to Westphalia Gardens to visit Grandma Helen.

By 3:20 P.M. Jeannie and Lizzy had pulled up in front of the stone entry to Westphalia. It had a good reputation. The nursing home had made it possible to cope with Grandma Helen's diagnosis of Alzheimer's disease. Lizzy had a song ready to sing to Grandma H. But it was always hit or miss as to whether her grandmother would recognize her. Sometimes she would talk and talk and have a box of candy ready. Sometimes she would be just as sweet and talkative, but had no idea that Jeannie was her daughter-in-law. At those times Lizzy knew her mother would drive home in a funk. Once she put her hand on her Mom's and said, "Don't worry, that won't happen to you." Her mother pulled over to the side of the road and hugged her. The thought crossed Jeannie's mind that Lizzy might have Helen's genetics. She hugged her little girl tighter.

At dinner, Harold had the look he reserved when he brought home a present or a surprise. What he had was a brochure from Equestrian Meadows, a retirement community in Utah that was built around a world-class horse facility. He wanted to downscale and live in the equestrian condo. But with his boomerang generation son, his ten-year-old daughter, his Mom to visit, his mother-in-law to monitor, and his wife who seemed to have bloomed at menopause, all he had was the brochure. He hoped he could afford to stop working. Meanwhile, he thought he might take some correspondence courses to get a certification in computer repair. That way he could sort of semiretire and still run a small business.

Larry arrived from the airport at about 11 P.M. Lizzy was supposed to be asleep, but she secretly waited up for her older brother. She would be a wreck in the morning. Larry wasn't sure his plan would really work out. But at age 23, there was no rush. There was plenty of time to get a full-time job, settle down, and maybe have some kids when he was around 40, even 50. After all, Mom was 45 when she surprised everyone by getting pregnant. Grandma Peanut was up, too. She was thinking about a peculiar phenomenon that little Lizzy had learned in fourth grade science. For every year you live, your life expectancy goes up a year and a fraction. So she had not used up a precious day of her life, but had added a day and a little more. Grandma Peanut liked the math.

Introduction

What's Going on Here? How Longevity Is Affecting Our Life Choices

With Potato on My Face

As I write this book I have a raw potato on my chin. In Dr. Robert M. Gillers' book, *Natural Prescriptions*, I read that shredded raw potato helps get rid of black-and-blue marks. I have a big one from the silicon shot I took last week to make my Charlie McCarthy lines disappear. For my younger readers, Charlie McCarthy was the jowled ventriloquist dummy created by Edgar Bergen, Candice Bergen's father (you know the one that played Murphy Brown, and now plays every younger star's gorgeous mom or mentor). But I digress. I took shots because my television producer suggested it. He figured I'd be making lots of public appearances in a few months to publicize this book (God willing), and he figured that the "The Queen of Longevity" should look young. Of course, he didn't use the word *young*. He said, "Look good," which in today's culture is synonymous for young. Or is it? Candice Bergen is a beauty by anyone's standards, and Cathy Bates is cavorting naked in a hot tub with Jack Nicholson. So, maybe there's hope for a real change in how we feel, approach, and manage our aging. I sincerely hope so, because this potato on my face looks ridiculous.

But my love affair with the concept of longevity, our increasing life expectancy, is about a lot more than looks or even self-esteem. It is about recognizing how great things can be as we get older. In *Another Country: Navigating the Emotional Terrain of Our Elders*,[1] author Mary Bray Pipher discusses the pain of losing your friends as you age. But there is another side to advanced age. Anita Kramer's mother at age 87 (you met Commissioner Kramer in the foreword of this book) was just told by her doctor that her eyesight is good enough for driving. And my Mom is off somewhere getting her hair permed for her 86th birthday. No matter how many elders I meet, I'm still bowled over by their verve and good looks, despite their occasional depression and constant medications. These people are our pioneers. As Pipher reveals in her insightful biographies of our elders, it is a cultural crime to isolate them, and eventually ourselves.

I'm no Pollyanna. I know that death is still alive. My father died of a sudden stroke when he was only 40 years old. I was 11 years old at the time and his untimely death has informed my life ever since. I never thought I would live past his age. But when I hit 50 I blossomed, and I embraced being older. What struck me most was not that I was aging well, but that I seemed to be youthing. Longevity, physically and psychologically, did not mean that I would be old longer, but that I would be middle-aged longer.

And so I started an uncharacteristic scientific journey to learn about the effects of longevity on our bodies. Studies confirm that it is the middle years that increase with longevity. Gerontologists call it the "third age," not "old age." Anita Kramer calls us Generation B. In fact, lack of frailty in old age may be our biggest advance. Centenarians die healthy.

If you're a baby boomer you think you have a lot of life left, and you're right. We are making adjustments in retirement dates and definitions, in housing choices, in careers, and in marriages. We are starting new things years later in life than anyone would have dreamed only a quarter of a century ago. My dear friend and life coach, Dan Chayefsky, is reviving his father's play *Marty* on Broadway. In this Paddy Chayefsky award winner, written in 1953, the mother and her sister complain that they are finished, washed up. "What can you expect at 55?" they lament.

But if attitudes have changed so fast and so much, for my generation, what about my younger readers? Growing up with an expectation of living to over 100 will alter the course and timing of your important life events even more. Last April, when I addressed Yale college students on how longevity may effect their career selection, I talked a great deal about changes in the life event time line. It's a mega difference from when I graduated from college in 1968 to what they will encounter. The students asked me about postponing child-bearing, multiple careers, and of course the money needed to make it all happen.

Life expectancy, and how we conceive of it, has a direct effect on the order and speed at which we structure and pace our lives. The timing of our controllable life events, such as the beginning and end of formal schooling, marriage, childbirth, and retirement are a matter of agreement within societies, families, and peer groups. Each of us then decides how far we can comfortably stray from the norm.

Already we see a change. Children are being born less frequently and later in their parents' lives. In the next 30 years, while the over-50 population will grow by 74 percent, the under-50 population will grow by *only* 1 percent. This is partially due to the ambition and op-portunity of today's women. But the factor of longevity, itself, makes a difference. We can vigorously run after infants well into our 40s and 50s. That gives both men and women the freedom to work longer, es-tablish a career, and accumulate wealth before they diminish one parental paycheck or another. If childbirth can be postponed, so can marriage. Dr. Thomas Perls, in his study of centenarians published in *Scientific American* (1995), revealed that a statistically significant num-ber of women who lived past age 100 bore children after age 40. Other studies, too, show that the slowing of the aging process is a constant. Statistics support the domino effect that longevity is begin-ning to have on our life event time line.

This life event time line domino effect is also causing changes in our social policy, such as Social Security entitlements. If Social Secu-rity trends continue, it is clear that the official age of retirement will jump into the late 60s, then 70s, and then who knows? With the postponement of retirement comes a change in when school should end and work begin. Questions are open. Will we simply work longer, and therefore start work in our 20s as we are expected to do today? Will we school for two separate careers at once as we enjoy a two-ca-

Longevity effects the length of time we stay in our schools, in our jobs, in our marriages, and in our homes.

reer lifespan? Or will we pause between careers to retool in accordance with the wisdom and self-knowledge we have gained after our first 40-year or so stint?

The answers to these questions are no slam dunk. They will evolve from our own voice and preferences. They will at first be as sloppy as the concept of childhood when it peeked from behind a curtain of child labor and voluntary elementary school education. And make no mistake, even though longevity affects us no matter what our current age, if you are a baby boomer, it's you that will eventually have the most influence on the lives of all our children and effect the longevity of generations to come. Laws will eventually be codified, policies set, buildings built, and university curriculums created according to our demands and our usages. But in view of ageism in our culture, especially media marginalizing of anyone over 50, we must meet the challenge by consciously voicing our opinions and asserting who we are as we grow older. We will be defeated by this challenge if we opt to make old age pretty instead of powerful. Luckily, they are not mutually exclusive.

If 18 starts college, will 22 still end it? If childhood starts at birth will 13 start our teen years? Some of this momentum, the time we take in life to complete life's phases and move on, depends on biology. Childbearing time clocks are a matter of hormones as well as work schedules. Puberty created the sweet 16, not vice versa.

There is already evidence that the longevity factor impacts on human biology from birth. Studies are ongoing to determine whether human growth hormones are remaining at high levels at later years, whether puberty is coming later and childbearing age is lasting longer. Such evolution is thought to take generations, but as a practical matter we are seeing rapid cultural changes. More and more students opt to take time off before settling down, people are marrying later and waiting longer to have children, and people anticipate working longer and selling established businesses later in life.

There is a generalized feeling among us that we have time to move on to the next phase of life. And we are characterizing life periods more minutely. The AARP has divided aging into 50 to 64, 64 to

Longevity is the "silent giant" at the core of our life choices.

75, and 75-plus. The advertising agencies still looking for that 18 to 49 demography have nevertheless accepted that age 50 is different from 70 and the 30-somethings have claimed their own adulthood crisis. Sociopsychological researchers are already identifying three midlife crises: one at 30, the other at 45, and the last at 60 or our pre-retirement age. And this last midlife crisis has become subdued and merged with longevity planning as we enter our postretirement future. Do we finally have a chance to make wisdom the measure of successful aging? We do, if that's the way we see it.

As we increase life expectancy we also increase the pace at which the moments of our lives are experienced. This concept is counterintuitive. If the life event time line momentum is about the big things, pace is about the day-to-day little things. These are the activities, no matter how trivial, that inform the moment-to-moment experiences of daily life. In his seminal biography, *In Memory Yet Green*, Isaac Asimov tells us "Life goes on minutia by minutia."[2] And so it does. In the days when I hosted my radio show, my program directors invariably told me not to take phone calls that lasted longer than four minutes because the pace of the show would drag and I would lose listeners. Even interviews with celebrities were to be short and snappy. This was so for my radio show, but not for NPR, nor, for example, the PBS interview show hosted by Charlie Rose. The same audience who would not tolerate more than four minutes per segment on "hot talk radio," will hunker down to 40 minutes with the director of a classical ballet company on public television or radio. The difference is context. And it is context that dictates content.

If time of day, expectation, and channel changing can affect pace, how much more can universal longevity? We cannot assume that the pace of our days will be slower because we have more of them. On the contrary, so far we have speeded up pace since the turn of the century. It is easy to blame this on technology. Planes get us across country in hours not months; faxes and e-mail give us instant communication. We complain we have lost the excuse factor of snail mail. The best we can come up with now is, "The computer is down." Even then it is an item under our control and we are expected to buck up and get the job done in minutes.

One fortunate revelation that many seniors have after retirement is that they can learn the new technology. The Internet, coupled with extra time to study investing, has made postretirement millionaires of many average investors. There are second acts in the

United States with regard to work, love, and health, but also with regard to investing acumen. Give yourself a chance to enjoy the fast pace of technology at a time of life when big events (momentum) come farther apart, and who knows, you may never have to worry about going broke at 102! But be warned, in this fast-paced world it is unlikely that you will settle down to a peaceful old age, unless you work at it. You will still be slave to the tyranny of the multitask and have trouble staying in the present moment, as every thought rushes to the future. We are already programmed to cram in all we can, and longevity seems to have made no difference.

What can we make of the odd result that as we can live longer we are compelled to act faster? Actually, it makes perfect sense. The same technology that increases our longevity is used to create the World Wide Web, electronic music, and supersonic flight. Our scientists are brilliant, and every discovery is a ripple in the stream with multiple and unpredictable results.

Ultimately, this book is about money and what it can buy in the form of added years, health, lifestyle, independence, and peace of mind, all buzzwords of financial planning. But the subtext is an ethical question: What if they find the immortality gene? Or more likely, what if we discover how to create one in the laboratory? Who will be able to afford it? No, I don't see UFOs. But I do follow biotech stocks with a fine-tooth comb. I have written in my stock newsletter, *Wealthbuilder*, about longevity being a separate investment sector, about companies whose business it is to grow worms for DNA experiments, about cloning, about the Methuselah gene already isolated and potentially reproducible in the lab.

If we have the imagination to transform aging as we wish, to reconsider its impact as a fact of life, we also have a grave responsibility. We need to be very careful and thoughtful as to how we use this power. And we need group consensus. If the logic of aging is that older people no longer work, and we plan to work, we will work. Soon the logic will be that older people do work. Our transformation of old age will inevitably start with rejecting the obvious, that is, infirmity, forgetfulness, obsolescence, and replacing these outdated handmaidens of aging with vitality, sharpness, and contribution.

Since 1987, when the journal *Science* broke out of the disease framework and redefined successful aging, we have begun to disconnect old age from illness.[3] But we have not gone far in replacing admiration for fear. There is a distinct prejudice that the old are different from you and me. And we turn away from what we are loath to become. Where is it written that seniors like wolves should live in packs? Yet, even the best-intentioned attempts at acknowledging our aging seem to isolate us. We have begun to create assisted living facilities with continuing care to supply our health needs and a new circle of friends as old ones pass on. Small towns and suburbs provide trolley and shuttle buses for seniors. And, of course, there is the ubiquitous senior discount at entertainments. All of these things are useful (I like a discount as much as the next guy), but they merely create a better "what is." Not a different "what can be."

Ultimately, aged-based living solutions may create a natural setting for depression. People around you die and you suffer constant loss of friends and loved ones. Your social structure is torn from you daily. Researchers wonder how to treat aged-based depression which is a common problem. There is a growing trend toward integrating even those in need of care into an age diverse community. That's one reason why seniors going back to college or seeking higher education always inspire me. I am fascinated with the concept behind such places as Lasell Village at Lasell College in Newton, Massachusetts, which offers crossgenerational learning for residents. Retirees must agree to take courses and follow fitness and health programs. This provides a retirement option for those who would rather swing a book bag than a golf club.

If we can count on anything when it comes to baby boomer home and lifestyle preferences after retirement, it is that they will be diverse, but trending toward full integration into a mixed age community. Pulte Homes, Inc. (owner of the Dell Webb brand, the nation's leading developer of active adult communities) conducts a "Baby Boomer Report, Annual Opinion Survey" each year. Results for 2003 revealed that of those likely to relocate in retirement, "7 percent chose an age-qualified (over 55) community as possible for their new home." But 75 percent want a mix of all ages, and the remainder wanted either a community over 45 years of age or another type of community.[4]

And those over the age of 55 can benefit from the educational and economical travel provided through Elder Hostel, started in 1975, and one of the most venerable programs for education after retirement (or before). Chairman of the Board Harry R. Moody, also on the advisory board of Lasell, tells me that the costs are as low as they get ($700 for a week in New York. I am impressed.) Participants spend 21 hours of their week in serious classroom learning.

"University Retirement" will proliferate. We have embraced early learning for children, and more than a select few seniors will seek late learning. Fifty thousand Americans over the age of 50 are in degree programs right now. We can create a society that has high expectations for its seniors, a society that rewards us for our contributions as well as reprimands us for our sloth during our advanced years. The MacArthur Study of successful aging lists contribution and a feeling of being needed as one of the top three indices of long life. The better we are at achieving life long "relevance," the longer we stand to live.[5]

We must stop being the authors of our own ageism. If we do not, how can we make better laws, and demand respect in our advanced years? We clamor for flextime in the workplace, and other accommodations so that we have an enriched future, and simultaneously equate aging with obsolescence. And, we can't blame the young for their callousness in viewing the aged. What we teach our children makes all the difference. According to Children's View on Aging, 35 percent of fourth and fifth graders thought old people were scary and 12 percent thought it would be fun to be old. Negative or positive, 62 percent of them got their views from their grandparents and 22 percent from their parents. Only 16 percent were more influenced by the media than their own family. When it comes to our future positions in society, we are truly the captains of our fate.

Sex, Lies, and Videogames could well be the title of this book. My friend and classmate, Nancy Akbari, a nationally known attorney for her work on the influence of cults in our society, has encountered a new cultural phenomenon: the refusal of courts and families to believe in true love after 70. She detects an unspoken presumption that the transfer of money from an older person to another is almost always caused by incompetence and undue duress. In one case, an 86-year-old man made a $150,000 gift to his 78-year-old paramour after a decade of her taking care of him. In fact, his daughters were so used to her taking full care of him that, when she herself was in the hospital for a few weeks, their father became depressed, failed to eat properly, and became dehydrated—all without the daughters even checking in on him! He himself would have died were it not for her calling the front desk of their apartment complex when he failed to show up for a visit with her. Yet, his family was able to obtain a temporary restraining order prohibiting her from utilizing the monies she was gifted and are suing to reverse the gift, all because of the unspoken presumption. At what age do we lose our right to zest? When are our lives to be relegated to knitting, watching television, or in this technosenior age, playing videogames? If we are successful in achieving everlasting wealth, on what will we be allowed to spend it?

Why have we made so little impactful preparation to enjoy old age, while coveting our extra years so passionately? It is because we tend to view longevity and even the specter of extended life span as just more years added to old age, and not very good ones. Baby boomers spend agonizing amounts of time, emotion, and money shepherding their parents to nursing homes, puzzling through assisted living contracts, and minding multiple medications. Generation Xers see their parents' strain and their grandparents' fragility. By this example alone we wonder sometimes if long life is worth it. We sign our living wills so the "plug will be pulled" as soon as possible. We eschew long-term care insurance equating it with nursing home confinement, and exclaim, "Shoot me first!" It is inevitable that a culture that equates age with obsolescence finds it hard to embrace ever-greater aging in a joyous and constructive way.

Even death has a greater panache than old age. Studs Turkel states he had no trouble asking people about their view of death. They wanted to discuss it for his new book. But even octogenarians will not acknowledge aging for its value. When the most vigorous among them are asked what it's like to be 90, they are likely to answer, "I don't feel like I'm 90, I feel like I am 16." Is it possible that 16 is also what 90 feels like? Is it possible that we have preconceived aging in such negative terms that we have failed to grasp its rewards? People claim to have come back from the dead to tell us what that's like and we have been riveted with attention. Yet, few display any interest in listening to the anecdotes of the aged. We either ignore, or patronize, and in doing so we lose the opportunity to create any fiercely different possibilities for our own future.

Chapter ONE

The Longevity Revolution

*T**he first fellow to say that life is a marathon, not a sprint, didn't know the half of it.* As we look forward to the real possibility of living past 100, it's time to admit that life is long and we need to plan for it. As I write this book, a multitude of faces pass before me. Sometimes I'm writing to an Asian American woman about 65 years old. She has just sold the family store and is wondering if she should consider the Malaysian second home program for her retirement. Sometimes I'm writing to a 30-year-old man in middle management who is wondering whether he and his wife can wait another 10 years to have their first child. Other times I see an African-American couple doing well in their careers, wondering whether to retire early. Most often I see my friends, the centerpiece of today's longevity mega trend, the baby boomer, age 55 or so, looking under 40 and feeling like 14 or 90 depending on their mood.

It was Eubie Blake who said, "If I knew I was going to live this long I would have taken better care of myself." That's the pitch of this book. You will live long. Take better care of yourself spiritually, physically, and financially. All three are so interrelated that we cannot separate our money decisions from our life fulfillment, from where we plan to live or the healthcare we insure for our families and ourselves. Ultimately, this book is neither about aging nor money, but about self-reliance, independence, dream fulfillment, and above all, social and personal relevance during the decades ahead.

Money does count for happiness, health, and fulfillment. But it also causes unhappiness, want, and health-robbing stress. My life has been the test case, the lightning rod for all the financial woes and triumphs that average folks can experience. Consider me the crash dummy of personal finance. I have watched my own health and happiness rise and decline over my financial status. I have shared the financial journeys of hundreds of clients, radio listeners, readers, and seminar attendees. This book comes from our collective fears, worries, triumphs, and dreams. This is more my credential than my law degree, my financial background, or my research training.

We are all pioneers in longevity. Longevity gives us the time to really learn from our past mistakes and carve out an incredible future. In 1900, the average life expectancy was 47 years old. Imagine how different your thinking, decisions, and basic emotions would be if you anticipated dying before 50. The image of living past 100 has an equally powerful effect on your psyche. Although we consciously start thinking about our "end game" somewhere in middle age, longevity informs our decisions almost from the moment we are born. We decide to postpone or interrupt college, take several jobs, try out a career and sometimes try out marriages, postpone childbearing, get into debt and get back on our feet, delay

Of those who were 65 years old in 1940, only 7 percent lived past 90. By 1960, this had doubled to 14 percent. Today, at least half of all Americans will live well past 85. And since 1960, the number of Americans over the age of 85 has increased by 274 percent. The number of us over 100 has more than doubled since 1980. In the next 30 years, this statistic is expected to double again. My Generation-X readers will become middle-aged in a world where one of every two people will be over age 85.

"Census 65+ in the United States," Frank B. Hobbs with Bonny L. Damon, U.S. Bureau of the Census, Current Population Reports, Special Studies pp. 23–190 (1996).[1]

spending, and invest more. Because, instinctively we know we are making history.

Ten Questions You Deserve to Have Answered

1. As a Baby Boomer with a 401(k) and a Good Retirement Plan, Haven't I Done Enough Not to Go Broke at 102?

Probably not. In 2000, the American Association of Retired Persons (AARP) researched the attitudes of current baby boomers about their futures. They compared their attitudes with those who were of a similar age group in 1974, to see what differences appeared in their concerns. Significantly, today's boomers found fewer prob⁻ lems in all areas.

- Boomers have very ambitious plans for their future.
- Boomers are less hung up on specific age as on the specter of physical and mental decline.
- Eighty percent expected new treatments and cures and only 40 percent were worried that they could not afford them.

But boomers do worry about money.

- Money as a personal problem or future concern ranked number 1 for young people ages 25 to 39 in 1974. By 2000, it was those ages 50 to 64 that worried the most.
- Seniors are more sanguine.
- Those moderately worried switched from ages 40 to 49 in 1974 to those ages 65 to 74 in 2000; in the lowest range of worry were those ages 75 to 89.

The study also revealed that boomers still rely on Social Security for their major source of retirement income, and most have never met with financial planners. Exercise physiologist and personal trainer, Risa Olinsky, comments from experience, "My mother rarely spends money without thinking about tomorrow. As for my husband and myself, we are so active and so busy we put our future on the list, but day-to-day activities take precedence over things we know we need to do for tomorrow. My clients whom I personally train act the same way. But, my clients who see me for physical rehabilitation exercises after an illness or accident are very different. They are often caught short by the sudden fact of vulnerability. It often takes a physical wake-up call to make a difference."

My intention is to sound the wake-up call for all of us. There's a dumpster in my backyard right now, removing years of paraphernalia so that I can downscale and get rid of the possessions that possess me. None of us have done enough, but it's far from too late. That's the beauty of longevity.

2. What Differences in Thinking Does It Take to Plan for Longevity Than for Financial Planning in General?

There is a significant difference between retirement and longevity planning. In fact, there is now a certification for financial planners and insurance specialists called financial gerontologists. For example, inflation has a different impact when your salary and benefits are not indexed along with it. We have almost forgotten about inflation, as it has been so low: about 3 percent in the 1990s, 5 percent in the 1980s, compared to 7 percent in the 1970s. But at 4 percent, buying power halves every 15 years. It is a serious issue on a fixed income. Inflation is less of an issue in your working years as salaries are often indexed for inflation, and raises and bonuses take out some of the sting.

Further, a financial plan focuses on wealth accumulation, acquiring a home, and saving for retirement. A longevity plan focuses on decumulation, downscaling, and ensuring that your retirement savings last as long as you do and beyond. Attitude and outlook are also different when you are in the decumulation as contrasted with the accumulation phase of personal finance.

It seems to me that the beautiful words of John F. Wasik in *Retire Early and Live the Life You Want Now*[2] apply to longevity planning as well as early retirement:

> Finding a new prosperity is a matter of balancing our aspirations with our failures, our spending with our savings, and our hopes with our abilities. In balancing our lives for an early retirement, we discover other dynamic lives within us, like turning over a log in a forest and finding life in hundreds of forms, teeming, recycling, and growing.[3]

In with the New. Out with the Old.

In

IRA, 401(k)

Saving money

Wealth decumulation

Risk management for living benefits and healthcare insurance

Independence

Philanthropy, volunteerism, and relevance

Trophy lifestyle

Investment leverage

Annuities

Out

Defined benefit plan (except for the lucky few who still have one)

Consuming

Wealth accumulation

Denial of long-term care needs

Job dependency

Trophy house

Self-centered business

Consumer debt

Short-term strategies

3. Why the Age 102?

According to many actuarial tables, if you are currently 65 years of age you have a life expectancy of 82.9. At age 100, this jumps to 102.6. I didn't want to use a fraction in the book title so that's how I got 102. Longevity is a moving target. The longer you live the longer it slates you to live. If you are 60 you have 20 years actuarially to go. If you live past that to 85.1, you have over 10 more years to 91.5; if you make it to 100, you have an actuarial life expectancy of 102.6. See?

4. I'm 25 Years Old and I Still Don't See What This Book Has to Do with Me. What Is the Difference between Longevity and Aging?

It's important to absorb three definitions to get the distinction between *aging*, *longevity*, and *life span*. They are related, but they are not the same.

Aging starts the moment we are born as a natural biological process. At some point in our lives we begin to feel it. Feeling our age is a matter of our personality as well as our biology. When we do feel age we often say so or at least mutter to ourselves about it. I have felt old since I was a teen. My mother often told me, "You have an old head on your shoulders." And indeed my seriousness did make me feel less joyous and spontaneous. I hear my baby boom friends call lapses of memory or forgetfulness "a senior moment." Forgetting the keys engenders a wistful shake of the head as an acceptance of the inevitable end, a rueful tip of the hat to the aging process.

Aging can also be chronologically quantified with precision. One person is 25, another is 75. We know how much any of us have aged with a valid birth certificate. We know when aging ends with a valid death certificate. There is no guesswork to this aspect of aging. So aging is a feeling and aging is an objective, quantifiable reality. Whether you feel and look like a boy of 16 and have the back muscles of a 20 year old, you are still whatever age you really are. Whatever that age, it relentlessly increases day by day. How you feel about aging changes with your mood, your attitude, your circumstances and, I hope, the coming positive changes in our culture. But nonetheless aging is continuous until life itself ends.

Old is different. While aging is immutable (so far) the definition of *old* is for society to decide. According to *U.S. News & World Report*, (1997) "on average, Americans say middle age ends and old age starts at age 64." But according to the Baltimore Longitudinal Study of Aging[4] (a 39-year-old ongoing study funded by the federal government to determine how healthy people grow old), old age really starts at age 30! It is then that muscle tone, bone density, hearing, and vision begin to deteriorate. Hormone levels drop, the aging process begins, and its path is infinite in its variety. People do not change their personalities after age 30. Contrary to the curmudgeon myth we do not become cranky as we age, unless we were cranky when we were young. By contrast, demographers from the United Nations Population Division say elderly now means 85 and older, not 65 plus. So old can be 64, 30, or 85. It depends on the context.

But like the Groucho Marx song from the move *Horsefeathers*, one thing is clear, "Whatever old is, we're against it."[5] The negative spin we put on aging rubs off on its positive sister longevity. This is unfair to the concept of longevity and misleading to those who try to understand it. Longevity is not just a euphemistic, cleaned up version of aging. Unfortunately, it is this aging/longevity nexus that creates our love/hate relationship with its notion. That, in turn, leads to our pitiful refusal to make accommodations for longevity in our own life, and demands the necessary changes in the world around us, right now.

Longevity is a concept, not an inevitable biological process. It refers to our expectation of how long we will live. Our expectations vary by country, gender, race, wealth, and personal attitude. Longevity is our *notion* of how old we can get. And that notion can be molded and controlled. Just as surely as we created childhood, adolescence, and the midlife crisis, we created longevity, collectively, and individually. There have always been eight-year-olds, but in the medieval times they were chattel farmers, sons of serfs traded for plots of land. It took centuries before the concept of childhood took hold. In its full form childhood has a recognized beginning and ending date, with social and legal imprimaturs. Even now, the concept evolves. As young people seem more competent, more sophisticated and more adult, we ponder whether to change penal sentences, review court procedures, and change driving and contractual ages. Childhood is a man-made invention, so we can rearrange its elements. Longevity itself has an impact on childhood. According to Germany's Max Planck Institute for Demographic Research, Human Life Databases (www.demogr.mpg.de/), one-third of children born today in developed countries will live past 100.[6] Will this result in a prolonged period of childhood, longer schooling, and changing adulthood rituals? That is up to us. Longevity is like that, too. We constructed it and can deconstruct it. Given all that power, why not make it terrific?

Life span brings us back to biology. It refers to the ultimate number of years that human beings can reach. It is fodder for science fiction, genetic breakthroughs, religious and political controversy. Scientists generally agree that our present limit is 120, but disagree as to whether and by what means that can be increased. Today, the challenge of antiaging research is to increase life span not just life expectancy. Right now the focus is on genetics. This is not science fiction. While we have not advanced greatly in actually extending life span, research and development have increased longevity in very real terms.

Statistics abound as to how far we have come and how fast. My personal favorite is: Of all human beings who lived past the age of 65 from the beginning of human history, two-thirds are alive today.

Whew! So if you are 25 now, prepare for many careers, longer marriages (or several short ones), children later in life, two or three periods in your life that you will be a full-time student, time to travel between careers, and the need for a whole lot of money.

5. When It Comes to Longevity, Aren't My Genetics My Destiny?

If you're hung up on genetics, consider a Swedish study done with 350 separately raised twins and 400 twins raised together.[7] The researchers compared the life spans of twins raised together with those who were raised separately. They concluded that genetics explained about one-third of the differences in longevity. Other scientists go farther and posit that a whopping 75 percent of longevity is due to non-genetic factors like environment and attitude. Yes, attitude! Believe in

---

Everlasting Wealth

The Time Power of Money   Albert Einstein once said that man's greatest invention was compound interest. He was not too far off. Money earning interest and that interest, in turn, earning its own interest, all over time, makes money grow at an extraordinary rate. At 10 percent interest, money doubles in 7.2 years and triples in 11.6 years. At only 5 percent, interest, it doubles in 14.1 years and triples in 23.2 years. To calculate your own doubling, use the rule of 72. Divide your interest rate into 72 and the result is the number of years it will take your money to double. To find the tripling time, divide your interest rate into 116.

100. If you embrace your aging and accept it, you will live longer. Unlike Elsie the protagonist in a song from *Cabaret*, you may not be the prettiest corpse in the cemetery, but you may be the oldest. According to a Yale and Miami University Study, "Life span is reduced an average of seven years just by harboring a negative attitude about aging." The Yale/Miami Study (2000) cited attitude toward and self-perception of aging as more important to increased life span than body mass, not smoking, and a tendency to exercise.

We begin to internalize stereotypes about aging from childhood, and they continue to the end of our days. Psychiatrist Lyn Mac Beath in her article "Calling All Elders: The Vital Importance of Role Modeling" recalls a patient with terminal cancer, who at age 83 refused to be seen by her devoted son because "Nobody wants to see an old lady." Mac Beath calls this, "Ageism against the self."[8] I am reminded of the character played by Bette Davis in the movie "Mrs. Skeffington," who is happy to find that her former husband was blind because he would never see her in advanced age.

6. Is This a Women's Book?

No, but it certainly could be. Longevity is a leading women's issue, on several counts. Women do have a longer life expectancy. In 2000, a conservative estimate by the National Vital Statistics Report of the Department of Health and Human Services showed it as 76.9 (up 0.2

Everlasting Wealth

Several websites guide you to a ballpark idea of your longevity based on your life care style. Visit www.livingto100.com for the test developed by Dr. Thomas Perls in *Living to 100*, or visit www.wealth102.com. Click on our health button; go to the life expectancy section and voila! You'll be prompted to answer a series of personal questions concerning your life, lifestyle, and health. When you are done, the program will return with your life expectancy. The powerful lesson of these sites is that the sooner you appreciate the elements of longevity, the more control you have over actual life expectancy.

years since 1999) for women, contrasted with 74.1 for men (also up 0.2 years since 1999).[9] If this seems low, remember that this is measured from birth. Longevity increases by more than a year for every year you live. In 2003, the average expectation for girls born that year is that at least half will live past 100. But no matter whose chart you study, women live a little longer.

More important, women earn a lot less and work for fewer years. The 2001 national median salary for women is $26,592, for men $34,944. In 2001, income from salaries for women at age 65 was $19,348, for men $28,496. Older women have nearly twice the chance of being at the poverty level in advanced years than men.[10] No wonder the fear of poverty is called "The Bag Lady Syndrome," not "The Bag Man Syndrome."

This statistic is particularly true for single women, as 63 percent of them live on less than $15,000 in their postretirement years. When Oprah examines the bag lady syndrome, she's discussing more than a neurotic reaction, but a too frequent reality. Widows are over three times as likely to live at the poverty level than older women who are still married. And lifestyle needs are often not cut in half by the death of a spouse, but diminished by less than one-third. Many sources of income may be cut off, including pensions, unless the couple has planned for joint benefits or bought an adequate replacement insurance policy.

Then there is loss of earnings as women are the point person for both child and elder care. It has been estimated that lifetime loss of income for women amounts to $659,139. Couples suffer, too. If women must drop out of the workforce in their peak earning years to care for mom or dad, family wealth building often stops short.

7. Why Do Women Outlive Men, and Will This Continue?

So far, our medical advances are largely in the areas of heart disease, cancer, prenatal care, lower respiratory diseases, and in men, stroke. We have eliminated or prevented many of the causative conditions, rather than generally extending the life span for the species. These cures and preventions are accessed by caretaking. Men don't go to doctors, share ailment information, or stay in good general health through exercise and nutrition to the extent that women do. But, it's not only that. At least for the present generation of elderly Americans, differences are in part due to earlier and prolonged smoking by men. Women started smoking later in life because of post turn of the century mores.

8. Do These New Trends in Longevity Apply to All Americans?

Nice try, but no, you can't get out of taking salt from your diet or getting on the treadmill because you are a person of color. HIV and homicides, a tragic result of inner-city poverty, not genetic inevitability, influence most of the miserable statistics you see for minorities regarding longevity. Indeed, African American females have a higher life expectancy than white males. Among elderly African Americans, one in five were 80 or older in 1990. In 2050, this is slated to rise to 30 percent for African Americans and 36 percent for Hispanics. What's more is this growing population has a significant statistical chance of going broke in advanced age. The poverty rates for African Americans and Hispanics are greater than for elderly whites, in some areas by double.

9. OK, I Get It. I Will Live a Long Time. But in the End, Won't the Government Take Care of Me?

I start every one of my seminars with, "There's good news, and there's bad news." The good news is you are going to live longer. The bad news is you can't afford it! Today, we need $2.23 dollars for every dollar we spent in 1972 for the same standard of living.[11] We may need to generate two and a half times our present income during 30 years of retirement! The government knows we won't have that much and hopes that Social Security and our pensions will keep us afloat. But as our population ages, how much can the government tax us (and our children and our grandchildren) to keep up our support? Already, according to a 1984 University of Pennsylvania study by demographer Samuel H. Preston, the Federal government spends only one-tenth as much per child up to age 17, as it does per senior. In dollar terms, the difference is six times spent on the elderly than on our youth.[12]

In *Born to Pay: The New Politics of Aging in America*,[13] Philip Longman cites longevity, the baby bust that followed the baby boom, and nonmeans tested senior benefits as reasons that the government may cut back or disband senior programs just as the boomers and those coming after them reach retirement. One need only sit down with *Age*

Power, by one of the fathers of longevity thinking, Ken Dychtwald, and read it side by side with the probenefits material in *Longevity Revolution: As Boomers Become Elders* by Theodore Rozak,[14] to know that there is an important debate afoot. It has emerged in the press, in our personal discussions, in Congress and in worldwide arenas.

My purpose is not to argue the politics of government programs, but to make sure that you are self-reliant enough to be above the outcome. The way to do this is to be in control of both the accumulation and the decumulation phase of wealth management.

To many boomers, self-reliance means late retirement or working after retirement, or *rehirement*. This seems fine if the jobs are there. Going broke by outliving your money is a simple function of six variables:

1. How long you will live.
2. How much you will spend.
3. How much guaranteed income you can derive from your investments.
4. How extensive are your replacement ratios—pensions, Social Security, covered health benefits.
5. How long you work and how much you earn.
6. How much inflation will impact your buying power.

The point of this book is to help you maximize your control over all six.

10. Planning Is So Speculative and We Can't See the Future. How Will the 102 Planning Change That?

Yogi Berra philosophizes, "The future ain't what it used to be."[15] And indeed it is not. Time was when everything about your retirement was one of the great mysteries of life. How long will you live? What will your expenses be? How much will you have to spend? These were all questions that often went unanswered. Today, not only are all of these ascertainable, but they can also be individualized to a startlingly accurate degree. The net result is to eliminate the most frequently cited barrier to planning (and the most common excuse not to plan): *I'm not ready to craft my future.* But it is time for you to be ready. In the chapters that follow you will:

- Make guaranteed lifelong cash flow your goal.
- Discover how to assure yourself lifelong income.
- Choose retirement housing without compromise.
- Track the inexorable relationship between wealth and health.
- Meet the "sandwich" responsibility to your children and your parents, head on.
- Throw out a lot of junk along the way.

But most importantly, you will find your place among the revolutionaries that are changing the face and the place of aging in our world.

Part ONE

Longevity and Work

Work Longer, Live Longer—
The Clear Nexus between Longevity and Work

Logic tells us that if we are healthier longer, we can work longer if we so desire. But, now we are learning that we may be healthier just because we work longer. Puzzles keep our minds flexible and walking keeps our bodies supple. People who work longer tend to live longer. Studies that track the length of recovery after operations count a busy work schedule and a desire to get back to the job as aids to the healing process.

The extent to which people work through the physical problems associated with aging can be a measure of their longevity. In 1984, the John D. and Catherine T. MacArthur Foundation undertook an extensive scholarly study to develop a conceptual basis of a *new gerontology*, and to gather the knowledge needed to improve the physical and mental abilities of aging Americans. The findings that emerged, reported on fully in *Successful Aging* by John W. Rowe and Robert L. Kahn (Dell, 1998) showed that there was a direct and measurable connection between longevity and the degree to which work continued (and continued despite both minor and more significant medical conditions). Study subjects who were able to return to work (paid or unpaid) after taking medical leave had a more complete recovery from their condition than those who did not.

However, it is not merely work for work's sake, but positive work, and more important, satisfying work, that promoted healing. The MacArthur Report found a clear and convincing connection between health and longevity, on the one hand, and social connectedness, support, productivity, relatedness, and action on the other.

Work ⇒Self-Esteem ⇒Relatedness ⇒Successful Aging

If we are working longer years at satisfying work, it is less likely that health issues and chronological aging will impact our mortality. Having said all of this, the question then becomes where, when, how, and why will people work well into their longevity years? The answers lie in a complex combination of social, legal, and practical areas including job availability, benefits, taxes, social mores, and attitudes. As the over-65 (and the over-75, -85 and -95) population expands, they will shape those factors that are of the greatest concern to all of us for generations to come. For now, it is awareness and preparedness that will empower.

The baby boomer especially is in an odd position—both ready to retire and ecstatic about life-fulfilling work. We want to work at what we love. We may just now be discovering what that is, at a time when our age makes us expensive and sometimes unwelcome employees. Yet, with such a small workforce behind us, we are needed, often in the jobs that we plan to leave. And so we are undergoing an internal and external tug of war. We want the money and prestige of top-flight jobs, often in different or related fields. We are after all the elite, experienced worker. Conversely, we cost companies a comparative fortune in benefits. In addition, ageism, much of which we ourselves fuel, makes us less attractive in the workforce.

So, how do we proceed?

First, we recognize that this is not a life stage marked by compromise. The world will compromise us enough. We do not have to give it a helping hand. Most of us are stuck in a job selected by an eighteen-year-old—ourselves—when we were young and for decades we couldn't or wouldn't change.

Sigmund Freud concluded that life is at its best when "Liebe und Arbeit" (love and work) are the pivot points of existence.[1] Freud would get a big surprise today. On the one hand, we are walking resumes, producing our business cards as fast as we can shake hands. On the other hand, we are likely to feel unfulfilled and uninspired by our work, itching for early retirement and career changes. The word *calling* has virtually disappeared from all but the worlds of art and clergy. Work for many is merely a means to make money; money that we spend before it even hits our wallets. Our love-hate relationship with work is magnified at different times of our lives: when we graduate and take a first job, when we are fired or quit, and always when we contemplate retiring. This is not the type of job satisfaction that nurtures longevity.

We believe that if only we had enough money to be free of work, we would find the work we really love. Someday, maybe, we'll have enough money. Until then, it's only a day-to-day life of earning more. And with longevity increasing, there are just more somedays. This condition is not, however, a good enough excuse for not doing what we love.

If you are one of the fortunate among us that has truly found your calling, congratulations, you have cause for celebration and pride. It's an achievement beyond financial measure. Hold on to it. Do not be deflected by the money pressures of the end game. Keep yourself tooled for the new technologies of your job, and don't allow your head to be turned by the early retirees with their eye on the clock.

The end game is afoot. We must have the courage to find the work we love, regardless of money. Marsha Sinetar in *Do What You Love, the Money Will Follow,*[2] encourages us to live the work life we want and forget about the rewards. She says the rewards will come. From my observation, more often than not, she is right. But more important, for those that are doing what they love, it really doesn't matter. Fulfillment and calling can complete all gaps, including money.

And, it is never too late. Our longevity can be the very thing that gives us the time to retool and make a better choice. When she was 40, the mother of my daughter's classmate lamented that she had wasted her college education by never working. Now at 45 she is happily ensconced in school, working toward her masters, and ready to teach. Another mother, at 50 became an interior decorator and opened her own business. A busy attorney friend now sells crafts. And yes, my examples are all women, but they certainly don't have to be. My own husband, a labor lawyer, is finding his long elusive fulfillment in providing families protection and security through insurance and tutoring college and law school applicants. My best friend's husband went from biochemist to public school chemistry teacher. And it's never too early. My 21-year-old son is taking a year off after college graduation to work on the 2004 Presidential campaign, and then decide the next course of his work life.

Why not? Most of his age group will have at least three careers. The thought is exhilarating. But if we don't give ourselves the freedom to choose what we love, it can also mean just more years with one eye on the exit door. If past history is an indication, we have a pretty good chance of taking the career bull by the horns and finding job satisfaction. Boomers, especially, were never ones to wait 40 years and retire with a gold watch. And Generation Xers exceed their model by job jumping a minimum of seven times in their career. In fact, one of our financial difficulties comes from job mobility, leaving unvested pensions behind, or cleaning out and spending embryonic 401(k) plans.

When most of us graduated, we had limited career choices. Even I, who was primed it seems from birth, to be a professional at a time when many women were just beginning to have that choice, could choose from the career of lawyer, doctor, or teacher. That was it, and even having that much choice was very, very lucky. I was truly ignorant of any other of life's paths. Maybe that is why I have changed careers so often, being both so elated and so dissatisfied and finding true satisfaction in trying everything. My 11-year-old daughter has come up with everything from forest ranger to zoologist just by surfing the Net. The world is open to her from the beginning.

Now that we have the time for multiple careers and not just several jobs, it behooves us to give thought to what we love, and then let the money follow us. You may be thinking, "But I don't have the money to take the chance." A favorite aphorism of mine is, "the definition of insanity is to do the same thing over and over and expect to get a different result." If all of your years of working have not made you free to live the life you love, it's doubtful that another decade of the same work will accomplish anything different. If we try, most of us can make a more than acceptable compromise between our money and our life. One thing that longevity research shows is that you will probably work in one way or another for years to come, with or without money as the motivating factor, so you might as well let your dreams take over now.

Work, Relevancy, and the Cult of Busy

Two men meet for the first time at a party. What do they talk about? In France, it's politics; in the United States, it's work. We bond, identify, and categorize ourselves based on our work. Women are not immune. We have become master networkers. We can easily lead with a business card instead of a family picture. Our jobs describe our status and are a kind of shorthand for who we are when we meet people for the first time.

Helen Gurley Brown, publisher of *Cosmopolitan*, in her book *Late Show: Having It All* (New Star Media, 1993), writes that work is our life and our supplier of self-esteem. And for many that's where the truth lies. What, God help us, will we do with retirement? I know many financially successful, early retirees who apologize to perfect strangers for their decision, by launching into half-hour dissertations on all the volunteering they do. And if you think that seniors and even super seniors are not compelled to be busy, busy, busy, consider the 1991 Harris Poll that surveyed 3,000 people over the age of 65 and found 27 percent working, 26 percent volunteering, 42 percent helping children and grandchildren, and 29 percent assisting disabled friends and relatives.[3] Add that up and you'll get over 100 percent. Multitasking does not stop at retirement.

Social workers and gerontologists call this *productive aging*, a postretirement continuation of the work ethic. They consider this healthy, and a further contributing factor to individual longevity and successful aging. In a related study by the Commonwealth Fund of retired people over the age 75, more than half of the subjects reported themselves "in excellent health," and over one-quarter were active volunteers.

Volunteerism is especially popular among the early baby boomers now contemplating retirement, as well as among retired professionals currently in their 70s and 80s. For example, Samaritan House in California is a clinic staffed by retired doctors, including an immunologist age 78, a radiologist age 82 and a young, 61-year-old cardiologist, as well as nurses, well into their 70s.

Identifying the trend toward volunteerism, the San Francisco–based company, Civic Ventures, has begun to explore the opening of Life Option Centers, one-stop locations for financial, personal, and career centers for retirees. Says Marc Freedman, founder of Civic Ventures and author of *Prime Time: How Baby Boomers*

Will Revolutionize Retirement: "There's a population out there all dressed up with no place to go. We need activities that would capture [their] imagination, use their skills and give them a sense of purpose."[4]

We so identify the work ethic with virtue that it's hard to accept leisure life and feel that we remain relevant. This expanding view of the relevance of the aging population will, of course, have an impact on society as a whole. Without a major shift in the way society views the older population, their increasing numbers will become drains on the assets of the social structure instead of vital additions to it. Advertising, for example will have to change. As described by Edie Weiner of Weiner, Edrich, Brown, Incorporated in New York City, a prominent trend analysis firm, today's picture of the older American "tends to show these people in leisure activities or in retirement. These messages reinforce the irrelevance of elders in the serious business of day-to-day life. In many businesses, they feel marginalized, as their technical skills are often outdated or not superior."[5] As baby boomers

The Federal Government Tries to Make Us Rest: The Profile of a Little Known, Aborted Government Project

Thirty years ago, our government tried to make respect for leisure a national characteristic. It met with dismal failure. In 1971, at the White House Conference on Aging, it was concluded that our "society should adopt a policy of preparation for retirement, leisure, and education for life off the job—to prepare persons to understand and benefit from the changes produced by retirement." Fat chance. In today's "age of retirement," it remains fashionable and acceptable to work part time, to volunteer, to "do do do." Retirement itself has become an activity to be worked at and must be validated based on the cult of busy. A Harris Poll of retirees revealed that an amazing 95 percent wanted to work at something meaningful, even if they don't get paid.[6]

become more and more active, this will not continue. The public, says Weiner, "will come to recognize them for the assets they can be, because they are willing to work."

A review of 94 life histories of active volunteers showed no interruption in advanced age. The *Pathways to Life Quality Study in Upstate NY*, conducted by the Gerontology Institute at Ithaca College and the Bronfenbrenner Life Course Center at Cornell University, found that:

- The 30 percent volunteer rate was about the same for married women and men, and single women.

- All had fairly equal volunteerism and club memberships.

- Married men were consistently more likely to volunteer than unmarried men (a desperate attempt to get out of the house?).

- Most started to volunteer after age 75.

- Consistent volunteers do not necessarily have higher health and energy levels than nonvolunteers. They like to work.

- Most that stopped volunteering did so because of health reasons, not for lack of interest.

- Most were motivated by social participation and volunteerism increased immediately after moving to a community care facility.

Yet, despite the clear indication that advancing age does not equate with decreased work, whether paid or not, those working full time after the age of 50, often wish for early retirement. When people are asked why they work, their answer is most often related to money. For example, a Department of Health and Human Resources Study[7] of 1.9 million people still working at age 50 or older (one of the largest study samples in retirement data gathering) revealed:

- Sixty-seven percent of the men age 51 to 54 said they would retire as soon as they had enough money, and

- Thirty percent said that when they retire they would stop working all together.

Some of us struggle with our own internal paradox. We want to work. We want to stop working. This is easy to explain: We want to work at what we want to work at. We see retirement as our best chance to stop work without being criticized and to start living. *Retirement, like money, is a great cover-up.* With our newfound longevity, this is no longer the case. Our best chance to flourish may just be our second career.

Chapter TWO

The Aging Worker Paradox

The issue of work in the longevity years is nothing less than a tangle of conflicting ideas, values, goals, and expectations. This tangle exists on three distinct levels, and within each level is another labyrinth of seemingly irreconcilable forces. Whether on the level of society, government, or the individual, there are as many opinions and viewpoints as there are people to express them.

Simply put, the paradoxes of the aging worker are:

- If society, government, and individual values prize the retirement years primarily as an opportunity to enjoy the fruits of past labor predominantly through leisure, freedom, and recreation, there are insufficient public and private financial resources to allow for the majority of retirees to carry out this vision.

- If for our individual, financial, or health reasons continued work is our choice, that choice cannot easily be fulfilled if our societal focus is kept on making leisure retirement a priority.

- Laws, mores, and practices aimed at protecting retirement seem to be in conflict with lifelong continued productivity and work.

- The desire for lifelong independence, relevance, and productivity seem irreconcilable with protectionism, ageism, and the youth cult.

The resolution is being developed baby boom style, simply because that group is still in the workplace in overwhelming numbers. We are the bosses and the policy makers. And whether we are the employer or the employee, we are facing:

1. The baby boom generation is fast approaching that time when all of the social, governmental, and personal values associated with retirement age will be confronted—probably in the manner baby boomers have approached every issue, with spirit, determination, and resolve;

2. The generations following the boomers are of a lesser number, and face a financial and social burden unprecedented in history, and placed on them by their parents; and

3. As science and medicine advance, the likelihood is growing that the boomers will be staying around for an increasingly longer and longer period of time.

The question "Will we find work?" may paradoxically be put, "Are we too ageist to hire ourselves?" For those older workers looking to stay on or even move on, the issue of job availability will be ever present. Do you remember the days when you had to fight off the competition for a job or to get into the school of your choice? My baby boomer readers will, because there are so many of us. Will it be "déjà vu all over again?" We are about to go into competition with each other, again, this time for second and third jobs, and even for the plum volunteer positions. Younger readers may experience just the opposite in years to come because the baby boom was followed by a baby bust. Going across the generations, there is a *boomlet* occurring right now. But you can't count on lack of competition to provide you with a job for as many years as you choose, and certainly not the perfect job or even one in the field of your choice. The reason is simply a combination of ageism and our laws. Yes, the very laws created to protect the experienced worker and stop discrimination has created an elaborate system of early and forced retirement, at least in the larger corporations.

Social Security and Similar Statistical Nightmares

In simple raw numbers, the increase in eligible Social Security retirement recipients will so far outweigh the number of those paying into the system that the government will necessarily have to reevaluate the Social Security structure. In the year 2000, workers over the age of 55 comprised 13.1 percent of the workforce. By 2015, this percentage will be 19.6 percent. It will be over 20 percent by 2025. But the percentages are deceiving. In raw numbers, between 2000 and 2015, the total number of workers over the age of 55 will increase from 18 million to nearly 32 million. The *dependency ratio*, the measure of the number of workers currently paying into a benefits system compared to the number of workers slated to retire and take benefits, is woefully inadequate.

In 1900 there were 14.2 active work force participants for every retiree, in 1970 there were 5.3 workers for every retiree, in 1999 there were only 3.4 workers per retiree to back up Social Security. By 2030, the prediction is that the ratio will be totally reversed, with fewer than two employees for every three retirees.[1]

The serious downtrend in the dependency ratio is often used to sound the death knell for Social Security, as we know it today. But is it also a manifesto for better and more jobs for older workers? In Japan they are already asking the question, "If not the old, then who will work?" Here, at home, we are witnessing a demographic change as the number of us over age 65 grew by a factor of 11 since 1900, while those under 65 increased by only a factor of one! If you are among those age 50 to 65, who have both dependent children and dependent parents, you probably need to work at least part time, past the normal retirement age. If you are already financially independent you may want to work to stay relevant. The burning question is—If you are an experienced worker and need or want to work, can you rejoice over the workforce statistics?

Many say, yes. According to a report by Watson and Wyatt, *Demographics and Destiny: Winning the War for Talent*, "workforce demographics are about to implode," as 11,000 people per day turn 50.[2] The *Atlantic Monthly* stated that we will be a nation of Floridas by 2025.[3] There is already a 30 percent shortage of young workers. Can companies overcome the idea that high performance means youth? Are they wrong? Do we fear that they are right?

If ageism in the workplace persists, from where will we get what corporate planners call our "renewal of human capital?" One answer has been from other countries. Those in the technology field know only too well that our immigration laws were loosened to bring in highly educated information technology (IT) workers to fill a shortage some years ago. But, will that happen again in other fields, even if we have experienced workers willing to work?

I think it will if we continue to price ourselves out of the market. It surely will if we don't recognize that our skills can get rusty and keep on top of our profession. We know we are at the top of our game, but we must be prepared to show. If we really want to work into latter years, we may have to prove we can do the job. Let us not weep that after all these years we still have dues to pay.

The Unintended Effect of Antidiscrimination Laws

In 1978, age-based forced retirement was rendered illegal under the Age Discrimination in Employment Act (ADEA). Section 4(a) forbids discrimination with regard to workers age 40 and older with respect to "compensation, terms, conditions, or privileges of employment" and forbids employers to "limit, segregate or classify . . . employees in any way which would deprive or tend to deprive any individual of employment opportunities or otherwise adversely affect his status as an employee because of such individual's age." But, while discrimination is illegal, a company can set a minimum age for early retirement and can incentivize early retirement with the so-called *golden hand-shake*. That is what makes the older, experienced worker a high maintenance worker by law!

Here are some of the provisions of the ADEA that make the experienced worker less cost effective to the company than a younger worker, at least by strict benefit costs: A company with over 20 workers:

- Cannot refuse participation in benefits because of age.
- Cannot discriminate in benefits on the basis of age.
- Cannot decrease benefits because of increasing age.
- Must satisfy life insurance, health insurance, and disability terms that are an equal benefit or an equal cost standard (that is, the employer must give a benefit that is either the same or costs the same, for all workers, regardless of age).
- Must vest employees in pension benefits by age 65 or after five years of participation.
- Make early retirement voluntary. (If an early retirement incentive is offered, the plan must be offered for a limited period of time.)

The result of the ADEA was to eliminate forced retirement. However, it also inadvertently gave companies reason to downsize whole divisions of older workers, and offer incentive packages with the implied threat of downsizing or euphemistically right-sizing. For example, the cost to the employer of healthcare group benefits doubles for employees after ages 55 to 59, compared to ages 20 to 44. The cost of a defined benefit plan for a 64-year-old as compared to a 25-year-old worker is more than double. At age 28, the cost of a worker's pension is approximately 3.25 percent of the total compensation package. At age 52, it is nearly 9 percent and by age 63, it is almost 12 percent. As for defined contribution plans, older workers average a 6 percent contribution of their of salary and younger workers 2 percent, making employer matches more expensive.[4]

But it is illegal to make an adjustment in benefits because of employee age alone. And we wouldn't want it any other way. Or would we? Many of us would just like a job. We are tired of hearing that we are *overqualified* as a code word for *too expensive*. In bad times, when we need to work most, we are protected out of earning a living.

Longevity Itself, Costs Employers Money

William Mercer Inc. took a study of the difference in benefit costs to them if life expectancy increases actuarially by one year. For an

Cost Effect of Added Life Expectancy on Corporate Pensions

Category	Typical Company		
	Original Mortality	Revised Mortality	Change (%)
Life expectancy at age 65	18 yrs	19 yrs	+5.5
Pension liability			+3
Annual pension costs			+11.6
Annual postretirement medical benefit			+5.4

Source: Wealthbuilders 2003.

employee retiring at age 65, the annual pension benefit cost rises 11.6 percent, and the health coverage cost by 5.4 percent.[5]

The unfortunate outcome of these likely added employer expenses is to eliminate us from consideration for many jobs. Those of us who have been told that we are "overqualified" know that this is a code word for "too expensive." Fortunately, many major employers as well as the U.S. government, are on a campaign to have us better prepared to take care of ourselves when we retire. There are more aggressive campaigns at work to suggest that we save by contributing to voluntary plans. Here are a few of the ideas on the horizon:

- Defined contribution health plans may replace the present system of employer-paid insurance. Current medical savings plans are an example of a system that gives you tax benefits and more discretion over your healthcare, but limits the employer's cost of coverage.

- Aggressive on-the-job communication to employees about buying annuities and the importance of creating lifelong income.

- Required annuitizaton of part of the 401(k) as is now part of the British system.

Chapter THREE

Recent Innovative and Progressive Workplace Solutions

I n today's early stages of planning and thinking about the future of the aging workforce, some corporations and employers are starting to look at and experiment with new ideas and innovations for the experienced worker. These include new concepts in work arrangements as well as new thinking in the area of benefits.

Flexible Work Schedules and Locations

CVS, the retail pharmacy and drugstore chain, has instituted a plan under which workers are being permitted to transfer their work between locations in the South and in the Northeast, allowing the so-called *snowbird* (the retiree who stays, for example, in Florida for the winter, and New York for the summer) to work part time in one location and part time in the other. The company has found itself with happier workers and a solution for its problem of seasonal transfers of business, geographically.

In another example, one worldwide communications company has begun a program for 750 of its interested employees whereby potential retirees are transferred to company locations and ventures in foreign countries. The experienced workers are given custom-made retirement locales and the company has a ready-made staff for its new operations. A win-win solution.

Other similar plans have been popping up. In its 2001 study, the General Accounting Office (an auditing and reporting arm of the U.S. Congress) found the following kinds of arrangements:

- A needle manufacturer allows its older workers to choose their workdays. The average age of the company's workers is 73!
- A temp agency with 25 percent of its workers over age 55 has been so pleased with older workers that it has undertaken a major re-cruitment drive.
- A space design company has a formalized plan to allow its retirees to return to work as independent contractors.
- Companies in many areas, including the aerospace and chemical industries, are establishing a 999-hour rule (to avoid increased ben-efit costs for full-time workers) under which retirees are rehired as part-time workers working less than 1,000 hours per year.

The study concluded, however, that the incidence of these flexi-ble programs is not yet widespread. Most of the flex programs already in place have been open only to white-collar and profes-sional workers.[1]

Innovative Compensation Plans

Adjusting the way salaries are calculated and paid is another longevity trend. It requires a willingness to let go of traditional (and, to many, sacrosanct) ideas of seniority-based rewards. One of the most entrenched beliefs in this area is the notion that pay should au-tomatically increase based on years of service. Annual raises have be-come the norm and are expected. Of course, the annual raise, year after year results in a huge pay differential (sometimes for the same level of time and competence) between the senior worker and the newcomer. It is no wonder that companies are anxious to replace the long-tenured employee.

Labor Unions in the Mix

One logical stumbling block to the widespread implementation of these innovative compensation programs may be labor unions. One of the most cherished benefits won by unions over the years is the se-niority-based compensation plan under which pay increases are given almost solely on the basis of length of employment and tenure. Tinkering with this is heresy to organized labor. Unions will not be quick to recognize any benefit that would warrant a change in the hard-won seniority system. It will be up to the aging membership of each union to convince their leadership that alternatives are what they want and what they need. For union members, it is not too late nor is it too early to begin exploring this.

For example, one of the newest innovations in the area of compensation is the performance-based pay scale. Ironically, to call this concept an innovation is not quite accurate. It is a throwback to the old concept of piecework, payment by the item produced. However, the new idea is not tainted by the bad connotation associated with the piecework *sweatshop*. Rather, it is based on the notion of partnership; putting the company and the employee on the same conceptual and practical track, that of increasing production, increasing efficiency, increasing profit, and, of course, increasing pay. The consulting firm of Watson and Wyatt is a particular innovator in this area, working with companies to design compensation plans that engage workers and encourage both them and the company to maintain the relationship well past the traditional retirement age.

New Ideas in Retirement Plan Funding

Cash Balance Plans

The cash balance plan is a breed of qualified benefit plan, which differs in one important respect from the more traditional, more widely used defined benefit plan. Under the latter, pension benefits are determined by years of service. Under the cash balance plan, pension benefits are determined by the amount in the worker's benefit account. Basically, instead of having to fund a benefit, the employer makes a defined contribution to each worker's credit, which is the same for each worker, each year, without regard to years of service. This will guarantee a base distribution for life.

Cash balance accounts allow you to set aside a percentage of your salary, and guarantee you an interest rate below, which your earnings cannot go. But, unlike the defined benefit plan, cash balance accounts are not dependent on how long you work, and there is no reward for tenure. Their value does not inflate in the last few years of service, but grows steadily. Cash balance accounts do not penalize workers who change jobs frequently, or whose salaries do not rise significantly.

By contrast, the traditional defined benefit plan or old-fashioned pension accelerates in the last few years of service by basing it on a multiple of the salary at the end of your work span. When employers switch over from the traditional plan to the cash balance plan, tenured workers get cheated instead of rewarded for their loyalty. As a result, age discrimination cases have been brought against companies that make the switch. Some experienced worker advocacy groups have questioned their legality under ADEA, but the switches have upheld in court proceedings, for example, *Eaton v. Onan Corporation.*[2]

However, because of the concern over age discrimination, new rules will be emerging from the IRS and the Department of Labor, which will make the cash accounts more attractive to older workers. Among those rules are some that will make combining the defined benefit and the cash accounts beneficial to workers with long tenures. Coupling this with the cost savings to employers makes the cash account innovation a boon to the encouragement of post-retirement continued employment.

Pension Equity Plan

Watson and Wyatt has developed an innovative pension product called the pension equity plan (PEP). The PEP plan has been successfully adopted by such companies as RJR Nabisco to the pleasure of both its younger and its older workers. Based on the idea that a company pension is as much a current benefit as it is a future one, this plan combines aspects of both traditional, defined benefit, and cash balance programs so that benefits accrue more evenly throughout a career. Under the PEP plan, a worker can elect either a lump sum contribution or an annuity based on the lump sum. This permits the choice of a lump sum with many years to grow for younger workers or a lifetime annuity for workers closer to retirement.

Defined Retirement Option Plans

Defined retirement option plans (DROPS) are a form of attracting the older worker adapted from a plan that has grown in popularity to the public sector. These plans permit participants to accumulate extra pension credits in the form of added interest after maxing out under a defined benefit formula. Defined retirement option plans provide a lump sum payment at retirement or a lifetime monthly income.

There are benefits in DROPs to both the employer and the employee. The employer gains both fiscally and administratively because DROPs require an absolute, fixed amount of contribution and cost per employee, thereby providing a degree of control and certainty. The employees benefit because they can contribute additional tax-deferred dollars that augment their pensions, which they can choose to annuitize or take in a lump sum.

The DROPs pension is designed to encourage work into later age because it creates immediate annuity benefits. However, workers cannot collect on this pension if they are still working, even part time. Many DROPs require retirement by five years after entry into program. Although DROPs have been around for at least 20 years in the public sector, their legality in the private sector has been questioned as a form of mandatory retirement, and may be in conflict with Employee Retirement Income Security Act (ERISA)'s nondiscrimination and mandatory funding requirements.

Pension Plan Comparisons

Type of Plan	Best for Experienced or Younger	Sector (Public/ Private)	Lifelong Annuity Available	Long-term or Short-term Employee
Defined benefit	Younger	Both	No	Long-term
401(k)	Both	Private	Yes (rollover)	Both
403(b)	Both	Public	Yes (rollover)	Both
Cash balance	Younger	Private	Yes (rollover)	Long-term
Pension equity	Both	Private	Yes	Both
DROPs	Older	Public	Yes	Short-term

Source: Wealthbuilders 2003.

Chapter FOUR

Making Rehirement a Reality

With all of the debate and discussion over laws, social values, innovations, and changes in the arena of elder work, the most significant factor in the mix is personal. With the help of the remedies, solutions, and equipment, we enjoy increasing control over our work future. Despite the policy changes and the debates, you get to decide based on all personal factors of health, wealth, attitude, and desire, if, how, and when to work, knowing the pitfalls as well as the benefits. Rehirement is in your hands.

To make *rehirement* a reality for you, be aware of and take actions in the six key areas:

1. Pretool.
2. Consider careers in government and teaching, seek out smaller firms, or start your own business.
3. Fulfill your dream.
4. Compromise.
5. Find an end run job if you need a pension enhancer.
6. Embrace neotony (the retention of youthful qualities by adults).

How to Pretool

You must be prepared for the new jobs and activities of your longevity years. Rehirement takes preparation. It takes training in both the skills of new work and in the anticipation of the changes in the social and financial life to come.

People of all ages are going back to school to get certificates instead of diplomas. Although many of us already have a career and even a college or graduate degree, we want to recreate our career path. Others need to stay on top of the new technologies. Don't wait to retool after retirement.

Start now. If you have a career dream, pursue it. Check out *Peterson's Guide to Distance Learning Programs* (Peterson's Publishing, 2003) and visit www.detc.org. It is never too late. If you still can't decide what you want to pursue, check out www.overview.com/colleges to research over 900 career fields.

Anyone at any age can use the secrets of career hunting taught to college students by their placement office. Here are my four favorites:

1. If you think you would like a particular job or profession, find someone who already has it and shadow them. Interview them about their work. See how they really spend their day. If this sounds weird, it may mean that you haven't caught up with the new freedom to pretest your work life and take it out for a spin, before committing.

2. Join professional clubs that relate to the job or field you seek. That's where you will meet people in the career loop, make friends, network, and learn the issues faced by the profession.

3. Subscribe to the leading newsletter in the field. Eventually you may even write a piece for it. You are building a resume without even having a job.

4. Get active in the charity supported by your profession, you'll learn about these in the newsletters and at the organizational meetings.

Government, Small Firm, or Your Own Business

These options must be considered because you may be too expensive to hire at a large corporation. But, you will never be too expensive for the government, for a small company, or for yourself.

It's no surprise that an AARP study showed that 41 percent of

companies employing 1,000 or more people have early retirement incentives plans, and 37 percent with 500 to 1,000 employees have
such plans.[1] But of companies with 100 or fewer employees, only 4
percent have such plans. Remember, the ADEA, the age discrimination law, does not apply to companies with fewer than 20 employees.
So the devil is in the details when it comes to how expensive you are
to companies that cannot discriminate.

For a final example, if you are over age 65 and are working,
Medicare will not pay if covered by a pension at work. So, even if you
are Medicare eligible, a large firm cannot take you out of their healthcare benefit system. Smaller firms are not covered by ERISA, and can
offer you a job without health benefits.

Why Government Work and Teaching?

Both these arenas are models for phased retirement programs, many
of which began with the notion of a tenured faculty, and innovative
benefits like the federal government's pioneering offer of group long-
term care insurance. Further, government and the manufacturing sectors such as auto and steel still offer defined benefit plans. But those
jobs are often physically difficult assembly line jobs.

Why Not Hire Yourself?

Here is another best-kept IRS secret like the real estate IRA (see Chapter 11)—*it's the self-employed 401(k)*. If you own your own business
you can contribute up to $40,000 a year, $42,000 if you are over 50,
in this plan tailored for you and you can start it at any age. It is the ultimate end run because it permits a higher level of savings than in
any other government plan for the self-employed. Only an insurance
program allows you to defer taxes on more, and those are after-tax
dollars. The plan doesn't even have a brand name yet, like ROTH or
SEP. Some call it the solo 401(k) others the uni-k or personal k.

The plans are for real Mom and Pops, one employee or a spousal
business with no employees. Siblings and parent/child businesses
merely open a separate uni-k for each owner. These plans allow for
borrowing out of the 401(k) penalty free, not recommended, but at
least you have the same rules as the big boys.

And guess who makes the employer contribution? You do. And
guess who makes the employee contribution? You do. And guess who

decides on how much the match should be? You do, at the end of the year, unless of course you've fired yourself by then.

The *uni-k* (my favorite name for it) is created as a catch-up plan for boomers who want to save more and have pretooled for their own business. You can contribute 20 percent of your self-employment income, plus $12,000 yearly ($14,000 if you are over 50), so long as the 20 percent plus the additional contribution does not exceed your total income from self-employment. Once your self-employment income exceeds $200,000 the cap changes to Keogh rates, but until then the program is far more liberal.

You can set up payroll deductions to fund the plan. This brings me to the most critical aspect of using your business as a longevity tool—be scrupulous. Have a business plan, even if you expect to earn pennies. Pay yourself by check, don't fudge your income tax by taking personal deductions on the business. Your purpose is to have as much legitimately earned income as possible, so you can make the greatest contribution possible. It helps if you or your partner is detail-oriented. If that's not the case, get an accountant to be careful for you. At this writing, the companies that allow you to open the uni-k are rare as hens' teeth, but not as hard to find as real estate IRA custodians. They are:

Fidelity, www.fidelity.com

AIM, a family of mutual funds, www.aimfunds.com

BISYS Retirement Services, www.individualk.com

Pioneer Investments, www.pioneerfunds.com

Scudder Investments, www.scudder.com

The format of your company, sole proprietorship, S corporation, limited liability partnership, is unimportant to opening the 401(k). But it's very important for other reasons, like tax and estate planning, and limiting liability from lawsuits, and even applying for small business loans. Checkout the wonderful guidance in Judith McQuown's classic book, *Inc. Yourself.*[2] You can then see an attorney, or call long-time Wealthbuilder resource Jacques Luben. He runs INC Plan USA, an incorporation service provider that creates a wide range of entities in all 50 states, including Delaware.[3] (Delaware is known for its ease of incorporation, low state fees, low tax, and confidentiality.

Chapter FIVE

Dream Fulfillment and Compromise—
They Are Both Okay

How many marvelous things would you like to do, see, experience, or become that you have postponed until tomorrow? Whenever tomorrow starts for you, one thing is certain: *It is never today*. The trouble with waiting until tomorrow is that our future unfolds moment to moment. Life starts right now, and it keeps on coming until it is over. There is no intermission, no time out after which the future officially begins. We owe it to ourselves to be ready for the future as it becomes the present, and before it is dissolved, bit by bit into the past.

Come back with me to that marvelous day in kindergarten when you were assigned your first arts and crafts project. It was the time before that papier-mâché panorama with the erupting volcano that really counted for your science grade, the time before you cared even one bit about coloring within the lines. You were riveted to your desk with excitement and focus. Every moment counted to finish your daisy chain, clay cat, or finger painting, before your mom or dad came to pick you up from school. The bell, signaling the end of the day, startled you. You did not want to put your brush down. But alas, you had to go home.

Somewhere along the way creativity got confused with self-worth, approval, and competition, and things weren't so much fun anymore. But, it doesn't matter. It takes no more than a new box of crayons to revitalize your primal urge to scribble. Utilize that primal urge and get that dream career, now, in your longevity years.

My friends call me the Phoenix, and I thought that it was the right time to share with you my simple technique for rising from the ashes in my own life. Four years ago when I turned 50, I declared it the best time of my life. I had never been fitter, busier, or more enthusiastic. I found my friends and many of my clients equally turned on by their mounting birthdays. But there was a subtle undercurrent of trouble that was tough to define in that very prosperous time.

Even though we had the money to fulfill many of our lifelong dreams, we continued to tread water, to do more of the same in turn getting more of the same. There was no adequate explanation.

One friend went looking for her dream house by the shore, and ended up sinking a ton of money into redoing her kitchen instead. An executive client, who had spoken of early retirement for five years, refused a terrific golden parachute deal and kept working. My long-time buddy, who swore she would start her own business as soon as her son went to college, never got around to it.

My 50th birthday party took place in a fancy restaurant across from Lincoln Center in New York City. First, we all had cocktails in my new *pied à terre*. Afterward, I treated everyone to a climbing wall experience in the atrium of the building. It was a brash statement from all of us, "We're 50, we're headed upward, and we're terrific."

Less than four years later, the world had turned around. Five people at the party were out of work. One was struggling with office politics to keep his job. One couple had divorced, and one close friend had been diagnosed with breast cancer. With September 11 and the economic downturn, most every one I knew was seriously hurting, and many of them were just plain scared.

But what struck me the most was how all of them regretted not having taken advantage of the recent good financial times to realize their dreams. There were so many, "I should haves," that I knew it was time to loudly declare what I know to be true. "It's *not* the economy, stupid!" What we do with our lives is not a function of what we have in our wallets. It is a function of our own self-created stop signs and red lights.

No matter what your life is like right now, I bet you are making plans for tomorrow, when the really good stuff will start. For big dreams, like traveling around the world or starting a business, tomorrow may be sometime after retirement, or when an early pension kicks in, or when the kids graduate from high school or college. For the lesser dreams, like traveling or pursuing a hobby or learning to play an instrument, tomorrow may be next summer, or when the kids are in camp, or when the slow season at work starts.

If you don't refresh your vision with occasional action, eventually the great achievements become stale. When you finally make room for them in your life, they have been reduced to the realm of fantasy, too difficult to pick up with any significant results. Here is the action to take: Write it down!

What have you tucked away in your dreams? Will you be equipped to take it out and fulfill its promise as soon as you retire? When you reach 60? 80? 100? 102?

As you make your written list, your mind will inevitably start the process of conjuring dreams—the things you have always wanted to do but saved for later. Not all the entries are positive. Many times you will want to consider *negative* entries—things you want to stop doing, like smoking or traveling so much for business.

Write down these goals in simple sentences, without elaboration. Don't skip this step. By clearly expressing your desires and creating an object (paper with the description words), you have brought your desires into a new realm, and made them tangible. This is a most significant step toward fulfillment. At a recent seminar, I asked the audience to do this exercise. One woman nearly began to cry. "What I want is not possible," she said. I saw that it was hard for her to express her desire. It turned out that she always wanted to travel to China, and because of her health it was impossible. I asked her if she had heard of a travel agency that specialized in disabled travelers? She had not. But there are such specialists, and I have no doubt that by clearly expressing her wish she will reach what seems to her like an impossible dream.

Unfortunately, the list is so simple and so easy that you are probably in danger of dismissing it as a useless gimmick. As you will see, even I often use it without much hope for the outcome, but it always works. It embodies the concepts and findings of decades of self-actualization, habit formation, life-planning and self-fulfillment research. Most important in this frenetic world of ours is that it works in practice. It costs nothing, and it can be done on the fly.

For each positive or negative goal, answer the following seven questions in writing (I use index cards) next to each.

1. *What are your dreams large and small?* This is both the most fun and the most important part of the creation. Be specific. *Travel* is not enough. Where do you want to go? Don't hold back because you think your wish is impossible.

2. *When do you want your dream fulfilled?* Give yourself a date, a season, and a time line in which the dream will fit. Milton Gralla, my co-author in *How Good Guys Grow Rich*[1] and one of the world's leading philanthropists, taught me that in business you must always set a date by when a task is to be done. He considered this the centerpiece to success, with personal life planning, as well. This is just as true in dream fulfillment as in business.

3. *Why won't you perhaps realize the dream?* List every barrier of which you can think. I am sure you can imagine many of them. In the chapters ahead, you will relate to many of the barriers, but the five most often expressed are money, looking good, family obligation, time, and lack of know-how or ignorance.

4. *How can you overcome your barriers?* Who can help? What would help? Now, comes the magic. You will start with a blank page. Maybe a germ of an idea will come to you, or 100 far-fetched ideas.

In a recent finance course I taught to high school girls, I asked them to list one way they could become millionaires before the end of the class hour. At first, they thought this preposterous. Then one raised her hand and said, "win the lottery." Another said, "maybe someone will leave me money." Another thought she might get discovered for a movie, and another that she might find a foreclosure property in the real estate section of the newspaper. By the end of class, we had a long list of the nearly possible and nearly impossible. But *nothing* was 100 percent impossible. The listing and the writing attracted solutions.

5. *What will you do next (and by when) to take the steps you need to overcome your barriers?* "When the student is ready the teacher will come," is undoubtedly correct. As you allow yourself the freedom to make tomorrow happen today, several resultful ideas will emerge. The more specific the task and the more pinpointed the deadline, the further you will move forward toward your fulfillment. In his biography, the prolific science fiction writer Isaac Asimov writes, "Life goes on minutia by minutia."[2] So, too, do our dreams come true.

If you are stumped and cannot come up with ways to overcome your barriers, ask yourself the sixth question.

6. *Is there an acceptable compromise?* In these highly aggressive times, compromise has gotten a bad rap. It is tantamount to defeat for some. But acceptable compromise is not really second best; it is another outcome. You know in your heart when you are unhappy with your compromise and when you are excited about the result.

You may have heard the Zen aphorism, "The strongest tree is the one that can bend." Acceptable compromise is not about bending, but it is about moving to another forest where you can stand just as tall as you like.

Our family recently suffered the death of my mother-in-law, Evelyn Bochner. Before she retired she owned a dry cleaning and tailor shop. She did not have a life one would mark as extraordinary in terms of fame or money. But even her children were amazed as person after person filed into the chapel to pay their respects. Three hundred people gathered after only one day's notice. Many flew cross-country to attend. What could bring such a crowd to honor a human being that had never had her 15 minutes of fame? Her daughter offered a deeply affecting and amusing eulogy. She shared, "My mother, who lived her life adjusting clothing, taught me one thing. If you can find a top you like, you can always make the bottom fit."

Compromise with joy is an art and a gift that you give to others. So many people had been touched by my mother-in-law's acceptance of what each day provided that they needed to pay respects to their teacher. If you can't find a way to realize a dream and no compromise that suits you, you should consider whether you chose a goal you really want.

7. *Do I really still have this dream, or is it a hanger-on from the person I used to be?* This is a profound question that I needed to ask myself. In August 2001, the radio station from which I broadcasted became an all sports station, and I was off the air. An agonizing year ensued. My quest to get another show was thwarted at every turn. The industry was consolidating, financial advertisers had a tight budget, and people were fed up with the bad economy. Not only did I lose my life's calling as a communicator, but most of my income as well. With that went my husband's income, as he publishes a financial newsletter largely sold to my listeners.

Meeting fans that begged me to go back on the air only made it worse. I had no control over whether I went on the air. It was all up to other people. Joan Lunden, the TV talk show host often speaks of months by the telephone waiting for it to ring. I know exactly what she means.

But, I had this technique I just prescribed for you. No matter how many times I used it successfully in the past, I still approached it with skepticism. I was in a defeatist mood, but I forced myself.

Despite my love for radio, there was one thing about it that I did not love. Because of my broadcasting schedule, I was not able to travel for more than five days at a stretch since 1992. I took out my trusty index cards and wrote *world travel*. I made my list of what I needed to do and by when which was to travel to the place of my dreams for free. This included attending a travel writer's convention (for which I needed a resume), cultivating at least three magazines, choosing story angles, and contacting tourist boards until I got the gig of my dreams. Yes, I put in the dates. And, no, I did not think it would work. I was wrong. I left for Malaysia a week later. This is a critical point. You need not believe in the technique. It doesn't need your blessing to work, just your thoughts and actions.

Yes, the world is abundant, but we are stingy. Be generous to yourself and dare to list even the seemingly impossible. And don't wait. Not even for one moment. I started my journey by taking notes on a commuter train.

As you get adept at postponing your life's aspirations, you learn how to do just that. So many people come up dry after retirement that they become stagnate. It's no wonder that 25 percent of retired seniors go back into the job market and many more wish they could. Fifty-three percent of baby boomers expect to work a second job. Will that job be more fulfilling than the first?

The July 29, 2002 edition of *BusinessWeek* reported on a Harris International poll of 1,022 individuals with salaries of $85,000 or more, who planned to continue working after age 65. Of those polled, 83 percent chose to work because "I want to stay challenged and stimulated."[3] A July 2002 NBC survey asked beleaguered baby boomers what they planned to do about the recent (at that time) huge dip in the stock market and their own nest eggs. The survey revealed that the most common response was "to work another five years and postpone retirement." Very few planned to rethink their financial needs, be creative, scale down, or take any action other than postponement.

I believe that this willingness, even eagerness, to keep working stems from a lack of commitment and excitement about a postretirement future. So here is the crux. We harbor plans for the future that move and inspire us. When given the excuse of money, we retreat back to work. We don't break through our patterns to make any real difference in our futures. But we must. Solely by dint of our longevity, our prospects for the future are different from our parents' and grandparents'. We cannot coast into retirement, or whatever new word we will invent for the new Sage Age. We need some preparation. Not retooling after retirement, but pretooling long before.

Do You Want Fries with That?

There's an old song that's called, "When I'm Not Near the Girl I Love, I Love the Girl I'm Near." Somehow I always think of that song when anyone makes fun of the spate of McDonald's commercials that show a senior citizen sheepishly taking a job at the counter and finally fitting in. This was McDonald's attempt to recruit seniors, much to the horror of my colleagues, who gasped at the come down that some old man must feel in slinging fries. Too bad about my colleagues. It's honest work. And some of us want or need to work, and not much else may be available depending on the competition and the neck of the woods we call home.

Sure, I want to have your entire healthcare paid for, and a healthy annuity with lifelong cash flow. But let me be the first to pat you on the back and say it's just fine if life has caught up to you and you need to work at whatever honest work you get.

But what about all this poetic, "do what you love stuff?" Let me share a little story. In 1993, my son, then eleven years old, and I were on a book tour for *The Totally Awesome Money Book for Kids*. (Newmarket Press, 2002). I was pretty sure that the little man would be an MBA some day, running his business from his yacht. Or at least that was my fantasy.

As we went to the curbside check in at a Midwest airport, we noticed that one of the skycaps was attracting attention. He looked to be over 60, and he was in such a whirl of activity that the old Handy Andy commercials came to mind, five arms and all movement. He wore a belt that he obviously crafted himself, from which dangled every type of rope and paper cutter, scissor, opener, plier, and tape you could imagine. As each traveler approached, he neatly cut off their old luggage tag, replaced it, booked their seat, and took their bag. It happened in a matter of seconds. We heard one passenger say, "I never check my bag. But with this guy I feel safe." And indeed the very act of his efficiency made you a believer. Your bag would never go missing. And maybe he was a walking good omen. Luggage tagged by him was like a little blessing; your plane would not go down either.

My little boy stood in rapture, riveted to the spot. He couldn't take his eyes off the whirlwind of competence. And then my son said a strange thing, "That's why I want to be the President of the United States." I didn't get the connection then, and I'm not sure I understand it now. All I know is that since he was 15, my son has interned in Washington. He's there right now. Next year he will graduate early to work on the next Presidential campaign. Then who knows? What is clear is that when he searches for his place in government leadership it is not Gandhi, or Martin Luther King, Jr., or even Abraham Lincoln that is his model of excellence. It's the curbside check-in guy at a commuter airline. If you end up working at a job that the world sees as less than you had, never mind. Bloom where you are planted, and be the finest flower in the garden.

Chapter SIX

Securing Your Retirement with An End Run Job

I f you could create a creature willing to live the first half of its life in preparation for the second, you would develop a civil servant, who would marry a civil servant, both of whom would have no children, and trade every vacation and sick day for hard cash. The truth is that a police officer in any city in this country probably has a better fix on retirement than the physician or businesswomen making three times the salary. Why? Because the police officer has secured a guaranteed pension that can allow him or her a replacement ratio after 20 years on the force. Most of my pensioned clients are now landlords managing real estate. Others are simply retired (of course, they are very busy) at well before 50. In short, many people, not working the "job" for all of their years, must scramble later in life to secure a pension benefit.

This is done with an *end run job*. On the edge of your retirement, take an end run job that has only one purpose. It fills in the blanks left by earlier, pensionless work.

An end run job should make up for the permanent benefits you failed to accumulate during your past work years. Most notably they are: pensions, health care, company stock, profit sharing, defined contribution or 401(k) plans, and, if you are lucky, a defined benefit plan. And any program that is inflation sensitive is worth more than richer programs for its effects on your future buying power. That makes whether the employer adjusts benefits for inflation, one of the biggest questions to ask in evaluating an end run job.

Make Sure That the Pension Will Be There When You Need It

If you plan to make your end run for the guaranteed pension, be sure it's there when you need it. Ask:

1. Is the pension insured by the Pension Benefit Guarantee Corporation?
2. Is there any plan to terminate the pension?
3. If a standard termination takes place, will a replacement annuity be bought to replace it, even though it will stop building?
4. If a distress termination takes place, will the Pension Benefit Guarantee Corporation (PBGC) intercede?

Check out your company's ranking with Forbes, the Better Business Bureau, and any trade associations.

Be comforted by the existence of the PBGC. The agency is part of the U.S. government that deserves your attention as it is the insurer of defined benefit pensions. The money comes from insurance paid into pension benefit reserves from dividends, not from tax money. There is no 401(k) or profit sharing protection. If you are missing a pension and can't get information because your company went out of business, or for any related reason, write to PBGC at 1200 K Street NW, Suite 240, Washington, DC, 20005, call 1-202-326-4999 or 1-800-877-8339, 1-800-400-7242 (Spanish) or visit *www.pbgc.gov*. They may be able to track down your former employer and vindicate your rights.

Be aware that even if you have a defined benefit plan, after age 55 an additional year of work may not tack on a full year of benefits. The Dolitzky study done in 1999 of Fortune 500 companies found a trend to incentivizing retirement before age 65, by not increasing benefits by an actuarially fair amount.[1]

Make Sure That You Stay Long Enough—
A Word about Vesting

Whether you are a young worker ready to jump at a better job as soon as you can, or an experienced worker making an end run at retirement, the date that you become entitled (vested) in your pension or 401(k) program is called the *vesting date*. Do not confuse vesting with the date that you can receive benefits. That comes with death, disability, and reaching age 65 or whatever other date is specified in the plan. Vesting has to do with entitlement, not payment. There are two types of vesting based on length of service: *Cliff vesting* and *graduated vesting*. Both define the period of time you are required to work before the pension benefit becomes yours. With either program, you are usually not vested if you have worked two years or less. In a graduated vesting plan, vesting starts at 20 percent of your entitlement after three years of service and increases to 40 percent in the fourth year, 60 percent in the fifth year, and 80 percent by the sixth year. By the seventh year, you are fully vested. As for cliff vesting, you are not vested during your first four years of work. Once you hit the fifth year, however, you are fully vested. The message is clear; if you plan a short-term stint go for a graduated plan. If you won't even be at the job for three years, take a better salary.

Social Security and the Longer Work Life

When calculating your needs, don't forget Social Security and taxes. Taxable income can reduce your Social Security benefits. So, you may want to use your qualified plan money to live on if you are not yet on Social Security. Then once you start to collect, you can use savings and allow the remainder of your 401(k) and 403(b) or IRA to build.

The 401(k) End Run

Forget flowers—these days we are singing, "Where Have All the Pensions Gone?" They've been replaced with 142,000 401(k)-style plans, each with an average of six investment choices that we have to make on our own. A 401(k) and its sister plan, the 403(b) which is mostly used for healthcare workers and teachers, require us to make a contribution, invest it, and even allows us (heaven help us) to borrow against it. There are no guarantees that we can count on if the stock market has a bad year, or we are too much in debt to sock money away.

Pity the poor corporate worker stuck with a defined contribution plan, the 401(k), that requires him to contribute money or none will be there for retirement. Julia R. Vander Els, vice president, retirement education, Delaware Investments, laments of longevity: "These projected time horizons (our long retirements) will prove unsettling to the generations of 401(k) plan participants who have been told that they are responsible for paying for their future."[2] This is forcefully dealt with by the acknowledged inventor of the 401(k). Ted Benna, who describes what he considers to be a good 401(k) plan in light of longevity and reminds us that at 3 percent inflation you'll need 2.42 times your income or $2.42 for every dollar you spend to live at today's level after 30 years of retirement.[3] He concludes that any program indexed for inflation and guaranteed is better than any discretionary program you are offered.

The best programs are ones in which:

- Participation in the program and employer matching start as soon as you begin to work. Many require 30 days, while other programs require up to one year.
- Employer contribution does not rely on your making a contribution (very rare).
- The highest employer matches allowed by law are made when you do contribute.
- You receive a definite percentage of your salary plus a match of your contribution.
- An employer contribution is made without you contributing (which is better than one with a big match).

How Much Can You Contribute to Your 401(k) Plan?

$12,000 in 2003

$13,000 in 2004

$14,000 in 2005

$15,000 in 2006

To aid us in our end run, recent legislation now allows those over 50 years of age to contribute an extra $2,000 in 2003, $3,000 in 2004, $4,000 in 2005, and $5,000 in 2006. The total maximum contribution is $40,000 or 100 percent of pay. This is a great benefit for late starters or those with enough base income to sock away the maximum.

Your employer can contribute from 1 percent to 50 percent of your contribution, but the usual matching program is 50 cents to every dollar you put in, up to a limit. The common limit is 15 percent of the total you contribute, but do ask your employer.

Always take the free money and never lose a portion of the employer match. Be sure you contribute during the pay periods in which the match occurs. That may not be a calendar year. If you diligently make all your contributions by January, you may get only one quarter's worth of match. If you don't trust yourself to make periodic contributions, set up an automatic contribution program with your bank. And check whether the percentage you can contribute is based on salary only or if overtime and bonuses are included.

As for investment choice and expense, it is better to have a large number of choices, some of which are guaranteed, others which help you stay in the market. As with any other investment, don't invest in what you don't understand.

Costs and Services

There are several costs of contributing to a 401(k). Each mutual fund you buy has an expense ratio. How is it paid? Will expenses be deducted from the allocation to that fund or taken off the total? Will you be able to see which are the expensive funds from reading the statement?

Then there are the administrative fees for plan participation. Costs are about $500 per participant in a large 5,000 participant plan. The employer and the larger accounts support smaller accounts. Wrap fees (all expenses in one charge) for smaller funds run from 0.5 to 1.5 percent of your account value.

Finally, do not forget service, online support, and access to planning. According to the International Council of Benefits Services (ICBS), the single most requested job perk by employees is more information about their investments and other related issues.

What to Do with Your 401(k) When You Leave Your Job

I had never seen famed Wall Street doyenne Muriel Siebert upset, until she heard my speech at a New York Financial Expo. I reported that most young workers not only take out the savings in their 401(k) when they move to a new job, but they pay the tax and spend what they withdrew. Muriel was being interviewed on radio from the floor of the Expo. She exclaimed her heartfelt concern that young workers would never be able to retire. "What can we do about it?" she asked me after her interview.

My response is that you can leave your 401(k) with a former employer until you are age 65, if the amount is over $5,000. But 57 percent of those that leave roll over the kitty to their IRA, usually for greater control and sometimes lower expenses. If you are eligible to make a contribution into a new employer's plan immediately upon starting work, you can also consolidate the account with your new 401(k).

If you do roll over the money, make it a plan-to-plan rollover. Don't distribute the money to yourself then redeposit it. You can do this, but if you fail to redeposit within 60 days (no excuses) you'll pay tax, a 15 percent penalty, and forfeit the right to make the deposit. But even if you deposit on time, without a plan-to-plan rollover, the custodian of the first account must withhold 20 percent in tax.

Similar to 401(k)s are 403(b) plans. If you are eligible for a 403(b), you can make tax-deferred contributions while you work, and make withdrawals without penalty at age 59½. But, the subtle differences between the 403(b)s and other qualified retirement plans, that is, pension, profit sharing, 401(k) and Keogh, can't be ignored without hurting your future.

If you are a teacher, healthcare worker, or work for a nonprofit organization, the likelihood is that you have a 403(b) plan rather than a 401(k) plan. Most planners favor transferring 401(k) assets into IRAs in order to expand control over the investments. But, don't rush to judgment if you have a 403(b) plan. You may be best off rolling the money into an independent 403(b) instead of an IRA. In this way, you retain the ability to borrow up to $50,000 tax-free and to defer withdrawals until age 75 for deposits made and interest earned prior to January 1, 1987. A 401(k) does not provide the same opportunity.

Evaluating Your Exit Package

When you retire, whether early, late, or at age 65 with a defined benefit plan you may have to decide if you want to annuitize your benefit or take a lump sum.

With a lump sum, you will have three choices: roll it over into another qualified plan with no present tax consequences; use the funds to buy a private annuity; or (heaven forbid) spend it. Carefully compare the monthly annuity income with the yield on investing the lump sum, using a reasonable rate of return. To do this you will most likely need to use a planner. But you can start with the calculator (our own) on www.wealth102.com.

Everlasting Wealth

Longevity and Early Retirement   To retire early, you may have to tap your IRA at a 10 percent penalty before age 59½. The challenge is to find a sensible way to get the money out with no penalty. Section 72(t) of the IRS code allows penalty-free withdrawals from all IRAs and from 401(k)s if you are no longer working for the company. Here's how the section works:

• You make a schedule of substantially equal periodic withdrawals for five years or until age 59½ whichever is longer.

• You must continue the same withdrawal program without interruption and pay the yearly income tax even if you don't want the money.

• If the money is in a Roth IRA and has been for at least five years prior to withdrawal, there is no income tax or penalty to pay.

• Don't confuse this section with others that permit a hardship early withdrawal from qualified plans or those that deal exclusively with 401(k)s. The 401(k) requires that you be at least 55 years old, and that the money is not rolled over into an IRA, and that you leave your job. Section 72(t) can be applied at any age and is usually used with IRAs.

With an annuity, you can usually chose a lifetime payout, a joint lifetime payout, a sum certain payout or time certain payout. Ask if an annuity will be indexed to inflation and, if so, which index will be used. If you are a member of a union, will you participate in any new or additional benefits negotiated by the union after you retire? Once you know these answers you can begin to determine where you are best off.

THE WORK CHALLENGE THINK AND DO LIST

Do you plan to work after retirement?

If so, describe your ideal job in writing. Take your time. Describe your workday, the people you are with, and the compensation you expect to receive.

Pretend you are getting an award for your work. For what are you being honored?

As of right now, what is your "replacement ratio"? How much in lifelong pension is coming to you? In Social Security?

What health benefits do you have from your present job? Include prescription, dental, and mental health and physical therapy benefits.

How long will the health benefits last after retirement? Can you pay and keep the benefits longer? How much would this cost?

Will you need to work to establish health coverage? If so, add that to the description of your ideal job.

Contact your union and/or human resources office to learn more about the postretirement benefits you will get, even if you are years away from retirement.

Are the benefits adequate to replace at least 80 percent of your current expense? If not, add pension availability to build a salable business to the characteristics of your ideal job.

Do you need to retool (get additional training or degree) for what you would like to work at after retirement?

Contact the online universities that can fill your need.

Visit nearby colleges and educational institutions to see what they offer.

Join trade associations and subscribe to newsletters that help you connect with your ideal profession.

If you would like to teach, contact your local school system to see how to apply. Get information from the Peace Corps and other organizations about teaching abroad.

If you would like to own your own business, log onto www.sba.gov and start thinking about small business development.

If you have a 401(k) or 403(b), investigate the choices, costs, and the amount you can contribute. Resolve to max out. Make that the first priority of your savings goal.

If you have an IRA, contribute the maximum allowed. Work toward that goal if you have not done so in the past.

Make it a family matter, and do not let the goal out of your sight.

Part TWO

Longevity and Your Home

The American Dream Is Alive and Well But with Fewer Stairs

When my mother and father got married they moved into my grandmother's two-family home. They lived downstairs and my aunt Rose (the RN) and my grandmother lived upstairs. Even if my father had lived, I doubt that my parents would ever have moved. When I was three, my grandmother had a stroke. It left her totally disabled, except for the ability to sit up. Every day for three years her daughters bathed her, fed her, and changed her. Every day grandma sat up in a straight, hard-backed chair, which was most comfortable for her. We all talked to grandma, even though she could never answer us. It sounds pathetic. But it wasn't, it was typical, and now archaic.

As I write this chapter there are three brochures spread across my desk, all designed to sell longevity housing of one type or another. The first is an action-packed flyer for Solitude, in Cottonwood Canyon, outside Salt Lake City, Utah, explaining how you can buy a ski condo and rent it out for part of the season to defray your costs. This buy-and-rent plan is a sure trend in the upscale boomer and early retiree second home market. The second brochure is an over-sized glossy from Green Hill. You may know it because it is the assisted living facility used to film the hit HBO series *The Sopranos*, when Tony Soprano's mother needed long-term care. The third is a price list for Summit Ridge Center, a top-rated nursing home owned by the Genesis Eldercare Network. Summit Ridge is a full-care facility with highest government approval, the kind of place you would choose if you needed help 24/7.

What strikes me first is price. The daily nursing home rate at Summit is $252 a day for a semiprivate room. It's the same price to stay over for a day and try out your new skis at Solitude. The second thing that strikes me is that Green Hill is trying valiantly to reckon with the nuts and bolts of longevity, as it stands today for many seniors. Neither fully independent nor fully dependent, the residents get their share of "busy, busy, busy." But they do so in an age isolated facility. The staff works hard to get the gifts of seniors to spill out into the community, but does the community recognize all they have to give?

Side by side with these new housing alternatives are legion of statistics finding that we want to stay put, or age in place. So part of this independence-for-all housing movement is universal design, adult daycare, and the reverse mortgage, all in the service of keeping us home, if we can swing it.

The National Association of Home Builders (NAHB) now presents Icons of the Industry Awards to those designing and building universal housing. In 2003, the corporate award winner was Honeywell for the Easy to See Thermostat developed for those with decreased vision and limited hand strength. The NAHB has built a 6,400 square foot longevity show house in Mableton, Georgia, that boasts no thresholds, an ADA approved toilet, and total technological smarts, at a cost of $1.3 million. Richard Duncan, professor at North Carolina University at Raleigh, helped create a new credential achieved through an NAHB training course—the Certified-Aging-In-Place Specialist.

Local governments are getting into the act in unexpected ways. There the new word is *visit-ability*, requiring that whatever age you are, your home be accessible by your significant elder. City ordinances in Pima County, Arizona, and Naperville, Illinois, were the first in the nation to require that all new private homes be built for handicapped visit-ability. They must be wheelchair accessible. Six other counties throughout the nation have these requirements on the drawing board. The federal government already provides tax breaks if you plan to increase the visit-ability of an existing home.

Then there are the active adult developments that depend on

longevity for its youthful effect. If old age is longer and healthier, middle age is twice as long and downright disgustingly robust. We dream of first and second homes where we can rock climb, ride horses, or play golf. To accommodate us, new forms of ownership like timeshare, seasonal, and fractional share and the buy/rent model, make the fantasy come true.

Margaret Wylde's *Boomers on the Horizon: Housing Preferences of the 55+ Market* (National Association of Home Builders, 2002) surveys what boomers want in retirement housing. The report's cover page sports a buff silhouette of a man carrying a surfboard into a moonlit ocean. This is not a guy who wants to believe that he'll ever need a grab bar in his bathroom.

Yet, as we age, even megadeniers begin to see the connection of our present self to our self yet to be. We grasp the continuum. Housing developers are trying to accommodate the ebb and flow of our capacity without making us feel old. So, they soldier on, merging independent living with custodial care to help us achieve our highest level of independence without ever leaving the facility. And there's the rub. No matter how we look at it, today's retirement housing is age isolating. Yet, more and more of us assert that we want age diversity throughout life, and that goes for today's seniors.

Age isolated retirement developments are not new. They started in the 16th century in the Moroccan desert. The Romans built the town of Timgad for retirees of the 16th Legion. After 25 years in the army, retired military persons were encouraged to stay on. It was a reward and a bribe that extended colonialism, but also an attempt to ease the pressure on Rome. From then on, most housing for retirees was charitable or religious. Then, *bang*, it was 1960 and the DelWebb Corporation created the famous Sun City, introducing the concept of a separated life of leisure in an affordable community. Today, we are at a new frontier of age integration. Lasell Village is the first continuing care facility located on a college campus, Lasell College in Newton, Massachusetts.

Companionship, the developers tell me, is the new amenity. Gay and lesbian adult communities are being built in converted high rises by Fort Lauderdale developer, The DeLeo Company. Fifteen hundred applicants were on the waiting list after publication of their first brochure.

As for the Solitudes of the world, the resort-type communities,

Education As a Way of Life

Dr. Margery Silver, a neuropsychologist, and her husband Bob, a retired attorney, have chosen to live at Lasell Village, a retirement community. What sets her apart is that she is not retired—and she is the co-author of *Living to 100: Lessons in Living to Your Maximum Potential at Any Age* (Basic Books, 1999). She, together with co-author Dr. Thomas Perls, is one of the leading proponents of the connection between mental stimulation and longevity. If anyone understands that cognition and learning are ageless, it's Margery. She completed her doctorate at Harvard University in time for her 50th birthday. Her postgrad education was completed at age 60. She is my poster girl for longevity. Living at Lasell allows her to continue her research on centenarians at Boston University Medical School, where she is an assistant professor of neurology, as it allows Bob, who has two doctorates, one in law and the other in sociology, to continue his habit of lifelong learning.

their health will depend on ours. If we can ski into our 80s, and many can, then a long-term commitment to vacation housing will be a fortunate by-product of longevity. If we find ourselves saddled with an extra mortgage, only partially defrayed by rental income, the tide may turn. In any case, the great real estate slogan, "location, location, location," is taking on a different meaning in the age of longevity. Throughout our lives it meant proximity to safe neighborhoods, good schools, and above all, jobs. Now, retirement housing is an industry with considerations of proximity to nature, man-made leisure facilities, and low taxes. Climate is more important than elementary school education. Price is more important than job banks. And whole neighborhoods are being created where none existed, with their own policing and medical emergency systems. In New Jersey, a monastery has been converted to an assisted living residence. In Maryland, a retiree can live on a simulated ranch with the bunkhouse as a common element. The ripple effect is massive: taxes deflected away from schools for our kids as taxpayers leave for low property tax states; a population shift to the Far West and Southeast; housing clustered around golf courses and hospital facilities, not work plants and industrial parks.

What is evident is that choice, and perhaps over-choice will be the watchword of longevity housing. In the following chapters, you will read of a smorgasbord of new offerings to choose from, and how you might best access them for yourself and your family. Then, in the next part, we will consider that a new American family is emerging together with a new American home, with intergenerational spaces reflecting the mutual dependency between the generations. If we as boomers are lucky, we will be held up to a high standard of wisdom. Guidance will be expected of us. We will be listened to, not just indulged, for the contributions we can make to younger generations when we take over the helm as our family's significant elder.

Chapter SEVEN

Aging in Place

The AARP surveyed people over the age of 45 regarding where they want to live in the future. Seventy-one percent strongly agreed when asked if they planned to stay in their own homes as long as possible. That means planning for modifications to be able to stay at home independently. Many had considered reverse mortgages and refinancing to pay for the freedom to live at home even if they had chronic disabilities. This is not surprising.[1]

We are a nation of homeowners. Seniors are no exception. A study by the U.S. Department of Health and Human Services and The National Institute On Aging[2] reveals that a little over three-fourths of those over 65 own their own homes. A whopping 91 percent of those couples where one or both are over 65 are homeowners. And even of single women over the age of 65, 67 percent still maintain a home. And of all senior housing, 72 percent are single-family dwellings.

The majority of seniors plan to age in place after retirement, and it's getting easier. For one, universal design is becoming more affordable and accessible. For another, long-term care insurance can be bought with a 100 percent benefit for home healthcare. The Medicaid Homestead Exemption does not count the home to determine eligibility if one spouse still lives there. A study at the prestigious International Longevity Center in New York City suggests that with so many elder-led and one-person households, policy-makers should consider "loan and subsidy programs to help stimulate landlords to modernize existing homes and adapt large spaces for single occupancy."[3]

As you consider alternatives for yourself, or help your significant elder make a decision as to whether to age in place, look at the demography of your home community. Determine who will remain in your community. Are new services available for those over age 65, such as food, home fix-up and other stay-at-home help proliferating? If so, you may be able to stay put.

The burning question for those of you that want to stay put is, "Can I afford not to sell?" You can if you are flexible and careful. Here are some of the staying put, real estate basics.

Downscaling without Moving

There are lots of ways to stay put and make your home more economical. Refinance if interest rates are currently low. Lock them in at a fixed rate for the long term. Don't take chances on low teaser rates with an adjustable mortgage. More than anything, a longevity budget needs certainty. If rates go down substantially, you can always refinance again. Be sure there are no prepayment penalties, and accept only a no or low closing cost mortgage.

When you refinance, take some money out of the equity of your home to make money-saving improvements, not to build a dream kitchen. Do the research. Would a new boiler save on heating bills? Can you close off a third floor to save on utilities? How can you find a cheaper way to mow the lawn or shovel the snow? I know one landscaper that emulates Japanese rock gardens. Very chic, no lawn. Are you willing to rent out a room or at least the garage to defray costs? These improvements would make a world of difference. But be sure you have the legal right to do so.

Selling a Remainder Interest

If you own a co-op or condominium, or even a private home, you may be able to sell the place and still live in it. The price, of course, is set low, discounted for the years you plan to stay. The buyer takes the risk of your longevity. This works most easily with family members, but many co-op and condominiums allow these programs with investor/buyers. In France, such arrangements are very popular. You get to stay put, and the purchase price is paid up front for your use, to maintain or carry the home.

Sale-Leaseback

A related strategy is to sell the house outright, and lease it back from the buyer. You get full, present market value, but you are responsible under a lease. In all cases, an attorney will negotiate the terms and protect you under the usual landlord–tenant laws. Of course, you also lose the upside potential for the growth of the home's value.

Life Estates and Life Leases

These are both traditional estate-planning strategies that allow you to transfer your home to a child or other person and live there without interruption for as long as you want. Done correctly, life estates and life leases keep the value of the home out of your estate for tax purposes but give the child a step up in basis.

When you transfer a home but keep a life use, you get the tax bills and you still get any senior tax breaks that your locale allows, and you are responsible for the upkeep. But, the property can never be sold without your written consent.

Everlasting Wealth

Step up in Basis   When transferring an appreciated home to an heir during your lifetime, remember that you are depriving them of the "step up in basis" they would get if you left them the home at your death. With the step up, they are deemed to have paid the date of death value of the property, or its value six months later, whichever gets them the lower tax when they sell. Sale-leasebacks for those wishing to age in place get the step up as of the sale date, and properly done life estates and life leases can still get the step up because occupancy does not pass until death.

Naturally Occurring Retirement Communities

As the name suggests, Naturally Occurring Retirement Communities (NORCS) are areas, often in major cities, but lately in suburbs as well, where long-term residents are already aging in place. In general, NORCS are created under a government program, and areas are designated as NORCS because of the age and economic character of the community. Residents get special benefits, like home repair and access to adult community centers.

But, many middle-class and middle-aged people are looking at NORCS as a private sector model for living. "Hell No We Won't Go" now refers to those that opt to stay in their homes and cobble together their own style of middle-class NORC. This has fostered a developing fertile ground for community services from catered meals on wheels, to reduced-cost house painting contracts. It has also fostered the "key exchange" with seniors looking out for each other. A daily phone call from a neighbor, "Are you still alive?" is enough to keep in touch.

Reverse Mortgages

Fundamentally, a reverse mortgage is an annuity collateralized by your home. The technical term for the reverse mortgage is the *reverse annuity mortgage*, because you can collect a tax-free monthly check for the rest of your life, no matter how long you live. The amount is based on your age when you take the mortgage, the value of the home, and the interest rate at the time of the mortgage closing. Reverse mortgage income is not taxable, and the real estate taxes are deductible. You don't pay the loan back until you move, sell the home, or upon your death. You do have the upkeep responsibility. In most states, you are not eligible for the reverse mortgage until you reach age 62. There are reverse mortgages available that give you a single lump sum payment instead of a monthly check. There may be a cap on the amount you can borrow ranging from $155,000 in a rural area to $281,000 in an urban area.

At your demise, there may be no equity left in the home, but not necessarily. If the home has appreciated, it's possible that your heirs can pay off the mortgage and have an inheritance left. I hope so, because of the $3 trillion slated to pass from today's seniors to their baby boom kids, approximately 70 percent is home equity. Longevity is an inheritance robber.

Reverse Mortgages and the Second Home

Some reverse mortgages allow you to take a lump sum instead of a monthly amount. Suzanne used her equity to take a lump sum and buy a condo in Florida. She had enough income from other sources to maintain the main home. While her home will go to the bank, the condo will go to the kids.

Is the reverse mortgage worth it for you? In a 2000 working paper by the International Longevity Center, *The Influence of Family and Community Ties on the Demand for Reverse Mortgages*, economist Kenneth Knapp studied 135 counties throughout the United States. He found that some determining elements in taking a reverse mortgage are the strength of ties to younger family members and a desire to remain in the community. Significant elders want to leave their home as a legacy. Similarly, elders were less interested in reverse mortgages

Interview: Insurance and the Reverse Mortgage

An insurance agent whom I know well has successfully used life insurance to help his clients age in place. Buying a simple whole life policy or a "second to die policy," that protects heirs at a discounted dollar creates a tax-free inheritance, which can be used to buy out a reverse mortgage. When your home is your largest asset, and you plan to stay there in your advanced years, it's nice to have the option to take the reverse mortgage if you need it, without inner conflict over providing a legacy. Here is what he had to say: "In recent years I have moved away from the traditional need-based planning. I strongly believe that individuals should have life insurance in the amount equal to or at least as close as possible to their human life value depending on the insurance company's underwriting guidelines. It is important to remember that wealth is not just an amount of money, but also the benefits, which the money can supply."

where their neighbors were migrating out, simply because they had less reason to age in place.

Your age determines whether a reverse mortgage is a good way to leverage your home. Few advisors recommend it before the age of 70, I go further to explore it after age 75, if you are able to stay put, and still want to. The viability of a reverse mortgage is age related because the lender buys an annuity, similar to an immediate annuity, that you can never outlive. The lender transfers the risk of your longevity to an insurance company. The older you are when taking a reverse mortgage, the better the deal will be. In the event that the property sells for less than the loan value, the loan is *nonrecourse*, the lender gets the property—that's all. You never take on any additional personal debt. Today, many elders use the reverse mortgage to supplement a too sparse budget, or to pay for unskilled care at home. The AARP helps you compare plans at www.aarp.org/revmort, and download the program, Home Made Money, or call at 1-800-209-8085.

Beware, as with any mortgage, that there are closing and initiation fees. You'll pay about 2 percent of the loan as insurance and 2 percent in closing costs. If you opt for a line of credit, you could be paying a great deal for money even if you do not use the line. Despite this, according to the National Reverse Mortgage Lenders Association (www.reversemortgage.org), lines of credit are very popular.

Chapter EIGHT

Downscaling by Moving

Even though most people plan to age in place, there is an ever-growing group of people who dream of being on perpetual vacation, or at least feeling like they are. For those, it means selling the family home and relocating for a different kind of life. Even those who simply sell and buy a smaller home in their own town are making a profound psychological change.

Leave it to the baby boomer to find a fancy name for this act of moving to a smaller, cheaper home, *downscaling*. Maybe we need to take the sting out of it. The act of downscaling itself is scary. We move an average of seven times in our lifetime. But this is different. Before, we have moved up in the world, bigger, better, more impressive, more expensive. The home is where the heart is, but also our most obvious physical symbol of success. You may laugh at the new McMansions and trophy houses built on tiny properties, but you probably conclude that someone with plenty of financial success lives there.

When the time comes that we are ready to take on less in maintenance, yard work, and steps, or the kids are out of the house, and it's just silly to live in a three- or four-bedroom home, we may feel conflicted about the step down in size and value of our next home. If we need to move, because we need the all-important cash flow generated by selling, we may feel like financial failures, even when we planned to downscale all along. If moving to a bigger home is a sign of upward mobility, downscaling is a sign of age, of transition to a new phase of life, perhaps the last phase. Be prepared for an emotional roller coaster of sadness, fear, elation, optimism, depression, and enthusiasm. And be prepared to have fights with your significant other over the most trivial of things.

I know. I had an open house last Sunday and I'm waiting for bids on my grand old lady of a Victorian. She's my 11th home, and my all-time favorite. When I decided she was too big, with my son out of the house and my travel writing taking me around the world, I knew it was time to go. I often wonder, will I ever own anything so lovely? I know every brick and slope of her.

I have spoken to dozens of downscalers, and followed them at their house sales, garage sales, and met them after their closings. Here's what they taught me: *Focus on why you are moving and keep that purpose in front of you at all times.*

Those of us shedding our large homes for financial freedom need not cash out all at once. We may double and triple downscale, depending on our age and purpose. Ask yourself: Why are you thinking of downscaling?

- To cash out equity.
- For greater convenience.
- To live near the children.
- To get away from the children.
- For a better climate.
- For adventure.
- Because of a divorce.
- To fulfill a lifestyle dream.

Whatever the reason, write it down and keep it near you. Make sure you stay with the program and buy only what is consistent with your goal. Focus and refine your point of view. If you don't understand your goals and why you want to reach them, no one else can. What's your purpose in moving? In choosing your next destination? How does what you are doing fulfill that purpose?

If you have a disagreement with your significant other:

- Listen carefully and completely. Are there easy compromises? Are there innovative compromises?
- Use the labor negotiation technique of "final position." Have each person write up their best compromise and put it in a hat. Pick one!

Should you take a mortgage on your new downscaled home? Contrary to the conventional wisdom during your accumulation years, when leverage helped you buy a house, during the decumulation phase of life, leverage may cause you to lose a house. If you can, live mortgage free.

If you do not have the assets to buy your new home outright, at least take the smartest mortgage you can. In my opinion, that's a fixed rate, 30-year mortgage with no closing costs and no prepayment penalty. Times change. Today's best deal is actually a five-year balloon mortgage. But even that can cause trouble if interest rates are up in the next five years and you have to refinance to keep your costs low.

As with most things financial, knowledge is power. Know about the kinds of mortgages available and the benefits and consequences of each. The following is a short primer.

Mortgages 101 So You Won't Go Broke at 102

The benefit of all mortgage loans is that the only collateral is your house. A conventional mortgage contains a fixed rate of interest of a period of more or less 30 years. The mortgage is amortized (from the root word *mort*), meaning a part of the principal loan is paid off (killed off) as the years pass.

Because lenders were often stuck with conventional mortgages that paid low interest, they are now offering variable-rate mortgages. The initial interest rate is often lower than that of conventional mortgages, but it is fixed for only a short period of time (usually six months to a year). An index is applied (often the Funds Index put out by the Federal Home Loan Bank). There is a cap, but no floor. In reviewing variable mortgages, compare the initial interest rate, the cap, and the index used to determine a change in the interest rate.

A balloon mortgage, by which more money is paid at the end than at the beginning, is possible. The average American family is mobile. Most of us move every seven years (some surveys show every five years). You are, therefore, likely to pay off a mortgage well before the end of the variable or balloon mortgage.

Some people find a short-term rollover mortgage meets their needs. The interest rates are low, but refinancing is needed every three to five years. The bank must engage in renegotiation. Here one need plan for uncertainty in interest rate.

Often a seller will take a second mortgage, particularly when he or she is getting a highly inflated price for his or her home. The seller may be happy to permit you to pay a portion of the purchase price in installments. You pay interest but he or she takes a mortgage subordinate to the banks. If you default, the bank is paid first.

Downscaling Your Stuff

A wise man once said that our possessions actually possess us. This becomes hideously apparent when we start to downsize. Personally, I am a collector with a pack rat streak, so I went through downscaling hell trying to get rid of my stuff. As I write this, there's a dumpster in my driveway. It pays to become a downsizing pro because in these days of longevity you are likely to get rid of stuff more than once. My dearest wish is that my kids have nothing to throw out when I'm gone.

There are two ways to get rid of stuff: the hard way and the harder way. Resign yourself to this being a nasty task, either way. But there is also satisfaction in getting rid of stuff. It adds to your wealth, it reduces your costs, and it helps sell a house that's too cluttered (all houses are too cluttered). So, abracadabra, here's how to go about doing the magic disappearing act.

The hard way. Give most of it away and throw out the rest. Giving stuff away and even throwing it out is not as easy as it sounds. In fact, it may even *cost* you money. To make the best of a painful chore follow these Everlasting Wealth rules:

1. Only give to a charity that gives you a receipt for your tax deduction with their IRS number as confirmation that the contribution will be deductible.

2. Make a simultaneous list when piling up old clothes, toys, books, and so on, describing the item, its value, and condition in case of an IRS audit. What you originally paid is irrelevant, as the deduc-

tion is based on the value of the object at time of donation. With most things, you will be the judge of value, and if you have the simultaneous record it's some proof. Get an appraisal for items worth over $500.

3. Don't waste anything; give it away for the deduction. Remember when former President Clinton took a deduction for his underwear? It was allowed. Charitable deductions can be taken over a period of years, so don't think that it's useless to you if your current income is low.

4. Know the charity's pick-up rules before you waste your time and theirs. Charities won't take stained or damaged items, and many require that all items be at the curb or at the least on the first floor.

5. For everything that is left, hold a downscaling party and let friends and family take what they want as long as they pick up the delivery charge. Play a George Carlin album with his monologue on stuff. Then give the album away.

The harder way to get rid of stuff—*sell it*. Unfortunately, your stuff is probably too good just to cart off or give away. You'll most likely have to take the tedious route of sorting through and making an elaborate multilayered selling plan. Having sold everything from vintage clothes to Old Master paintings I have advice, sympathy, and Dutch uncle words of wisdom:

1. Take the time to make as good an inventory as you can.

2. Take sharp photos and note the size and provenance (where you got it) for every item.

3. Divide your stuff into five categories:
    1. Stuff worthy of an auction sale or private collector.
    2. Stuff worthy of a consignment shop or dealer purchase.
    3. Stuff good for a house sale.
    4. Stuff for charity and giveaways.
    5. Stuff to throw away.

4. Understand auction sales. If you are new to auctions, you may find that the sale goes fast and ends in disappointment. Auctions are gambles, depending on everything from the weather to the stock market that day. The auction house takes from five to 15 percent of the sale price. If you have a representative to help you,

they may add 10 percent for themselves to that figure. If you set a reserve, you will get the stuff back if it does not sell, *and* you will have to pay the auction house a fee to boot. You will also have to pay insurance, usually $1/2$ to 1 percent of the estimated value of the items, *and* a shipping charge, unless you bring the stuff to auction yourself. The good news is that almost all of this is negotiable. The most negotiable is the insurance fee, especially if you have homeowner's insurance that covers off premise and shipping loss. I never pay if the item doesn't sell. I can't stand to take a loss for nothing. If the auction house won't waive that fee, I do not consign with them.

5. Avoid using an agent unless they can reach special buyers for a unique collection.

6. Check reputations, no matter how you sell. Auction houses are highly regulated and reputable. Get their license numbers and call the licensing agency to determine if there are complaints. If you use a representative, often the contract allows the house to send them the money. Ask how reputable are they? Is the representative a licensed appraiser, a long-time dealer with a long list of clients? Watch a few reruns of *Lovejoy*.

7. If you have the time and patience to make a private sale, read the magazines that deal with the stuff you want to sell (i.e., collectibles, art, antiques), and place ads in those magazines and newsletters. Use a local paper or place your ad in the edition of a

---

Everlasting Wealth

Smalls If you find that you have accumulated a ton of what the British call *smalls*, you may want to box them up, store them with a friend or family member, and start an antique business in your new location. In Culpepper, Virginia, I met the owners of a lovely bed and breakfast who add about $14,000 to their income by doing this and fulfill their love of hunting the flea markets. Your old vase can be your new merchandise. You'll see money back that you've been spending for years. And, of course, check out, *e-Bay for Dummies*, for it can start you on a new career.

national magazine that only goes to nearby zip codes, which will get you a discount, on otherwise expensive adds. By all means, use eBay and other auction sites.

8. Make the family part of the selling experience. Read *Collecting for Kids and Their Families* (Wealthbuilder Network, 2002), the best book on general evaluation and selling strategies, if I say so myself (my son, Arthur Bochner, wrote it).

9. Check out local consignment shops. Choose one that features the kind of stuff you own. You'll get about 50 percent of the sale price, and it may take longer than an auction, but you'll have greater control over the price and there are many items no auction house will take.

10. If you like the auction idea and your stuff is rejected, ask if they will take it as a box lot or Klondike Load, and sell it as a group. Personally, I prefer the consignment shops for such items, but sometimes speed is everything.

11. If you enjoy house and garage sales have one yourself. Check out *The Totally Awesome Business Book for Kids* (Newmarket Press,

---

Everlasting Wealth

Smart Dumpster Tricks   The trick is to have as little for the dumpster as possible. In our metro New York suburban area, dumpsters run $165 to $275 to rent (20 yards) and $55 an hour for labor, plus dumping fees of $65 to $80 per ton. But it's worth it if you use the dumpster *before* you put the house up for sale. Most people pay twice for the stuff they dump. Once for dumping fees and labor, but worse, for the lower price they get for their house because of clutter. Dump before you sell because the dumping fees become worthwhile by the higher price you get. Keep huge plastic sheets available in case it rains, or the water will soak the stuff and the tonnage will increase. Ask for the largest dumpster for the money; you can get more yards for the same price if you hit it right. And ask for a free extended stay. Your dumpster is your friend, you'll want it hanging around as long as you are still cleaning out.

2002), another book by (guess who?) my son Arthur Bochner, and initiate your children or grandchildren in business by having them run the show.

Put depression in the dumpster along with your junk. Apart from the move itself, you also may feel down about getting rid of stuff. Whether you are moving because you can't afford your old digs, have healthcare needs that cannot be handled at home, or are making a voluntary transition to smaller quarters, expect to suffer loss. If you are a couple, expect to react to that loss as you might a death of a pet or even a close friend. And no matter how much you are looking forward to the move, do not think you will remain untouched. It is usual and natural to feel bad about leaving and great about arriving at the new place.

In the heart-wrenching novel and film, *The Grapes of Wrath*, John Steinbeck depicted the extreme poverty and hopelessness of the dust bowl during the Depression with a single image. Grandma threw her lovely ceramic dog into the fire. She died soon after, homeless. The kids had to cover her body so the family would not be turned away when they crossed state borders. Are you depressed enough, yet? Get over it. You're about to move to a golden community and shed those unwanted pounds of stuff. Memories are cheaper to transport and they fit in well with any décor.

Chapter NINE

Where Will You Live
When the World Is Your Oyster?

One of the great rewards of our new longevity is the time to make our fantasy lifestyle come true. If school systems and job opportunities are unimportant, if a short commute and a convenient supermarket are not required, the sky's the limit as to where we can live. For better and for worse, states, countries, municipalities, and developers all know that. And they are asking one question, "What can we do to get you here?" You in turn are wondering, "Where is the right place for me, and can I afford it?" From active adult communities to isolated cabins in the woods, anything goes when it comes to retirement housing.

If you're confused about your retirement home, you can spend a weekend at the North Carolina Center for Creative Retirement, formed in 1988, sorting out who you want to be next, and where you should live to become that new you. Perhaps you'll join the 150 or so people from 26 states that go to Asheville to create their unique longevity experience.

North Carolina is not the only state putting out the welcome mat. Many states have retirement specialists designing programs to lure retirees with everything from tax savings to larger more readable highway signs. State planners call these *retirement inducements*. For example, New York State is planning an 11 yearlong highway renovation project to make roadways more drivable for seniors. Georgia is building state golf courses near religious institutions, presumably so retirees can pray for a better putt. And Delaware has made itself the tax relief champion of the United States for seniors. As they say on the airlines, states know that you can take your business anywhere, thank you for retiring in Montana, or California, or Rome, Alaska (or just Rome).

But, what constitutes a retirement haven these days? Low taxes and low cost of living? Great. But community, friends, family, and environmental health all make the difference. Lee and Saralee Rosenberg, authors of *50 Fabulous Places to Retire in America* (Career Press, 1991), surveyed people who moved to Florida to retire. Those interviewed regretted not renting for a while, so they could understand the neighborhood, or development better before they bought. With today's mobility, choices between New Mexico, Arizona, and Utah may not be as important as to which community within these broad areas you choose. Georgia, Florida, and North Carolina can offer Southern living and climate. It's the differences in the local living that impacts you the most. It comes as no surprise that numerous sources now rank livability of cities. Take another look at www.realage.com for a review of the health factors that make an area more longevity friendly. And check out the national and international rankings from *International Living*, a newsletter that a can be accessed at www.internationalliving.com. Take a look at the Appendix A for several ways to evaluate states, cities, and smaller locales for the big three in retirement living:

1. cost of housing
2. climate
3. healthcare

Next consider the nuances that make a difference to you that is, religious institutions, adult education, sports, and proximity to family, job possibilities, and the arts.

The best place to start your search is in the magazines that write about the areas you might like to live. And by all means, attend an expo where builders show off their developments and the Convention and Visitor's Bureau is on hand to answer questions. Of course, all major realtors have a full relocation service.

The "World Is Your Oyster" Quiz

1. Do you want to stay near the kids, or a second job, school, or location? If so, look on a map and circle the radius around that anchor.
2. How does your significant other feel about your answers? How does he or she differ?
3. Do you want to buy or rent? The answer should be based not only on money, but your comfort level at not being a homeowner.
4. Do you want two homes or one?
5. Would you like to travel without owning a residence for a while?
6. Would you like to live in alternative housing, like a houseboat or mobile home?
7. Would you consider living in a foreign country at retirement? If so, where?
8. How will you spend your time? Working? At what? Sports? Which ones? Volunteering? For what? Gardening? Painting? Writing? Sculpting? Describe and visualize your ideal retirement day.
9. Describe your ideal neighbors, such as taste, age, and degree of intimacy you would like to maintain with them.

Check all venues against these requirements. And if there are friends or family you want to be near, use a protractor to circle the target area on a map beyond which you will not move.

Moving Abroad

Don't give up on living abroad if that's your lifelong dream. I still plan to have a small place in Europe, although my first choice, the English Cotswold's may be out of reach. If you want to explore living abroad, at any age, start with a visit or phone call to the embassy of your choice for information on requirements for U.S. citizens living in their country; the Board of Tourism, for information on culture, transportation, and leisure activity; and the Consulate or Board of Economic Development for industry and economic information. Many countries have first and second home programs for U.S. citizens. For example, Ireland gives a dual passport for anyone with Irish ancestors; Malaysia has special tax breaks for those buying second homes there. By contrast, many Caribbean countries require a modest or substantial investment in the country, either in the form of a bank account or other assets placed in their jurisdiction. Tax considerations weigh heavily. Beware that the United States will tax income and capital gains made anywhere in the world. You will receive an

$80,000 income tax exemption and a foreign tax credit if you pay taxes in the expat jurisdiction.

When prosperity hits a region, real estate prices go up. If you ever intend to own a home in Europe you must act now or you may very well be priced out of the market. Fortunately, new technology has made the world smaller. Now, there are simple, safe ways that help you make the commitment.

Selecting a Location

- *Check out the exchange rate of dollars to the Euro.* The strength of the dollar will dictate how much home you'll get for your money. If, for you, a home in France, Italy, or Spain is fungible, buy in the area where you get the most for your money. Visit www.oanda.com, a website run by the foreign exchange firm of Olsen and Associates. You'll get daily quotes of the dollar comparisons against 164 currencies. They even give you credit card and other rates in case you plan to charge your down payment! In addition, knowing the daily exchange rates will help you choose the exact transaction date of your closing to get the best exchange rate.

- *Check out the cost of living in the local economy. The Economist* measures cost of living by the price of a Big Mac and other everyday expenditures. Check out their website at www.economist.com.

The Silver Hair Program

This is a profile of an Asian second home program, the Silver Hair Program of Malaysia, tailored for those with joint income of at least 10,000 RM ($2,630 per month) or individual income of 7,000 RM ($1,061), and are willing to deposit 150,000 RM ($40,000) in a Malaysian bank. Those that qualify can buy two houses and borrow up to 60 percent from local banks. To get full details check out www.mocat.gov.my. What's the temptation? Beaches, great climate, good food, and low cost of living.

- *Look for advertisements in the local newspapers for areas under consideration, and pay attention to travel costs to and from the area to your U.S. home.* If you plan to relocate permanently, decide how often you plan to travel to see kids or for pleasure. If it's a lot, skip remote places like Rhodes, the Azures, and the Hebrides, even though the locations are dreamy.

Selecting a Realtor That Focuses on the Area

Realistically, you won't be buying from the homeowner, unless you have a lot of time to actually look around in the area. The big breakthrough is the Web. But, even veteran Web users should be aware that it will take about three hours per country to search out the sites that are useful. There are lots of listings and dead ends that force you to call directly or bring you back to an American middleman. My trick is to do a United Kingdom search, no matter where in Europe I want to look. The sites are in English and the realtors usually offer housing in other countries. Once you have located the realtor, they will begin to send you setups on the type of property you request. A day on the Web will bring you face to face with at least 50 potential buys, with photos! If you are not Web savvy, I urge you enlist the help of the neighbor's kid, even if you have to pay for it.

Subscribe to the Local Paper

Before you buy, even if prices are rising, subscribe to local papers for at least three months. Reading the local paper will reveal the true concerns of the area, it's culture, it's crime and it's personality.

Know the Legal Aspects of Ownership

Every country has rules regarding foreign ownership, and it differs if you plan to be a resident, a part-time resident, or if you are going to apply for dual citizenship. In any case, the consulate of every country will tell you whether you need more than just money to buy property. While U.S.–style *fee simple* ownership is still the most prevalent, you may inadvertently be buying a leasehold that expires after 120 years rather than a free hold. To protect yourself, you must hire a lawyer in the area in which you plan to buy. I add $3,000 to the budget to cover research, attorney's fees, and other costs.

Getting Financing

Of course, you can always refinance a U.S. property and pay cash for your foreign purchase. But, if you plan to leverage that property, there is a wide variety of foreign mortgages. Three examples are *repayment, interest only*, and *flexible*. Repayment is like our traditional fixed-rate mortgage. Interest only is like our balloon mortgage, where the principle is paid up at the end of the term in a lump sum. A flexible mortgage is unfamiliar to us. Here, the interest rate is calculated *every day*. Overpayment reduces the interest charges at the beginning of the following month. You can also make deliberate overpayment to pay off the mortgage faster. There are also teaser rates, negative amortization, and variable-rate mortgages, all like our own. Watch for PMI (required mortgage insurance) and early redemption charges. In addition to application and appraisal fees, the United Kingdom, for example, has a stamp tax (hey, didn't we have an argument over that a while ago?). It's payable on purchases of £60,000 or more at the rate of 1 percent of the *total* price. Then the stamp duty increases to 3 percent for homes from £250,001 to £500,000 and to 4 percent after that. Revolutionary!

If you don't plan to use the new home immediately, you can rent it out through local realtors, or contact *The Caretaker Gazette* (www.caretaker.org), to find a free caretaker who may also do repairs and much more (i.e., animal husbandry). I plan to do this and be clear that I will also be using the premises during certain times of the year. *The Caretaker Gazette* is a responsible matchmaker bringing homeowners and caretakers together.

If you decide on most European destinations, you must qualify for permanent residence by showing a base income and be self-supporting. You will receive your Social Security, but you will not be Medicare eligible.

In buying a home abroad, heed caveats regarding financing and form of ownership. By and large, the only financing you can get is from a foreign bank, and they may require more than the property as collateral. And in some countries, notably England, you may not get fee simple, or full ownership, only a 99-year lease. A solicitor or no-

---

Everlasting Wealth

Long-Term Care Abroad   I have encountered many clients interested in portable long-term healthcare insurance. Companies differ with regard to these features and new benefits are added as the demand for portability gets stronger. New York Life will give you 100 times your daily benefit to spend during a stay abroad, and after that you must be in the United States to use any remaining benefit. The Hartford will extend you 75 percent of your benefits for four years, after which you must be back home.

---

taire will sort out and explain this form of ownership. Foreign real estate brokers with offices in the United States do a good job of explanation as well. Meanwhile, you can see thousands of properties on the Internet in any country you choose. For example, if you are seeking solace on the Riviera, visit www.vefuk.com, www.green-acre.com, or www.abodesabroad.net, which is based in Brooklyn, New York.

The Real Estate IRA can also hold foreign property, as you will see as you read on.

Finding Your Own Personal Tax Haven

One driving force behind your retirement relocation decision should be taxes. The wrong choice can eat up a whopping 40 percent of your cash flow especially with property, income, excise, gasoline, fuel, sales, and luxury taxes. Not to mention the estate tax and probate costs that form a merger between death and taxes.

Don't make the mistake of judging states (or foreign countries) by income tax alone. Some states with low sales taxes, for example, will have higher income or property taxes and vice versa. Striking a balance is necessary. For example, one of the least taxing states is New Hampshire. It has no sales tax whatsoever and the second lowest income tax of those states that have an income tax (only about $18 on every $10,000 in income). What's more, it does not tax retirement income. Many believe that New Hampshire has no income or

Everlasting Wealth

The Concept of Domicile The key to your tax picture is your *domicile*, or your intended permanent residence. It means more than just living there. You can have many residences, but only one domicile. Domicile is determined by the nexus between the elements of your life and a particular venue." It's practical and includes where you vote, register your car, keep your investments, establish bank accounts, send your kids to school, file your taxes, spend most of your time, affiliate with clubs and religious institutions, and even how you buy things on the Web or subscribe to e-mail. The government or courts can challenge what you call your choice of domicile. They look at the facts. Of course, it all starts out with you. You select where you intend to make your main home. Only if a taxing entity disagrees will you have to pull out the nexus card and prove you are right.

sales tax at all. In fact, it does tax food, and while there is no income tax on W-2 reported earnings or pensions distributions, you will be taxed on dividend income and certain other investment income. And it imposes a comparatively large property tax. This alone brought Concord, New Hampshire in as number 47th in a field of 50 state capitals in *Kiplinger's* survey, *Which States Give Retirees The Best Deal?* (www.moneycentral.com) in April of 2003. But, compared to its bordering neighbors, Maine and Massachusetts, and its almost bordering neighbors, Rhode Island, Connecticut, and New York, New Hampshire is truly the tax haven next door. You can move there, shop there, and educate your children there, or semiretire there on tax-exempt earned income.

Take the reverse case of Pennsylvania, which does have a high income tax. It, however, exempts Social Security benefits and withdrawals from public and private pensions. But, because of high property taxes, it comes in last in the nationwide survey. Florida, Washington, and Texas rank in the middle of the *Kiplinger* chart as tax favorites. (The survey makes its calculations and conclusions based on a hypothetical couple spending $20,000 a year on taxable items, living in the median priced home, and covers only state capitals.)

The advice must be tailored for you. For example, in 12 states a car tax tanked their score. (Something you won't care about if you plan to live in a big city and rent a car only once in awhile). New York City did well tax-wise, so long as property taxes aren't in your life.

If you've always thought Alaska was a tax haven, you might be right, or wrong, depending on who you are. Alaska imposes a severance tax on companies for taking raw materials, principally oil, from the land. This gives it enough revenue to dispense with a sales tax or income tax, and every year each man, woman, and child receives a check for their share of the excess of the severance tax over the state's expenses. Last year, that amounted to about $2,500 per person. But the housing costs and property taxes are high. Still, they pay you to live there.

Florida is just the opposite. They pay you to die there. . . . or almost. Florida has no estate tax. That is, they do not impose a tax on your assets when you die. You still have to pay the federal estate tax. There is no income tax in Florida, either, but there is a hefty sales tax, and a tax on intangible assets like stocks, bonds, and mutual funds, at a rate of $1.00 per $1,000 of value for people with the value of intangible assets in excess of $20,000. Annuities, insurance, and qualified retirement assets and IRAs are exempt. All things considered, *Kiplinger's* favorite tax venue was Dover, Delaware.

Tax Checklist

When comparing locations, use this checklist of taxes:

_____ Property tax per $1,000

_____ Excise tax

_____ Food and transient occupancy tax (TOT; when friends and family come to visit and stay in a hotel)

_____ Luxury tax

_____ Income tax per $1,000 yearly income

_____ Sales tax

_____ Car, gasoline, cigarette, or other special taxes

_____ Tax on assets (intangible tax)

Prioritize these from one to eight and see where your tax haven lies.

Busy, Busy, Busy, and the Envy of All Your Friends

After you have selected the state or general area that strikes your fancy, you'll want to choose between a development or an established neighborhood. If the number one amenity is friendship, it's not enough to focus on the grade of carpeting or shape of the pool or even the size of the house to make your decision. But that's what most people do. The material things can be pretty exciting, like any new toy. The more important factor is, who are the people? They will be your friends for many decades. Developers are now creating themed Active Adult Communities (AACs) on the premise that those with similar interests will bond best with each other. Do not confuse these with assisted living communities. These are nonhealthcare related, often gated developments, where residents must be age 55 plus to buy. They are built along the tastes for golf, fishing, and soft adventure like hiking and rafting. Exotic themes range from farming and ranching to perpetual cruise boat traveling. Although AACs are offered in all cost brackets, those with first-class amenities charge first-class prices. Here is where Harold (remember him from the beginning of the book?) finally can become a cowboy (not a joke, take a look at a Maryland AAC located outside of Bethesda), as developers go beyond pools and golf courses to help us travel on our condo boat or live in a university as perpetual students. The new Active Adult Communities are virtual realities made of bricks and mortar, where computer games come to life. It's like Sims in retirement.

Before you make a permanent move meet some people. *Really* meet them. Eat in the restaurants, go to the religious institution, even if you are not religious. Join a club like the Rotary long distance and get the newsletters for awhile. If it works out for you, rent. And be sure that lack of age diversity is what you want before you buy.

Chapter TEN

Affordable Lifestyle Dreams for Sale

Many people want a little of everything. They would like to escape to their vacation paradise, but still live at home, or in a smaller version of their family home. To accommodate them, new forms of ownership like timeshare, seasonal share, and live/rent packages are offered to allow an upscale, dual lifestyle on a limited budget. You may not have the time or money to ski all year long, but you may be able to own a week in Aspen or buy and then rent out a condo at Tremblant, Canada, using it for one month per year for yourself.

As I write this chapter, I am staying at Gurney's Inn at Montauk, New York, where I have owned three weeks of timeshare for the past 25 years. As a young attorney, I participated in converting Gurneys into one of the first timeshares in America. Since then, I have bought two others in Snowbird, Utah, and watched the industry change from a strategy to sell real estate in a down market, to a worldwide community of traveling friends using timeshare as a convenient method of fulfilling their travel dreams. From that core has developed numerous new permutations catering to the longevity market. One or more of them may be just right for you.

Timeshare—The Original

Timeshare is not an investment; it is a luxury item that can defray the costs of travel. More important, it eases you into a community of travelers who have emotional and financial attachment to their resort, eat in their own kitchen facilities, take cruises together, and share experiences. Go almost anywhere in the world and you have instant friends. Most every timeshare welcomes you with special activities where you can meet fellow guests. As we age, we like to belong. Timeshare breeds familiarity.

Timeshares are properties divided into units, usually a room, kitchenette, bath, bedroom(s), and closet space. Each unit can be sold 52 times, a week at a time. Marketing teams move into a new facility and sell on site. In its infancy, timeshare was pitched as a real estate investment—instead of buying a country or beach house, buy the right to live in a resort for one week a year. And some were only leases, which expired after a few decades. Others, like mine, are a form of condo ownership that can be bequeathed to children or sold. But, don't look at timeshare as real estate. It has neither the tax deductions, the leverage, the depreciation, nor the secondary market of true real estate. Mortgages and financing are available, but at higher interest rates than conventional mortgages, although recently the IRS has permitted interest rate deductions. What timeshare does offer is terrific flexibility and a great network of venues, cruises, and airlines discounts that keep you traveling.

Resorts Condominium International (RCI), a telephone and an online swapping service, permits you to exchange your week for another at one of the thousands of properties that participate in their program. RCI contracts with over 3,000 resorts in 90 countries. Although it is not the only timeshare vacation exchange, seven of 10 resorts are affiliated with it. Resorts are divided into Gold Crown and Resorts of International Distinction. I find these designations helpful. The former denotes the more upscale, full-service properties, the latter are resorts with many owner testimonials.

There is a fee for membership plus an exchange fee that ranges from $139 up every time you exchange. This is in addition to the yearly maintenance fee you will pay at your home resort. You should receive a useful magazine and catalogue describing each resort with a picture and a website to visit. Through the years, I have indulged my passion for travel through exchanging weeks for resorts in Malta, St. Martin, England, and many more. Depending on the value of your swap, which depends on the quality of the establishment, time of year, and size of the unit you own, you will have greater or lesser luck in getting the exchange you want.

In budgeting for a timeshare, remember that yearly maintenance fees can be raised, and improvements may result in an assessment. The managing company and the financials of the property must be reviewed prior to purchase.

Recently, timeshares have expanded in several ways. Companies like Marriott and Disney have branded their own resorts and offered internal exchanges. Now, timeshares can be exchanged for points toward cruises, airlines, and much more. For details on all of this look at: www.rci.com, www.century21-timeshare.com, www.timeshares quicksale.com, www.timeshare-realty.com, and www.timeshares-time shares.com for constant offerings.

Seasonal Share—A New Twist on Timeshare

In response to our growing retirement market, timeshare has evolved into *seasonal share*. In a seasonal share, like the timeshare, purchases are by the week. Here, though, you are buying three or more weeks in both high and low seasons. The weeks you buy are not consecutive. They are scattered throughout the year euphemistically called *flexible*. Every year you must work out the schedule you want. You may not necessarily get the exchanges in a single period or in the same unit.

An interesting foreign permutation, not yet offered in the United States is the Isle of Mann Holiday Project Bond, marketed by my colleague, Colin Bowen. In this arrangement, you own points to be applied to vacationing at various facilities throughout Europe (high-end proper-

---

Everlasting Wealth

Timeshare Auction Sales   You can buy timeshares at auction. Websites like e-Bay and newspaper ads lead you to bargains from owners or their heirs. If you have no allegiance to any given resort, one low-cost strategy is to buy at the cheapest possible price and the lowest maintenance price, so long as the property has good financials and a good management history. Then you can deposit your weeks and swap through RCI or another service. I know owners who have never visited the timeshare they actually own.

ties like castles and villas). The properties are held in trust for the benefit of policyholders. Your cost also pays the premium on an insurance policy. At your death, your heirs can continue ownership or the insurance death benefit kicks in and gives your heirs the premiums you paid, plus 10 percent. Of course, you have still paid your yearly maintenance fees.

Housing Clubs for the Equity Averse

The latest permutation on housing is a high-end luxury concept that I call the *housing country club*. For a once in a lifetime membership fee, and yearly dues, you have use of a suite in a variety of high-end properties and occupancy of high-end homes, usually for at least two weeks during the year. But there is no equity participation whatsoever. The draw is the exclusivity of membership, often limited to 500 members, and the quality of the amenities. You'll soon see many ads for this type of offering if they take off as packagers hope. If it looks good to you and you can afford it, just be aware that this is not real estate, nor does it come under the tax laws that permit timeshare financing to be tax deductible, or the real estate to be bought in an IRA. If the concept does catch on, I see it more like the popular private jet sharing. It's for the upscale individual who doesn't want to foot the entire bill for a sometime luxury, or the corporation looking for some executive perks.

Fractional Ownership—A Buy and Rent Plan

For those who insist on controlling which weeks they enjoy their vacation home, want to decorate them to their taste, and perhaps live there full time, the *buy and rent plan*, sometimes called the *fractional share*, has proven popular.

In this category of luxury living for less comes a true real estate purchase with a twist. You buy and immediately rent out the unit through onsite or affiliated managers. The rental income helps (but hardly ever totally) to defray the cost of mortgage and maintenance. The buy and rent plan, if you get in at a young enough age, may provide a free and clear second home by the time you retire. Present retirees may use it to downscale by using the equity in their home to purchase a smaller primary residence, and also a vacation condo that they subsidize through rental.

Many fractional share developments offer another element of timeshare, the exchange. For example, Intrawest a world-class ski property developer offers exchanges within their resorts to condo owners. I recently received an invitation from HSBC Bank to come and "discover the investment benefits and personal pleasure of owning a property in Tremblant." I know that if you buy in Tremblant, Canada, you can exchange for Whistler and many others, including European facilities.

You'll find fractional share developments proliferating everywhere the surfs up or the snow falls. Developers build these upscale facilities with common elements like swimming pools, ski schools, and spas. The properties may be apartments, townhouses, or free standers.

Be aware that there is no guarantee that you will get a renter, and for the most part you cannot count on the rental income to defray more than 20 to 50 percent of the carrying charges, especially if you have a high mortgage. Most rental companies take 25 percent to 50 percent of the rental income plus a monthly management fee. To make you less competitive with your neighbors, some facilities pool the rent roll and distribute it pro rata. Even if your individual unit does not rent that season, you'll get your share. Most of the projects are so new that they don't have an extensive track record of doing this, and those were in the bull market days of the late 1990s. It remains to be seen how these projects fair as they proliferate. My advice to to buy in top locations and only if you can carry the mortgage even when the unit is not rented.

Buying a Vacation Home and Renting to Others

A competitor to the fractional development is the second home plus outside rental agent. If you have fallen in love with an area, you can simply buy a property and contract with a management/rental company.

International Home Exchanges and House Sitting

Even if you never buy a vacation or second home, you can participate in a world of free adventure on a true shoestring. No mortgages, maintenance fees, or obligations. All you need is a home to swap or exchange and membership in any of the following:

www.exchangehome.com
www.ihen.com

www.gti-home-exchange.com

www.homeexchange.com

www.4homex.com

And before you take any action, make sure your insurance covers any damage that may result from nonresidents living in your house.

If you have no property to swap, you can still live in Australia on a sheep farm, or in New Hampshire at a mountain mansion for months or even years at a time, free. How? Take a caretaker's adventure. Publisher Gary Dunn of *The Caretaker's Gazette* has frequently been a guest on my radio show and is cited in my *Wealthbuilder* newsletter. In 2002, he was featured in *Reader's Digest* as part of their article on living well on less. The *Gazette* is like a matchmaker for homes and their caretakers. Both the owners and the caretakers are vetted for

---

Everlasting Wealth

When renting out property that you own in resort areas, here are some tips to increase your income and lessen vacancy rates:

- Decorate for the masses with contract designers. They use narrower couch widths and indestructible materials.
- Consider universal design. Put the grab bars in now and avoid the rush.
- Be a smart marketer. Even if the facility has an onsite marketing agent, check them out.
- Use flyers and send e-mails to those in your clubs, take ads in golf or fishing magazines, such as *Sunset* and *Southern Living* among other lifestyle magazines to offer exchanges.
- See a management/rental company before you bid on a property. They can usually give you a good idea of what you might derive as rental income.

Independent rental managers have a trade association and a website where you can easily compare properties nationwide. The president runs several properties in Tahoe, and emphasizes the lifelong relationships that he cultivates with renters and owners alike. Check out Lake Tahoe Accommodations at www.tahoeaccommodations.com.

safety and experience. Some recent postings are an Arizona horse ranch, a Massachusetts cheese farm, and a Georgia mountain estate.

House Sharing

If ownership is appealing to you but you cannot afford sole owner-ship, form a buying group. You can do so with some basic legal work. The expenses are low, the concept is simple, and the buying power potential is enormous. Plus, your most important feature, the amenity of friendship, is built in. An S Corporation or a limited liabil-ity corporation, which protects you against legal responsibility for the wrongdoing of your co-owners, is a good choice. The by-laws and stockholders' agreement must be specific as to who pays what, who owns what, and when each gets to use the property. It's a simple way to buy for a small group. It also permits for beneficiaries and inheri-tance rights within each owner's family.

When the property and the number of people involved get larger, a limited partnership is the way to go. For years, I have ad-dressed the concept of the family limited partnerships as a planning tool. This is the same, only among friends. One person or a few of you choose to act as general partners to run the property, hire caretak-ers, manage bank accounts, pay taxes, and collect maintenance. The limited partners own the real estate in their proportionate share; they are protected from liability and only the property can be attached if there is a lawsuit that occurs because of the ownership. Inheritance rights, rights of first refusal, and terms of eventual sale and profit splitting are addressed in the partnership agreement as they are in a shareholder's agreement.

Your group can create a written contract as to who uses the prop-erty and for how long, alternating high season and even renting the property and sharing the proceeds in the times when no owners want to stay.

Why Not Rent?

Reminiscence: I'm sitting at a table in the glitzy (now closed) Russian Tea Room looking at a gigantic bear centerpiece made of ice. My din-ner companion is one of the wealthiest men I know and an interna-tional lifestyle king. At age 80, he lives alternatively in Caracas, Europe, Eastern Europe, and Asia. His money never gets used up no matter how much he spends, and he always has time to travel. "Give us your secret," I say. I am as breathless as a teenager with a rock star. His words of wisdom were simple, "Don't own a home. Rent."

I blanched. Decorating is my passion. How could I endure the ordeal of buying curtains for someone else's property? "Get over it," he said. "After a certain age owning makes no sense," he explained. "Costs are uncontrolled. If rent goes up you can always move. It keeps you young. If your spirit moves you, you can always leave. Besides, the biggest problem I find is that my friends move, or die. Many people are so tied to their home ownership that they stay just for the house, when really their life has moved on."

"But what about real estate as a great investment, equity building, the American way?" I whined. "Don't get me wrong," he replied. "I own a lot of real estate. More than most of my friends, but I rent to others, pay my rent with the proceeds, take a depreciation, and I'm on my way."

The idea of owning solely rental real estate is not original and is espoused by many real estate experts. Colleague Robert Kiyosaki, of *Rich Dad Poor Dad*[1] fame, and I often speak at the New York Financial Expo. (He's the handsome one with the crowds around him, and the stunning wife in the baseball cap.) Robert asserts that the greatest barrier to everlasting wealth through property ownership is attitude.

Frankly, it took me a long time to come around to the idea of "rent not own," as a longevity play. My first mistake was passing up a brownstone on Manhattan's Perry Street because it had a tenant. It could have paid my mortgage, and with a value appreciation of $117,000 in 1972 and $4 million in 2003, that's a heartbreaking regret. The second mistake was my husband's aversion to being a landlord. "Too much work," he said. So we sold our loft on Union Square, instead of renting it for a whopping $72,000 a year! But don't despair if you have been blind to landlordism.

Downscaling is a great time to consider renting. You're giving up your fortress anyway; you have cash to invest in rental real estate. At least consider putting your equity into rent roll, instead of living in your bank. If the voice in your head is starting to chatter, it is probably saying: "Won't my high rents eat up my profit?" Not if you are willing to accept that cash flow makes you richer than trophy home ownership. Choose a rental for yourself well under the rent roll you get as a landlord. Many people rent small apartments in the same building in which they own big apartments.

Everlasting Wealth

Landlord and Tenant Questions & Answers

Won't I hate being a landlord? Maybe. If so, underestimate your rent roll by 10 percent and pay that to a property manager. Hook up with one through local brokers and be sure of the usual fee, before you buy.

Isn't rent taxable income? You bet. But depreciation helps save taxes as do mortgage interest and land tax deductions.

Why should I have a mortgage on rental property when I have a mortgage-free home? Leverage is what makes money. Everyone thinks that Willy Loman in "Death of a Salesmen" killed himself because he was washed up. Not true. Read the end of the play. You'll discover he had just paid off his home mortgage. Truly he must have realized that he no longer had leverage and couldn't take the thought.

Renting is also catching on in senior housing. Retirement development consultants, like Howard and Associates, warn builders to poll the neighborhood before they build. At the International Builder's Show, this year they asserted, "Some want the freedom and the money obtained by renting, while others see ownership as the American Dream." When seniors do rent, they spend 40 percent to 60 percent of their income monthly. That's because the services they get with the rental units include trips, security, meals, and housekeeping.

Chapter ELEVEN

The Real Estate IRA

How to Buy Real Estate Now, and Avoid the Baby Boom Rush

O f all the articles I've had published on the Web, the one that gets the most e-mail response explains how you can buy real estate with IRA assets. Many people have real estate dreams, but their money is tied up in their retirement plan. They have no wiggle room to jump on a good deal when they see one. Others would like to buy their retirement home or buy one to rent for income before the baby boomers rush in and inflate the prices. They think they must wait until they reach age 59$^{1}/_{2}$ to access their IRA.

But that's not so. A little-known section of the Internal Revenue Code allows us all, at any age, to purchase real estate in our IRA, so long as we do not currently use it for a linear family member, our own business, or ourselves. What's more, the realty can be located in any country or any state. It gives you a considerable edge if you have cash available in your IRA, or assets that can be rolled over into an IRA from a 401(k) or 403(b) plan.

The Real Estate IRA

The Real Estate IRA also permits you to receive rental income, defer the tax, and reinvest the income, tax deferred, or tax free, if you use a Roth IRA.

What Type of Real Estate Can You Buy in Your IRA?

The Internal Revenue Code approves the following types of real estate for IRA ownership:

Raw land

Condos

Office buildings

Single-family homes

Multifamily homes

Apartment buildings

Improved land

Timeshare in condo form

Co-ops

Townhouses

Note: For all of these type of real estate holdings, your IRA must purchase the property itself. An option to buy real estate is not approved.

The Real Estate IRA that I review here offers you a method of owning hands-on real estate, second homes, retirement homes, and rental residential or commercial real estate, in your IRA so long as you do not *currently* (while it is owned in the IRA) use the property for yourself.

How Do You Buy the Property?

The key to the Real Estate IRA is the custodian. A bank, and there are a growing number of them now getting into this business, acts as the custodian of your IRA, just as your brokerage house or bank does now. The custodian is your fiduciary in signing the deeds, getting appraisals, and listing it when and if you sell. You find the property. You give them your instructions. The custodian for the IRA signs all papers. The ownership is in the name of your IRA. When you sell, any profits are paid to the IRA. If you eventually chose, after age 59$^1/_2$ to use the property yourself, it becomes an IRA distribution to you and the custodian changes the deed to your name.

All expenditures including repair, maintenance, gardening,

property taxes, management and custodian fees must be paid from IRA assets. If there are rents, tenants make out checks to the custodian, in the name of the IRA.

What Does the Real Estate IRA Cost?

First, you will encounter a set-up fee, usually a few hundred dollars. After that there are two types of yearly custodian fees. Some charge a yearly percentage of the amount of your IRA, from 40 to 150 basis points. Others have an à la cart menu for each service they perform. Some will also hold and manage your other assets, like mutual funds, stocks, and Real Estate Investment Trusts (REITs). There are experts to help you select your custodian here and abroad. Yes, the Internal Revenue Code allows you to choose a custodian abroad especially if you plan to buy foreign real estate.

How Do You Carry and Maintain the Property?

Once the IRA owns the property, it pays the land tax, insurance, and maintenance costs. The rent it collects can be used to cover these costs, as can your yearly addition to the IRA, up to the legal limit. Your custodian distributes the sum to you if you have a company that acts as your own real estate manager, or to the management company you have selected. So, you must plan for enough income from your IRA earnings, rental income, or yearly contribution to meet the expenses of the property.

Prohibited Transactions

The policy of the Internal Revenue Code is to prohibit any transaction that might put your IRA in jeopardy. The government wants your money to be there when you retire. For this reason, there are two areas that are restricted, with regard to the real estate IRA: your personal use of the property while currently in the IRA, and the mortgage that an IRA can take. First, you cannot engage in self-dealing. The term *self dealing* means you cannot lend money, extend credit, and furnish goods, services, or facilities from your IRA to yourself or a disqualified individual. IRS publication 590 defines a prohibited transaction as "any improper use of your account" by "you or any disqualified person."

You cannot, I repeat, cannot, use the real estate to live in now! Nor, can you fool the IRS by buying from a relative or a corporation over which you have control, or renting it to them. That includes:

1. Linear descendants—children, spouse, the spouse of your descendant, and parents or grandparents (but not siblings)
2. A corporation, limited liability corporation, or partnership if you or a linear descendant or other disqualified person is an owner, directly or indirectly of 50 percent or greater of:
   - the capital interest of a partnership
   - the total value of all shares of stock of a corporation including all classes
   - the combined voting power of all classes eligible to vote
3. Your fiduciary—you are a fiduciary with regard to your IRA.
4. A 10 percent owner, officer, director, or highly compensated employee of an entity that would be disqualified.

With these restrictions, it may look like the real estate IRA would be useless in buying an eventual retirement home. But it's not. The key word is *currently*. Let's assume you have found your dream retirement home or the piece of property or the land on which you would like to build it. But you are not yet ready to move in. You can purchase the property in the IRA and eventually distribute it out when you want to use the property penalty free, after age 59$\frac{1}{2}$ Of course, you could sell the property outright at anytime. If you are over age 59$\frac{1}{2}$, you can distribute the cash as you would with any other investment.

How Exactly Do You Get the Property out of the IRA So You Can Use It Yourself?

When you distribute the property out of your IRA, you must get an accurate appraisal. That will be the basis of the income tax you must pay at distribution. The major drawback of IRA real estate ownership is that the ordinary income tax, not capital gains, is applied to the profit. That's why the best plan is to buy in a Roth IRA, if you are eligible. In that case, no tax is ever paid so long as the property stays in the Roth for at least five years after purchase.

When you reach April 1st after you have reached age 70$\frac{1}{2}$, you must make distributions from your IRA, no matter what your holdings are. This is the required minimum distribution (RMD), which the government mandates. If the property is in a Roth, the RMD will be tax free, but if the property is in a traditional IRA, you may be hit with a whopping tax bill just as you are ready to retire.

A better way to distribute the real estate is through shares in the property. To do this, form a corporation to own the real estate so that your IRA holds shares in the corporation that can be distributed to you a few at a time until you are the 100 percent owner. Each distribution requires an appraisal of the value of the shares. For example, let's say your corporation issues 200 shares, owned by the IRA. Starting at age $59\frac{1}{2}$, 10 percent or 20 shares are distributed to you. The property is worth $100,000 at the time. In that case, you pay tax on $10,000. If the value changes up or down next year, an appraisal will set the basis of that year's tax. With the Roth Real Estate IRA there is never any tax to pay.

Can Your IRA Take a Mortgage on the Property?

Yes and no. The *strict* rule is that the IRA can only take a *nonrecourse* loan. That means the lender can only have recourse to the property and no other assets if there is a default. Neither you nor a disqualified person or entity can guarantee the loan. Unless you get top professional advice, I suggest you pay all cash as the consequences of taking a mortgage and disobeying this strict rule can bust your IRA, and result in immediate tax consequences. You'll need a cooperative lender and a property that appraises well and constitutes strong collateral, against the amount you borrow. However, as the Real Estate IRA becomes more popular, developers are beginning to finance their own

---

Everlasting Wealth

Limited Liability Plan The limited liability corporation (LLC) is often used to prevent major loss in the event of a lawsuit regarding real estate ownership. Your IRA can own the shares of an LLC that owns the real estate, rather than the real estate or shares of an S corporation.

sales through nonrecourse loans. Many custodians now allow you to finance at least 50% of the property.

Traditional mortgages are disallowed because a default would leave you or other IRA assets vulnerable. The lender must be an arm's length entity—not you, a linear family member (siblings are acceptable), or an entity like a corporation in which you are a 50 percent or greater owner. You may not personally sign for the loan.

The tax downside is that there is no depreciation, land tax deduction, or business expense deduction. And if you take a loan to purchase the property, there is another tax downside. Leveraging can result in taxes on some of the income that must be paid by the IRA. These taxes are often higher than on income from property you finance on your own. So, you need enough liquidity, perhaps in a money market fund in your IRA, to pay off the debt. IRS Form 990T gives you instructions.[1]

Ed Slott is a colleague who has been a guest on my radio show and on my *Money Talks* television show many times. We agree on most things, but not on the importance of the Real Estate IRA. Ed is a powerful voice in IRA education, and he does not like the Real Estate IRA. He is concerned about the lack of stepped up in basis for heirs, and capital gains treatment for you. Nor does he like the idea that real estate can become a money pit, and you could need money that the IRA simply does not generate to maintain the property.

Here is where I differ; I have encountered many middle-class people of all ages that have amassed upwards of $200,000 in their IRA, and not much else in ready cash. They see a golden opportunity to buy raw land, or an underpriced property, and they just can't. They could if they understood the Real Estate IRA. Real estate profits are made largely when you buy, not when you sell. If we can't buy at the right time, we overpay. It's happening right now all around us. Interesting places are being developed and sold at low prices for the time being. Take a look at www.pocketrealestate.com for real estate eye candy under $75,000. Many of us would have much more freedom and flexibility if we could buy our downscaler early, rent it out for tax-deferred income, and then distribute it out after age $59^{1}/_{2}$.

Integrating the Real Estate IRA with the New Amenity

You and your friends, your family or your spouse, can join together to buy a single piece of property or raw land through several different

---

Everlasting Wealth

Some Custodians Will Now Allow You to Act as Your Own Property Manager You may collect a reasonable fee for this service from your retirement plan. You will receive a 1099 at the end of the year for these fees. Any income from the property must be returned to the retirement plan as a profit of the plan, less any expenses incurred. The plan assets may pay administrative and recordkeeping expenses as well. Conversely, you may hire an outside property manager to perform this service, provided they do not fall under the disqualified person(s) definition.

IRAs. If you come across a wonderful buy and have several friends with the same lifestyle dream as you, why not noodle together how you can create a buying group? If one or all of you do not have ready cash, the property can be bought in an LLC and each can pay for their share with IRA assets, if they choose. The deed names both individual owners and IRAs.

Chapter TWELVE

The Link between
Housing and Healthcare

Blurring of the permanent residence and the long-term health-care facility is the real estate hallmark of longevity. There is a dizzying array of housing geared to keep us independent as long as possible and allow us to access just the correct level of care we need. Continuing care communities, assisted living developments, nursing homes, and adult homes meld in our minds as to which is which. Architecture, decorating, healthcare, and safety mesh to make our homes also our healthcare centers.

With all this choice, it is no wonder that only 5 percent of those over age 76 live in nursing homes, a figure that has been declining since 1982. But even for those living at home, the line between personal residence and healthcare facility has blurred. Pity the poor real estate developer who can't decide whether to put a ramp or a hot tub in his latest project.

There are, at last count, five types of longevity housing, and variations thereof. So-called only because of certain government created distinctions for licensing. No one choice is right for everyone. Where you land depends on:

- availability
- familiarity

- referral
- taste
- temperament
- money

Five Types of Longevity Housing

When you or your family consider the possibility of continuing care or assisted living, legal and financial issues often take a back seat to the emotional and family matters at hand. That's why it behooves you to understand the legal ramifications of this new kind of advanced life housing, well before you are in the thick of decision making. In doing so, you get a better understanding of which might be the correct alternative for yourself and those you love. The watchword of the new longevity is *choice*. Continuing care and assisted living gives you the freedom to choose the level of extra help you need to live the life you want. The five types of continuing care housing are:

1. *Active adult communities*—These may be high- or low-end recreation-oriented retirement developments. They require residents to be over the age of 55 and do not allow children.

2. *Adult homes*—These are independent living apartments in a group home setting. They are often unregulated and are not a combination of healthcare and housing, but one of mild supervision, joint meals, and activities.

3. *Continuing care facilities*—These are developments where varying levels of healthcare can be delivered. You may begin with independent living in a single-family home or condo. But as greater assistance is needed, you'll get escalating levels of care. And with this comes more complexity in the form of care contracts. Continuing care communities generally offer several types of contracts:

Extensive contract: monthly costs are higher than for others, but they remain steady even if you eventually need as much as 24-hour assistance

Modified contract: monthly costs increase according to level of care

Fee for service: monthly fees are generally the lowest, but there are à la carte charges for many services. While state regulations differ, choose a facility that is accredited by the Continuing Care Accreditation Commission.

4. *Assisted living facilities*—These offer different levels of care, but you usually enter already in need of some assistance. If you are in a continuing care facility, *assisted living* means an area within a health center where residents are provided with a coordinative array of supportive personal and health services, available 24 hours a day. Assisted living includes long-term care services. From The Annual Disclosure Statement 2003 of Winchester Gardens, Maplewood, New Jersey (an assisted living community).

5. *Nursing homes*—These provide 24 hours of care for those in such need. The care may be either skilled care provided by a registered nurse or intermediate care provided by a practical nurse.

Home, Health, and Companionship

There is a clear nexus between your housing and your health. Not long ago, the choices for those over age 80 were threefold, age in place if you could manage it, stay with the family, or go into a nursing home. Developers saw the mega trend of longevity coming and sought to partner with the healthcare industry to create continuing care and assisted living communities, to allow for maximum independence and flexibility. But they underestimated the health and independence that we would enjoy.

Despite the aging trend (by 2020 those over 85 will double in number), there are vacancies in the now overbuilt assisted living market. Why? One certain answer is the confusion between these facilities and nursing homes. Another is the lack of consumer understanding of ownership. Our population stays independent longer than expected.

Everlasting Wealth

Know your neighbors

Assisted living residents

62 percent have graduate degrees

77 percent have income over $45,000

20 percent moved from outside the local area

And most of us want to live among people of all ages. The rub comes when there are few people your own age in your immediate community. In that case, companionship, a major requirement of healthy aging, is missing. If companionship is your goal, here are some relevant statistics. While it isn't exactly raining men in continuing care or assisted living facilities, by contrast to nursing homes they are hunk tanks. One of every three in nursing homes is over 85 and female. Only 1 percent of those between the ages of 65 and 74 are in nursing homes. This jumps to 6 percent for those 75 to 84, or 24 percent of these over age 85. In short, residents in nursing homes are older and predominantly female. For spirit and companionship, this new type of living often makes sense against nursing home living.

Level of Care

Continuing care and assisted living communities meet the special health needs of our growing longevity. Many of those over age 65 (the minimum age for most assisted living facilities) can live independently but do seek services, like meals and laundry. The flexibility to move back and forth over many levels of care matches up with the realities of health in advanced age.

Most facilities provide a clinical staff that offers at least three levels of care. Their expertise is at the threshold of your inquiry when judging a facility. At its lowest level of assistance, you may want only housekeeping and food services. If you are independent, you may be concentrating on decor, activities, transportation, and location. But the nice gym is only part of the selling point. Know who will care for you and the extra cost if you need additional assistance.

At the mid-level of care, costs rise as do services. They usually include laundry and bed making, medication management, assistance with activities of daily living like bathing, toileting, and mobility. At the highest level of care, professionals will be expected to administer medication, assist with all personal hygiene, and supervise continuously in cases of lack of cognition, like Alzheimer's disease. Ask for a typical day plan for a fully dependent resident with and without lack of cognition, even if you presently feel healthy as a horse.

The best facilities also offer flexible Special Care services. For example, Gregory Rogerino, director of Winchester Gardens in Maplewood,

New Jersey, suggests that you inquire of the director of Health Care Services whether a facility offers a neuropsychologist, cognitive therapist, psychiatric social worker, or certified recreational therapist.

The following items might be included in the monthly fee at an assisted living facility:

- Meals (you choose the meal plan and pay accordingly)
- Residential unit (like condo prices these vary by size and location)
- Use of community rooms
- Weekly housekeeping
- Bed linen laundering
- Scheduled transportation and recreation
- Snacks
- Building maintenance
- Security
- Activity programs
- Emergency response system
- Dietary monitoring
- Monthly wellness visits
- Telephone and cable (may be individual but basic cable is usually included)
- Parking

The Assisted Living and Continuing Care Contract

Note: Your state will regulate the terms of any continuing care or assisted living contract with regard to disclosure requirements, liability, escrow, and appeal procedure. Check with a lawyer or at least have the facility director give you a copy of pertinent legislation. The remainder of this chapter highlights the terms of most assisted living facilities in most states. It is general information, so check out specific differences before you make a choice.

Ownership and Management Is a Primary Consideration

You are buying a hybrid between real estate (like a condo), a health facility, and a hotel. Management expertise is key. Management must be adept at marketing. Check out their vacancy rates. Don't be fooled by long waiting lists. Many people put their name on the list with no intention to follow through. Ask how many beds are available at any time in the past two years? Even a wonderful looking place can get dreary if business is bad. We want an assisted living community that stays fresh, filled, and vibrant. Ask:

- Who actually owns and runs the facility? What is their track record and background?
- Who sits on the board of trustees?
- Is there an affiliation with other nonprofit organizations, religious groups, or healthcare providers?
- Have the key players or organizations been sued? By residents? For what? What was the outcome?
- What is the level of debt, financial balance sheet, and funds on reserve or in escrow?
- Is there planned expansion? How will that be funded?

Entrance Fees and Monthly Charges

Assisted living facilities require both monthly payments and an entrance fee. But, when the facility is no longer needed, either through deteriorating health or death, this fee cannot be passed on to heirs. Many facilities offer several entry fee programs. For example, a 90 percent plan gives the family or resident 90 percent of the amount back upon termination. It is a legacy preserver. Another typical plan refunds

---

Everlasting Wealth

Nursing home entrants should inquire about "deficiency rating." Adam Parton, director of Summit Ridge, part of Geneses Eldercare Network, suggests that you inquire of the Alzheimer's Unit of the Department of Health and the ratings given through the State Department of Health Survey. ("Summit," he proudly states, "got a rating of *deficiency free*, which was awarded to only 8 percent of the nursing homes in New Jersey last year.)"

only 35 percent. No interest accrues on the entrance fee, and yet recent tax changes may impute interest. Still, you are better off with the 90 percent plan if the cash is there to pay the higher up-front amount. The monthly fee is dependent on the level of service and care, but also on factors such as land taxes. This fee is adjusted for tax assessments or tax base changes, just like a condo. The remainder of the monthly amount is based on the type of unit you choose in size and location.

When you sign your contract, you may be asked to pay a nonrefundable application fee of a few hundred dollars and a 10 percent deposit, which is credited to the entrance fee and refunded if you rescind (cancel) the contract within the statuary period which is, usually 30 days. There may be, however, a recision fee. Ask how much this might be and under what circumstances it is required.

Cost Adjustments

If you temporarily require a higher level of care, the contract can state that the difference in cost can be deducted from the entrance fee and adjusted upon refund. If a couple takes up residence and one leaves the double occupancy for a higher level of assisted living, the monthly charges may remain the same and the higher cost may be

Green House

This profile introduces you to a project, not a person. The Green House Project, which opened in Tupelo, Mississippi, in May of 2003, studies and assists organizations that want to open Green House living centers. These are six- to eight-room homes that make use of assisted technology and provide skilled care at a lower cost than nursing homes. The concept started in New York at the Center for Growing and Knowing and is partially funded by the Robert Wood Johnson Foundation, a leader in healthcare innovation. This is a radical approach to long-term care and a melding of environmental design with medicine and universal design. Check out the details at www.edenalt.com.

deducted from the entrance fee. If you want a different arrangement ask *before* you sign.

If one of a couple dies, the remaining person can stay on and one monthly service fee is ended. However, if any money is owed to the facility, both entrance fees are available for adjustment. After the deduction, the remainder is halved, and 90 percent or 35 percent of that half is refunded when the second member leaves. If you eat out a lot, some facilities will give you meal credits against other charges.

What If You Get Married?

Residents do marry, and if so, they may move into either of their units. There is neither entry fee adjustments, nor a shift in monthly charges. But make sure there is no penalty either.

Health Benefits and Government Entitlements

If you are entitled to government benefits that would reimburse the provider, you must apply for them. If you fail to do so, you are responsible for the costs. The provider may require you to name its representative as your attorney in fact, so it can apply for the benefits on your behalf. You must cooperate. If the provider gets recovery and you have already paid, you get a credit to your account.

If you fail to pay or are unable to pay, you can stay until your refund runs out. After that, the provider may make voluntary arrangements with your family and allow you to stay on; if not, your contract is terminated.

The point is clear. If assisted living or continuing care communities are your preference, check with your state for details on Medicaid coverage, and add the answer to the mix of factors you consider when deciding whether to purchase a long-term care insurance policy. See Chapter 18.

Insurance and Liability

There is often a surprising amount of liability that residents do not think about when they invite guests or hire outside caretakers. You are responsible for loss of property or injury to fellow residents. Therefore, most facilities require you to carry auto and homeowners insurance.

Interview: Stanley Diamond

Stanley Diamond, an attorney and pioneer developer of urban assisted living communities, reports, "The demand for assisted living facilities is extraordinary." However, in New York State and a few other states, only nonsubsidized facilities are being built. The general Medicaid provision excludes entitlements for assisted care unless in a nursing home or at home. Many states have requested and received a waiver of this "no Medicaid exclusion," but not all, nor is the waiver exactly the same for every state that applied. In New York, the assisted living facilities are unaffordable to many, since they are entirely on private pay. Further, residents must leave the facility if they cannot afford to continue payments during a long chronic illness. Stanley Diamond recalls with great distaste an incident where the Medicaid authorities lined up his residents and had each one show if they could walk. Those who could not were sent to nursing homes, even though many had been living at the facility without complication for several years.

If you are injured, providers have a "right of subrogation" through a grant of power of attorney, to sue for compensation on your behalf. The provider first gets indemnified for any costs to them, like extra services, and the remainder goes to you, or is credited to your account or increases the refund when you leave. Check the terms of the contact.

Privacy and Property

You have the right to privacy, but as with apartments, the provider can enter for your safety or to make repairs. You are in charge of your property and you usually waive your right to sue them if it is lost for some reason. However, if it is stolen because of the facility's negligence you may have a case. They will use their right of subrogation to go after the known culprit. You must approve all settlements. You can also be sued or your contract ended for a deliberate failure to disclose aberrant behavior, or misstate your condition or addiction to drugs or alcohol.

What Are Your Legal Rights to Ownership and Use?

Once you sign your agreement, the rights are a hybrid between apartment rental and condo ownership. You have an unassignable right to
live in the space. You have full use of the common spaces. You have
no term lease; leaving voluntarily, death, or breach of contract termi-
nates the agreement. You can renovate only with approval of the facility. There is no refund of your renovation costs. You cannot sublet.

Involuntary Transfers

After consultation with medical advisors and family, the facility's director of health services can direct that a change be made to another
facility. Ask about this possibility and where they are affiliated before
contracting. Although this is rare, it happens in the event of a conta-
gious disease or mental illness.

What Happens on Temporary Transfer?

In most cases, you continue to pay the usual rate plus additional medical charges, supplies, and other services required on a temporary basis. Your health insurance or Medicare may kick in. Discover the exact
practices of the facility, since it is this flexibility of care that you seek,
and temporary added care for recovery (that is, after a stroke, heart attack, or fall) is a likely need in the new longevity.

Termination by the Facility

Most states require that in the case of an involuntary termination of
the contract the resident get the chance to appeal. This appeal is usually to the president of the facility or its director. But there are procedures and legal recourse if you are dissatisfied with the result.

The Housing Challenge Think and Do List

Do you and your significant other want to move after retirement or stay put?

Are you in agreement?

If not, start having discussions now.

Where would you like to move? Discuss and both of you describe in writing your ideal location, type of housing, and community.

Envision your day. Who lives in your neighborhood? Will you be working? Will you be going to school?

Check out details on the Real Estate IRA at www.wealth102.com if you want to start buying early with IRA assets.

If you want to stay in place, will your home need modifications? How will you finance them?

Are you planning to use the home as part of your children's inheritance? Is that a reasonable goal?

Do you have friends or family who may want to co-buy with you?

Do you want several households?

Where?

Will timeshare/seasonal share fit your need and budget?

Will you need to get rid of stuff if you move? Get ideas about value from auction houses, appraisers, and house sales now, and see what you can get rid of sooner rather than later.

Does a relative need your help in finding an assisted living or continuing care facility or a nursing home?

Will you be able to get cooperation from other family members?

Begin your search for the right facility.

Make an appointment with an elder law attorney.

Part THREE

Longevity and Family

Intergenerational Living: Significant Elders, Baby Boom Children, and Boomerang Kids

Baby boomers have been given the descriptive title, the sandwich generation, seemingly squeezed between their children and their parents. I certainly feel this intergenerational responsibility. My Mom is in our home, staying with us for a few days, and I wonder if she is bored. I am concerned about her health. But my 11-year-old needs the little attention I can give her while I am pounding out my latest magazine column or improving www.wealth102.com. Help!

There is some solace in knowing that I am not alone. In 1900, a 50-year-old had a 4 percent chance of having two parents alive, by 2000, it was 27 percent, with an 80 percent chance of having one parent alive. Today, the 60-year-old has a 44 percent chance of having a living parent. The impact on us as caretakers is just being explored.

Every generation, including that of today's seniors, cope with aging parents. But three things are different. First, of course, there are the sheer numbers. There are simply more older parents than ever before. Second, intergenerational living lasts longer. In the past, Mom might stay in an extra bedroom, or a first floor den might become a hospice. In the 1980s, suburban planners began to recognize that these sojourns would not be so short lived. They began to zone for

From Woodstock to Long-Term Care

It seems fitting that Dale Bell, one of the two producers of the Academy Award–winning Woodstock documentary in 1969, should also be one of the two executive producers (with Harry Wiland) of "And Thou Shalt Honor," the PBS project on volunteer family and paid caregiving. I first met him in the offices of PBS New York for a strategy session to plan for the dissemination to the public following the airing of the show. I was sure that this chronicler of modern culture had latched onto caregiving because of his natural instincts about my generation. But I was wrong. This time it was personal. Mr. Bell was a caretaker himself, and it affected him deeply. As he shared his experience, he found so much camaraderie and lack of knowledge, that he was compelled to bring this underground and unorganized but massive group together in the best way he knew how, through television and the media.

accessory apartments, separate wings with kitchens and baths, and elder cottages, freestanding structures on single-family lots. Today we find organizations like the Network on Environments Services and Technologies (NEST) for maximizing independence, a part of the American Society on Aging, bringing technology into the lives of today's high-tech seniors. The mother next door (or in the next room) now has a life! And third, seniors are financially and physically capable of making a contribution. I do not accept that the longevity of our elders is all a baby boom burden. While they live, our parents are still our parents, and continue to fill a parental responsibility to us, their children. Home merging may help the baby boomer make ends meet. Even where the senior is not asset rich, the second income from Social Security makes them a serious contributor to the household. Or an emancipated child in his or her 20s, or even 30s may decide on a career swing, and come home to make the change financially possible. Support may come from grandma or grandpa, or aunt or uncle. The younger generation may feel alternatively nurtured by their grandparents and deprived as Mom and Dad's attention is deflected from them. The longevity family dynamic is complicated and messy, our own personal sitcom, especially if we fail to recognize the huge contribution that our significant elders can make; and not just financially, but emotionally and physically, as well.

History professor Theodore Roszak of the California State University, wrote "*The Making of a Counter Culture* (1969)[1] about the baby boom generation. In 1998, his book, *America the Wise: The Longevity Revolution and the True Wealth of Nations*,[2] makes a plea to "free wisdom." He asserts that wisdom born of life experience must be viewed as a genuine contribution to our lives and our culture. If we play our cards right, longevity will make our family closer, if also a bit more burdensome and dysfunctional.

So, if longevity does not mean empty nests and smaller houses for you, join the club. Some of us have more people come home to roost than we had in our 30s. When Mom or Dad and an emancipated child both come to live with you, you know the true meaning of the term *sandwich generation*. You may need to quit work or slow down to take care of a parent, or pay unexpectedly for the support of a child.

Whatever the configuration, the intergenerational household impacts your health, your money, and even your decorating scheme!

Chapter THIRTEEN

Whose House (and Money) Is It Anyway?

Baby boomers intend on being in charge. They see no paradox or contradiction in the fact that they want to tell their aging parents what to do, how to live, and how to spend their money. And, they fully expect no one to do that to them when they are older. Marketing consultants Knowledge Systems & Research Incorporated (KS&R) compared the receptivity to advice in decision-making patterns of baby boomers to their expectations of their significant elders. They found that boomers are independent and relatively overbearing, that they expect to take over, and they expect that their significant elder plans to rely heavily on them.

In no case did the boomers anticipate that others would completely dictate their decisions when they were in advanced age. Yet, 18 percent said that they dictate the decisions of elders. They were willing to be equal partners only in 28 percent of the cases, but expected elders to be equal partnership in 46 percent of the cases.

Depending on your discipline, you can interpret the importance of this data in many ways. I'm a lawyer and one thing cries out to me, "Get it in writing!" For everyone's sake, I urge the family to formalize family relationships to be sure everyone knows their rights and responsibilities. In some cases, this is going to require legal help. Today, more and more people have access to lawyers. The elder law attorney will help you construct the new intergenerational relation-ship when families merge or remerge under the same roof. They are also likely to have relationships with geriatric care managers, medical facilities, and healthcare workers.

In the old days when I helped found the National Academy of Elder Law Attorneys, we could not have guessed the proliferation of services we would eventually offer. If I could sit you and your family down for a consultation here and now, these are the issues and legal documents that I would recommend you consider for prevent-ing trouble.

Power of Attorney

Seniors and boomers should have a Power of Attorney usually, but not always, naming competent spouses, then children, as their Attor-ney in Fact. Sometimes it's appropriate for a competent parent to be the Attorney in Fact for a grandchild or their adult child.

Powers of Attorney constitute the legal appointment of an agent to carry on your personal business when you cannot. There are five types. The first two depend on the scope of the Attorney in Fact's power. The next three vary by when the power goes into effect or is terminated.

1. The general Power of Attorney gives the Attorney in Fact powers over everything owned and all business transactions for the grantor of the power.

2. The limited Power of Attorney gives the Attorney in Fact control over only what is specified.

Both of these two can also be one of the following three types:

1. *Durable.* The power stays in effect even if the grantor becomes in-capacitated. This is the type you want, because your purpose is to have a trusted family member act on your behalf if you can't.

2. *Regular.* The power becomes ineffective when the grantor becomes incapacitated. You don't want this because that's exactly when you'll need to use the power.

3. *Springing.* The power goes into effect only if the grantor becomes incapacitated and a treating physician certifies lack of capacity.

Overcoming Senior Secrecy

Senior secrecy can hurt the family finances. If parents or significant elders refuse to sign a Power of Attorney or share their money-life information with you, I urge you to explain how terrible a conservatorship proceeding can be should they ever become incapacitated. Take a look at Appendix B and read all about it, then read it to them. It could change their mind. While a springing power is more of an ordeal to activate than a general power, at least get that from parents who want to hold back control until they really are dependent.

As for the details of a secretive elder's money-life, I have long discovered a solution. It's a notebook and a key. When parents refuse to share information, ask them to write out what, who, and where their assets, papers, and financial advisors are. Then rent a vault for them to store the information. Place the key with them but be sure that you have the authority to open the vault, to avoid having to get a court order for a marshal to open it. Often, when parents realize how much their secrecy will put you through, they cooperate. But in the end it's their money, and you must let go of control, whether you think it's best for them.

The Tragedy of Secrecy

Karen got a desperate call from her uncle. He was 92 years old and out of money. He was always the rich one in the family, giving gifts and living what seemed to be a fine life in Florida. But, he had truly gone broke. A single man, he never talked out or revealed his financial status, which consisted of a series of laddered bonds and certificates of deposit. He was doing fine before the interest rates went down, so he hired an expensive home healthcare worker, paying him from his savings. Through the years, he cashed in bonds, used principle, and his money simply ran out. Karen needed to collect the gifts he had given to other relatives, including jewelry and cash, to tide him over. She needed to take over the management of his remaining assets. But there was a question of capacity to sign a Power of Attorney. That led to a conservatorship proceeding.

Everlasting Wealth

Healthcare Proxy and Living Wills　These are important documents for all family members. When two parents are competent, usually they will be the designees for each other on the healthcare proxy, with adult children as successors. See Appendix C for a full explanation of the healthcare proxy and living will, and some examples of each.

Intergenerational and Family Agreements

Families are easily ripped apart when one or both parents merge their household with one of their adult children. It hardly matters whether the purpose is parental caretaking, downsizing, or support of an adult child by a parent. Whether divorce or Alzheimer's disease is the catalyst, a new relationship that transcends the childhood dynamic begins. Old and new animosities, conflicts,

As a veteran how-to writer, I suppose I should tell you a horror story of sibling fights over mom and dad's money. I bet you can tell me a few. I'd rather tell you a happy story. I counseled a 72-year-old widow about handling her finances after she moved in with her 43-year-old daughter. There were two other adult children. After making a Power-of-Attorney, she made a very special will. The will contained an *in terrorum* clause, which disinherited any child that contested the will. She then put a small lump sum for each of the grandchildren in a trust to be inherited when each reached the age of 30. All the children were advised of the plan. Through the years, she made gifts and contributed what she could to her daughter. That was 20 years ago. Recently, she called me. "I need a new document," she said. "Why, has something gone wrong with the kids?" "No," she replied, "I'm getting married, and I need a prenuptial agreement. I want to be sure nothing changes for the children." Happy wedding at age 92, to a younger man. He's 87.

jealousies, and fears are harbored in secret or on the table. The usual discord centers on money. So, it's no surprise that as a lawyer, I am a veteran of numerous litigations and family feuds, all of which are an emotional dance with money as such a clever cover up. It's difficult to separate money issues from the deeper issues of favoritism, betrayal, and love.

I cannot promise that grasping the legal end of the stick will make a world of emotional difference. But it may. Unfortunately, trusts and estates solutions like special will provisions don't bring families together to discuss and to find accord. In fact, they are created with confidentiality and a careful consideration of who the client is and where the attorney's loyalty lies.

Sibling Support Agreements

By contrast, the sibling support agreement is designed to create an atmosphere of full disclosure, airing conflicts before they escalate. Families under the guidance of an elder law attorney should create them. They do affect the rights of family members and in cases of unresolved conflict, an aggressive lawyer can have the agreement thrown out unless all sides were separately represented. Elder law specialist Daniel Fish includes a statement by all family members that they had been advised that they could hire separate counsel but chose not to do so. Still, without creating a war where there was none, I would put the financial relationship in writing including:

1. Who pays for what.
2. Who manages separate bills.
3. Who has access to assets and income.
4. Whose name is on the deed.
5. Who will inherit joint property.

The sibling support agreement is a contract that delineates the support responsibility of adult children when:

1. A parent comes to live with one of them
2. A parent is in need of financial support in their own home
3. A parent enters an assisted living community or nursing home.

In most cases, the agreement contains a waiver of some inheritance rights by the nonsupporting sibling, and a limited waiver of an accounting of expenditures of parent's money by the noncaretaker sibling, in return for consideration of the caretaker sibling's new obligations. The sibling support agreement can also determine who gets to take the dependency tax exclusion and any deductions for long-term care premiums. It can have a mediation clause in case there is conflict. In this way, all relevant family members know what is happening with Mom or Dad's money, and the suspicion that secrecy always brings is avoided.

The enforceability of the sibling support agreement may come into question if a parent dies disinheriting a sibling, or the noncaretaking sibling is critical of the job being done and wants to take over the tasks and the money management.

A conservatorship proceeding, or an action to set aside the agreement, might be brought. By law, *love* is not a consideration that makes a contract enforceable. If a competent parent sees a special problem on the horizon, there are two clauses that can be inserted in wills or trusts that make a difference.

In Terrorum and Advancement Clauses

When parents are competent and merge their households, assets, or in any way get financially closer to one child than another, they can protect both with two different clauses. The *in terrorum* clause is designed to disinherit a troublemaker. It requires the court to revoke the inheritance rights of any person that contests a will, even if they are successful. Most usually, this is used to be sure that the noncaretaker child does not make demands for money intended to compensate the caretaker child.

The advancement clause is used by parents who want to make sure that money given in their lifetime to the caretaker or needy child, whether in the form of cash, a home or other asset, is deducted from their inheritance as an advancement, so that they don't double dip.

The Caretaker's Agreement

Lay caretakers, mostly female relatives, provide 80 percent of caretaker services in the United States. In all, 54 million Americans in 22 million families, or 26.6 percent of our adult population give some form of care to a significant elder. The Assisted Living Federation of America and MetLife studied employer costs and calculated that $11 to $29 billion are lost because of caregiver absenteeism. Only recently has the *personal care contract*, become enforceable, and then it is untested in most jurisdictions.

Personal Care Contracts

A personal care contract is one under which a person agrees to provide care for life, in return for a lump sum amount. The purpose is to keep the elder at home or with the caretaker, and give the caretaker incentive to give their maximum effort, without fear that another family member (often their own sibling) will contest the payment as a gift under duress. It also protects significant others from facing an odious lawsuit after the death of someone they have been caring for for years.

In the past, these arrangements have been overturned by the Department of Social Services of most states, after an individual sought Medicaid. This is changing. The argument was that these transfers are merely to qualify for Medicaid, not enforceable consideration for caretaking services. These decisions have fueled family feuds and robbed caregivers of dollars morally, but not legally due to them. The system is beginning to come around. In *Matter of Carolla*,[1] the Medicaid agency denied eligibility even with an agreement between the elder and two children that was complete in describing the duties of the caretakers and the cost of their services at $15 an hour. The administrative law judge found eligibility for Medicaid because of the detail in which the rights and responsibilities were set out.

Within a family, caretakers deserve to be protected and noncaretakers deserve to be included. If Medicaid is beginning to recognize these agreements as enforceable, families should follow suit whether they ever plan to apply for eligibility.

Chapter FOURTEEN

Under One Roof—Selling the House and Building the Ancillary Apartment

At this point, the whole family should be on the same page with regard to:

1. Who will handle the parents' money?
2. Where will inheritances go?
3. Whether and how the caretaking child will account to the others?
4. Who will give respite to the caretaker?

Now, the rest is all about zoning! Yes, zoning. Don't presume that you can just build an addition to your home to accommodate Mom and Dad. Many people are selling both their and their parents' homes and *upscaling* because of longevity. Adult children and their parents pool their money for a bigger home in which they all live. Toll Brothers and other master builders are creating the mother-in-law suite in their top-of-the-line homes. Walk-out basements and second efficiency kitchens are often part of the sales pitch for new developments.

But, it is also possible to downscale and find room for Mom and Dad.

One of the best alternatives is finishing the garage so they can live on the street level. Give the kids the walk-out basement. But check your zoning, your septic, and your taxing authority. Figure the true costs of the renovation and compare the cost and angst of moving with the cost and angst of renovating before you make a decision.

Universal Design

Most of us still expect to make room for mom and dad in an extra bedroom. But if you do, be sure that they can take the stairs. Here's where your sibling support agreement or your long-term care insurance policy can really work wonders. If your parents have a policy and are eligible to make a claim, the right policy will allow for a cash distribution of typically $10,000 to put in a ramp, a grab bar, a stair lift and to otherwise *longevity fit* your home. Low bathroom and kitchen cabinets and even a tub that you can wheel into are all part of a new industry called *universal design*. Many retirement developments and active adult communities already feature such a design. Specialized interior designers and contract decorators are now able to add these features to custom homes and renovations.

If there is no long-term care policy, be sure your sibling support agreement allows for the distribution of Mom's and Dad's money to make a home renovation *and* for the money to remove changes if they diminish the resale value of the caretaker's home, although it will probably make it more valuable.

Everlasting Wealth

New Ideas For the Home

The following features will add value to your home and make it longevity friendly:

Wider doorways

Elevators ($30,000)

Adjustable height sinks ($7,500)

Thick plywood behind tiles if a grab bar must eventually be installed

Push button lowering of closet shelves

Motion detection faucets

When Johnny Comes Marching Home . . . Again

If you think that mom and dad are hard to live with, wait until your son or daughter comes back home. The boomerang kid can ruin the best longevity financial plan. There are some things you can do to prevent this.

One thing that many people, including many popular financial gurus, will advise you to do is say no. But those people probably have no children. To paraphrase an Art Buchwald quip, "An economist is

---

Everlasting Wealth

I promised you at the beginning of the book that not all the strategies would be based on conventional wisdom. Here's an example. Don't pay for your child's college; buy them an apartment, instead. Time and again I hear concerns from my friends that their post-college kids are coming back home to live because they need to save on rent money. These twenty-somethings are working, but can't manage city rents on entry-level salaries. Not only does this hold their parents back from downscaling, but it also breeds situations where it's all too easy to be tapped for pocket money. On the other side of the fence, parents have too much control over the lives of their adult children when they foot the bill for rent. No one is happy. "I wish I could afford to buy my daughter an apartment," one friend said, "But after paying for college, we can't do that, so Justin is living home now." Of course, if Justin had a student loan, he could pay it off at a very low interest rate, at far fewer dollars than a monthly rental. Imagine if he had a small paid-up studio or even a one bedroom, as a start in life. It would keep him out of the house and begin equity build up at a fraction of the total cost of renting. How dare you leave poor Justin with a loan? Well, I paid mine off when I was 32 years old. It taught me discipline and I never resented a minute of it. I did feel lousy when I couldn't wrangle the first down payment for a terrific condo on the Hudson. Think about it. One caveat. You cannot get a student loan discharged in bankruptcy, so before you decide to saddle a child with debt, be sure they are responsible.

like a man that knows everything about women, but doesn't know any women." Perhaps these advisors know about money, but they have never looked into their child's eyes and denied them. Age doesn't make it any better. If anything, it's worse. If your 25-year-old wants to come back home, he or she probably has a problem. If they just want to save a few dollars before they marry, go on to graduate school, decide on a career, and they are working, the path is simple. Make an agreement (you knew I would say that) just as you would for a tenant and or a roommate, deciding on chores, finances, and other responsibilities. I know that you will breach both. That's life. But it still gives you all a good framework.

But what if they have no resources? You must deal with this openly.

If you cannot without regret support an adult child, no matter how painful, you must say no. It then becomes your obligation to help them in every nonmonetary way possible. When you pick a rose, you are responsible for it for the rest of your life.

Chapter FIFTEEN

The New Family Financial Dialogue

It would be overreaching of me to say that longevity is solely responsible for the changes in the way families are handling and looking at money today. It would be an even bigger stretch to conclude that the new configuration of the American family is a result of longevity, alone. But, I'll take the risk of stating that longevity is the handmaiden of many changes in the way we think, act, and feel when it comes to family, money, and relationships.

A Big Batch of Family

For many years I was a divorce lawyer, then a divorce mediator. In my day, it was the era of the divorce lawyer bomber and barracuda. For me it was divorce wars among the rich and semifamous. The phrase *blended family* meant that the husband left his middle-aged wife for a younger woman and their toddler might see his teenager sibling from the first marriage once in a while. And while there are still many bitter divorces, things have changed. Some of the most loving families I know are a martini mix of two families, maybe four.

With multiple grandparents and difficulty in determining who belongs to whom, everyone belongs. Some of this has to do with cultural spin. TV sitcoms, cartoons, and in-school counseling have made what used to be an aberration, just another type of norm, and have provided us with some decent role models for good behavior when we separate. The weight of the numbers and our familiarity with divorce make divorce seem so much less drastic. Because we do not rush into dotage, but look and feel better, retool for new social lives, take on new things, one failed relationship is not terminal. Longevity gives us a better chance to outlive our animosity. Life is too long to carry a grudge. The law calls the heirs we love and want to leave our money to *the objects of our bounty*. With so many objects, however, what happens to the little bounty we have to spread around?

Elders Supporting the Young

We are pretty clear that longevity is postponing our inheritance, and in some cases wiping it out altogether. But there is a less quantifiable undercurrent of lifetime giving. Gifts are being made while seniors live, not just to transfer assets for tax or even Medicaid eligibility, but because the younger generation (mainly boomers) need the money, sometimes because of the burden of supporting two families.

Kurt Medina and John Migliaccio of Medina Associates and Maturity Mark Services Corporation are marketers in the mature market arena. They write, "Older parents are twice as likely to provide income for their children than to receive it." They remind us of the Harris Poll taken in 1940 when 36 percent of those over age 65 received their primary income from children. In 1990, that figure was less than 2 percent.[1] In the preindustrial world, children were born so they could support parents in their old age. As we strive and thrive through longer middle age and fail to save money, some of us rely on parents for a helping hand. And when the gifts are uneven among siblings, the family feels it. In the age of longevity, it's hard to keep financial secrets.

Financial Family Privacy, an Endangered Species

Part of senior independence is the desire to keep a close check on the bottom line and manage what they own by themselves. This frustrates adult children who tread a fine line between invasion of privacy and a genuine need to know what's going on in order to help protect family assets. Opening a dialogue about where the money is, charitable intent, distribution among heirs, transfer of assets as part of routine tax and estate planning, and competency to handle money are significant longevity issues.

The extreme cost of healthcare and caregiving may open that dialogue. In the past, concerns over taxation alone could not always do the trick to engage a family financial dialogue even among the wealthy, and certainly not among the rest of us who were little touched by estate tax issues.

Intrafamily Cooperation

Largely because of the escalating costs and our ill preparedness to give our parents long-term care, the family is often brought together by the needs of the parents. It's hard for siblings, even those living in different parts of the country, to stay separate and aloof in their own isolated world when a parent has Alzheimer's or a stroke. Longevity has brought us beyond seeing each other only at weddings and funerals. We may be brought together over a colostomy bag or a home defibrillator. This often brings out the best and worst of our relationships. And, the issue often involves money.

At a recent luncheon at the International Longevity Center Dr. Robert N. Butler, President and CEO and winner of the Pulitzer Prize for his seminal work, *Why Survive? Being Old In America*,[2] commented on the new family cement: long-term care. A discussion ranged around whether we would go back to the old way of family members caring for each other, and the usual observations were made that children don't undertake to care for parents as readily as they did in the past. I remember my mother saying, "One mother can take care of six children, but six children can't take care of one mother." (Of course, I'm an only child, so my mother's lament somewhat lacked impact, but I got her drift.) That's when Dr. Butler made a simple but profound comment. In the old days, he reminded us, caretaking rarely lasted for years. Caretaking was short-lived, because we were short-lived. The caretaking reforms we will make will not be a retrofit to the family and bring them back to a past that never was, but to create a new dynamic that would never need to arise without our current longevity. We rely more on family but also on friends.

Friends as Family

No man is an island, but many of us would like to live on one. If so, we need to bring a few things, mostly our friends, with us. One advantage the baby boomer has over the senior is that we are privileged to watch them in their advanced age. We have a better idea of where it goes and how it works. The clear pain of losing friends and the clear continued need for connectedness is already in our vision.

As we acknowledge the social and psychological dependency on friends, will we also start to consider joint housing? Second career partnerships? New financial reliance and dynamics?

I have been impressed from the day I left law school at how easy it has been for wealthy people to borrow from friends and include them in deals. I have rarely studied a major real estate development or a start-up company where friends did not contribute some capital. A client who was an entrepreneur once told me, "Friends are the rich person's bank." And he should know.

The rest of us find money pooling a taboo, at least until now. More and more, I am meeting up with a consortium of friends who intend to live nearby to each other after retirement, and are creating their own communities, timeshares, and shared housing. The topics around the dinner table are likely to be, "What can we go in on together?" Once they start to make it real, issues of their financial circumstances must be revealed, bringing everyone closer together and breaking the taboo of interfamily financial secrecy.

To Grandmother's House We Go

My children know their grandparents. Mine died too soon for me to know them; three of the four died before I was born. Similarly, I have several friends who need to look up their grandparents' names to remember them. By contrast, my mother is among the oldest of the grandparents at my daughter Rose's school, but she's the one that never missed a play or a soccer match. As for the baby boomer as grandparent—the mind boggles. I envision myself as some sort of Auntie Mame, wearing a turban and taking little Timmy or Janey on Safari.

Inheritance planning has changed radically—it's not tax reform or increased wealth, or even longevity itself that has made the difference. It's that we are likely to know our heirs. This may seem simple,

Profile: Carole Hedegren

Carole Hedegren is a skydiving, scuba-diving granny. I first met her on a familiarization trip for travel writers in the U.S. Virgin Islands. She's the one who encouraged me to Sea Trek wearing a 70-pound helmet on my head so I could walk on the ocean floor. She bicycles, cross-trains, and travels the world. For my 55th birthday she and I will travel to ecolodges across Panama, live in the Canopy Towers at the treetops, and explore the rain forest. This is the new grandma! I plan to learn a lot from Carole. To travel with us, keep up with our exploits at www.wealth102.com.

but it's at the crux of all inheritance decisions. Even the Latin phrases we use in making a will, like *per stirpes*, meaning your line of descendents, presupposes an ignorance of who may eventually inherit your money. At best, we named a grandchild or a minor as successor heir. Maybe that child was in their teens, and we hoped for the best for their future. Today, grandchildren grow to adulthood during our lifetime, they are in their 20s as we sit down to make or remake our wills. Boomers may know their grandchildren for 40 years. Our bequests are much more informed.

In 1980, when I wrote my first book *Moneythink*, I included what I still assert was the first personal finance material for opposite and same-sex couples pooling their money and planning together. In those days, they were called Persons of the Same (or opposite) Sex Living in the Same Quarters (POSSLSQs). To add to the innovation, my publisher, Pilgrim Press, was a small church press that never exorcized one word. Today, I scour the long-term care polices to find those that give same-sex couples spousal discounts, and there are many. As are these legal documents that give same-sex couples and unmarrieds of the opposite sex tailor-made inheritance and healthcare proxy rights. As for longevity, I sit on the advisory board of the Association of Single Americans, which lobbies for equal tax treatment and health benefits for those who choose not to marry, are divorced, or are widowed. I would be honored to be on the board of Senior Action in a Gay Environment (SAGE), the outstanding advocacy organization for the gay and lesbian community in the field of aging. (But they haven't asked me, yet.)

This new type of American family is leading the way by dialoguing about money, mainly because they must in order to protect their rights. As for longevity, they set new standards of friendship and affinity. But, the issues of outliving their money are the same issues shared by married couples. How do I stay relevant and connected in an ageist society? Where will I live? Who will take care of me? What will it cost?

The Law Facilitates the New Family Financial Dialogue

There are two kinds of lawyers: One committed to changing the law to make it as it should be and the other who is committed to using the law to make the best of what it is. I was always the latter of the two; not flashy, but easier on the blood pressure.

There are several legal entities, clauses, financial devices, structures, and procedures that hit the spot where new needs created by longevity are concerned. Yes, there will be new and even better solutions. For now, I'll put new wine in old bottles and limit myself to things you can do today to improve your family's financial dialogue and assure a happy ending.

Adriane's Top 16 Legal Longevity Ideas

Don't be alarmed, you've already read about the top five.

1. *In terrorum* advancement and will clauses
2. Caretaker agreements
3. Sibling agreements
4. Power of attorney
5. Healthcare proxy/living wills

And the other 11 are painless.

6. *The Family Limited Partnership (FLP).* The FLP is an entity run by a general partner but whose assets are owned by limited partners. (How do you like that legalese?) The FLP can own all types of personal property, real estate and securities, even a business. The tax savings can be great because the income flows to the limited partners and they may be at a lower tax bracket than the general partner. The FLP also serves to avoid probate and saves on inheritances taxes. But as a family strategy, it serves to keep parents in control of assets while allowing them to slowly transfer these assets to their heirs. For example, a family business could be transferred to an FLP, run by mom and dad, but owned by the adult or even minor children.

7. *The Family Bank.* The family bank is a clause in a trust that permits the trustee to lend money to beneficiaries. They must pay it back with interest. The trustee can collect for nonpayment or forgive the debt. The purpose is to help out heirs without permanently depleting the total trust fund, and to give help when needed while not giving more to one heir than to another.

8. *The Power of Appointment.* If you are not sure who you want to inherit, you can appoint someone to make the decision for you. This is used most often when you do have an heir, but they will not inherit all the money at once. If they do not use it all, especially if a trust pays them income, you need to name a successor beneficiary or appoint someone else to make the decision sometime after your death.

9. *Revocable Trusts.* A trust where you are the trustee and your inheritance wishes pass privately and without probate. This is excellent if your relatives are in many states, you own businesses, property or real estate in more than one state, or you seek privacy in your inheritance decisions. All trust and estates and elder law attorneys can help you with this, and check out my book *Gifting to People You Love.*[3]

10. *Irrevocable Trust.* The irrevocable trust was an important estate tax device, but with the changing tax scene it is now best used when you want to give up assets but still wield some control. Certain distribution clauses can make sure that new family members get their share and that blended families get equal treatment. Unlike the FLP, you do not manage any of the assets. Your control comes solely from the clauses you draft in the trust document and after that, management is in the hands of the trustee.

11. *Limited Liability Corporations (LLC).* If you join with friends or family to buy property or start a business, you must protect yourself from the wrong doing of each other. No offense, but suing is a national pass time and anything can happen. One excellent entity to help limit your liability is the limited liability corporation. If one owner is sued for their own deeds, co-owners are protected from being dragged into the suit just by dint of the relationship.

12. *The 529 Account.* Grandparents and parents can make gifts to a special account called a *529 account* that grows tax-free for college. The child is named as a beneficiary, but the beneficiary can be changed if the child does not go to college or does not need the money. Most states have partnered with a mutual fund or money management company to run the program. They are not all the same, differing mostly in fees and investment choice. But most programs are very good. You are not limited to the program of your state. However, some states give you a tax break if you participate in their program and reside in the state. See your financial professionals for the details of the programs they offer.

13. *Key Person Insurance.* The biggest mistake that people make in starting a small business, besides not maintaining cash flow, is lack of an exit plan. A simple way to buy out family members or partners, or even just close the company when one person passes on, is to insure the life of the entrepreneur as early a possible. Then enter into an owner's agreement as to what happens to the proceeds and the business when the key person passes on.

14. *Family Annuities.* You'll soon learn a great deal about annuity products bought from insurance companies, but another type of annuity is created within the family. Money is transferred to one or a few family members in consideration for a contract obligating them to provide lifelong income for the person who transferred the wealth. When properly structured, family annuities work well for early transfers and lifelong income flow. Primarily, your elder law and trust and estates lawyer has the credentials to work these out for you, and counsel you as to whether they are worth pursing for your family.

15. *Family Foundations.* Wealthy people have long kept even charitable donations under family supervision. Today, more of us can create family foundations for charitable purposes. This works well when there is a family business, but that's not the only time it may be worth the candle. Members of families can pool gifts, insurance proceeds, and even real estate for charitable purposes. Family members can run the foundation and make joint donative decisions and reap substantial tax rewards. Check your local bar associations for reduced consultation fees in the trust and estates field. Have a chat. And if the lawyer is young and hungry—good, you'll all learn together. Or, seek out the planned giving department of your favorite charity and they can guide you.

16. *Beneficiary Insurance Lapse Notifications.* Be sure that if you or a child of yours is the beneficiary of an insurance policy on the life of a parent, grandparent, ex-spouse or stepparent, that you are notified if the premium is in default. As families ebb and flow, and new families emerge, sometimes a policyholder drops the ball on paying the premium. *And the beneficiary is unaware of it until the person dies, and then it's too late.* The insurance company will inform you of lapse, provided they are instructed to do so on the application when the policy is bought. After a policy is in effect, the company will also accept a written instruction.

Transforming Your Money
Inner Monologue and the Effect on Family

Whew. That's lots of ideas and all or none of them may be of interest to you. What is likely is that the thought of taking action is exhausting and the inner voices begin their chorus. I have no time for all this! I have no money for all this! It's for someone else, not me! I can't understand it all! I hate working with lawyers/financial people!

If talking to others about money is important, how you talk to yourself goes beyond important all the way up to critical. If I knew then what I know now, there are two things I would try not to say to myself or at least dismiss as soon as I could after the thought arose. These are "I have time to do it," and "It's too late to do it."

This may seem contradictory, but it is not. I know the details of the financial lives of many people now in their mid 50s to mid 70s who are reaping the rewards of major financial success. I know how they did it. It was a combination of taking care of business as they went along and starting as soon as they could. It was never too early for them to save, buy a home or condo, and get their insurance in order. They paid attention to small details all their money life.

These are not people who have the highest education or grew a business or won the lottery. They just bit the bullet and made sure that the bank was authorized to send some money for automatic deposit to their 401(k) or IRA. Most started when they got their first job. It was never too early.

As for "it's never too late," this takes a bit of faith and a ton of self-confidence. How old do you think you are when you are too old to make a satisfactory amount of money? Is that a funny question? Some people feel it's too late for them at age 30, especially if they see many young hotshot successes around them. Others feel that money life begins at age 40 or 50 or 60. How about you? My friend's brother, the bum we called him, became a millionaire at 58, after getting his *first* corporate job at age 52. Something just clicked and he now runs the company. Except that it didn't just click. He got fed up with family handouts, left for a state where jobs were easier to find, and picked an industry that really interested him—refrigeration, go figure!

You may wonder why I put the inner monologue piece in the family section of the book. It's simple. We are always speaking to those we love, even when we are silent. Body language, the way we sigh or breathe, tells them a story about us. Our family absorbs our thoughts through our demeanor. They know every slump of our shoulder and twinkle in our eye. If you think your money attitude is a secret, think again. Children especially internalize your ways through your temperament, actions, responses, and mood.

Your immediate sphere of influence is your family. You owe it to them and your own future to start now, because it is not too early, and to start now because it is not too late.

What do you want to start now that you thought was too soon?

- Open a savings program.
- Open an IRA.
- Buy a home.
- Make a will.
- Get long-term care insurance.
- Get other insurance.
- Other.

What will you start now that you thought was too late?

- Start a business.
- Buy real estate.
- Open a 401(k) at work or an IRA.
- Start to make larger contributions to existing plans.
- Get an insurance review.
- Other.

THE FAMILY CHALLENGE THINK AND DO LIST

Will you have a parent or child or both coming to live with you?

If so, get ready for a family conference to honestly talk out the details.

If you will be hosting an elder, have these documents at the very least:

    Power-of-Attorney

    Healthcare proxy

    Living wills

And where appropriate:

    Caretaker's agreement—personal care contract

    Family limited partnership

    Family bank

    Rental agreements

If you are hosting a junior, have these documents at the very least:

    Chore and payment agreements

And where appropriate:

    An advancement clause in your will

    A loan agreement

Check out universal design showrooms, if you or a significant elder need modifications to the home for visitability and livability.

Check out your elder's long-term care policy, if he or she has one, to see what modifications are covered.

Work with local caregivers associations for support in your efforts. Find many at www.wealth102.com.

Take good care of yourself. And if you plan to work after retirement, investigate companies that provide on-site elder care, and add that benefit to your list of ideal job characteristics.

Part FOUR

Longevity and Health

"I'm Gonna' Live Forever. I'm Gonna' Learn How to Fly!"

As I write this chapter, I had a dozen health newsletters in front of me; most came from prestigious colleges like Harvard, John's Hopkins, and the University of California. Aside from the one that tells me how to watch for glaucoma (my Mom has it and it's hereditary), the one that caught my attention was a sell piece for the Life Extension Foundation newsletter. Now, I'm in the newsletter business, so I can tell you that these guys are good at selling. After mentioning alternative medicine and past discoveries, the sell piece throws us a little mindbender. It tells us that the Foundation believes it can reverse and stop aging in our bodies, also that its mission "is to conquer aging and death within the next 17 years. . . . It may become possible to program our genes to enable us to grow young biologically, instead of suffering the devastating consequences of aging."

With this information, my brain had become scrambled eggs. I knew about some of their research on mice. I knew that some of the Life Extension work is done at top facilities, and most has to do with life extenders not outright immortality. But, it bothered me that this cutting edge Foundation still saw aging as devastation, not a joyous natural evolution. I guess happy aging doesn't sell.

Although longevity is more and more about self-care and

prevention, not genetic destiny, we still look for an immortality magic pill. And hovering above all this is the ethical issue of who will pay for longevity whether it comes at the gym or in a bottle. If the fountain of youth is discovered, who among us should be entitled to drink?

Stories of amazing discoveries regarding cures, clones, and DNA breakthroughs hit the newspapers every day. We feel healthier than ever, but the face of the nursing home residents we saw on the minibus looms when we forget our keys. We want to take a colonoscopy to check for colon cancer, but our insurance does not cover it. We want to give our grandchild a big birthday gift, but we need the money to pay for our multiple prescriptions. Once upon a time, healthcare drove longevity. Now longevity is driving healthcare.

In the age of longevity, healthcare is not on the back burner, it's a current challenge to increase our life expectancy and be healthier throughout our added years.

We must be ready to consider the following issues.

- If we want the privilege (not a right, as yet) to live longer, we must be willing to voluntarily take good care of ourselves and decrease the financial drain on the healthcare system. My younger readers can make the most of our growing knowledge. They have the most to gain by the extraordinary technologies yet to come. Although it may seem counterintuitive, healthcare is a young person's issue. So, no matter how invulnerable you feel right now, make preventive care a top personal priority.

- As for the rest of us, we pretty much see the light. We have lived long enough to know that the vessel in which our mind and soul reside is worth more consideration and attention than the car we drive or the clothes we wear when we allocate funds.

- Healthcare today is more than about medicine. We want the major killers, cancer and heart disease to be abolished forever. But we also know that a good sewer system does more for a population's longevity than a good hospital.

- Aging is not a disease, and youth doesn't come with a facelift. Think about how deeply our mass media images suggest just the opposite.

- There's not enough money, not personally, not governmentally, to support all the advances and take all the care available to us, even now. Our ethical choice will be whether to leave out some people from some opportunities, or to eliminate some opportunities for all the people.

- More and more of our healthcare dollars go toward demedicalization, nonskilled care, equipment, and self-care.
- Healthcare is a women's issue. We are overwhelmingly the caretakers. Insofar, as we now have jobs and careers, our system of informal caretaking is in jeopardy.

So, Are We Going to Live Forever?

Well, not exactly, and here's why. As a species we were not meant for immortality. In fact, big bang species like the salmon that die after mating make more sense in the highly disposable world of evolution. Natural selection, or good genes, are not characterized by the ability to grow older and live longer. Darwinian high achievers are those with the best adaptive and reproductive mechanisms. So, is our ability to attain long years really separate from our individual genetics? Pretty much.

One of the guiding lights of biogerontology, Dr. Leonard Hayflick, calls our aging "an artifact of civilization."[1] Longevity is not linked to the genome. It is stochastic, random, but trackable. Oddly enough, stochastics is an analytic method that applies to the stock market, as well. Coincidentally, it is the one we use in my *Wealthbuilder* newsletter for over a decade to beat the S&P.

From stochastics we learn two things about our health. One, we can affect our longevity. And two, aging is not about disease. Centenarians die healthy. Dr. Hayflick forecasts that if we take our longevity as far as it can go, one day all our death certificates will cite *molecular infidelity*, a random process of *increasing molecular disorder* as cause of death. Basically, unlike the Energizer rabbit, we lose energy. Eventually, our body goes toward chaos, accompanied by a lessening of the strength to recover from a light fall or a heavy cold. In short, we cannot live forever.

Bummer.

But we can fly. At least in an airplane and that may be the state of longevity research some day; to find the immortality device that will artificially allow us unending life. But right now the inroads that have led to longevity are quite different. They include research and cures for disease, hygiene leading to lowered infant mortality, preventive inoculation as with small pox, and personal healthcare leading to prevention. The burning question is where will our next dollar be spent? There are so many longevity related choices.

If our goal is to prolong life among our young, we will divert money away from childhood disease research and give it to law enforcement. Accidents and homicides cause more deaths in adolescence than infectious disease. Or, as we break down the myth that aging means disease, our healthcare dollar may well be redeployed toward quality of life enhancement. That's where many of our personal dollars are already headed.

As a culture, we have the underlying suspicion that this growing longevity is much like the airplane; it can crash and burn if we are not vigilant. We cannot go helter skelter spending money on whatever seems fashionable at the moment. We are searching for a unique solution to universal healthcare. We are emphasizing general health prevention. But when we speak of specific health spending priorities, the fur begins to fly.

The Congressional Budget Office predicts that the cost of long-term care will grow by 70 percent over the next 20 years. ("DBO Memorandum: Projections of Expenditures for Long Term Care Services for the Elderly," Washington, D.C., 1999). But then again, the number of skilled nurses for acute care patients is dwindling. Perhaps dollars are better spent for the education and recruitment of geriatric nurses (Buerhaus, Staiger, and Auerebach, "Implications of an Aging Registered Nurse Workforce," *Journal of the American Medical Association*.)

Dr. Hayflick points out that the likelihood of dying from Alzheimer's disease is 0.7 percent, a low number for a high profile chronic disease. If Alzheimer's disease were eradicated from our population, it would add an average of 19 days to the overall life span. But the devastation to an individual family cannot be calculated so coldly. And the genetic advancements are so great that a single big push for research might erase it as a specter in our lives forever. As Dr. Hayflick concludes in many of his papers, "We have revealed a process (rapidly increasing longevity) that we were never intended to experience."[2] As my client, Jeffrey, concludes in choosing early retirement, "You cannot put the genie back in the bottle."

The genie is out. How will we pay for it?

Interview: Dr. Harry R. Moody
Financial Darwinism, the Survival of the Richest

Dr. Harry R. Moody, director of the Institute for Human Values in Aging at the International Longevity Center and author of *Ethics in an Aging Society*, (John's Hopkins University Press, 1992) is one of the foremost ethicists in the field of aging and longevity. I asked him how he saw the issue of medical rationing, and what he thought was ethical when the potential for continued life was a matter of money, affordable by some and not by others.

First, Dr. Moody wanted to quickly dispel any notion that immortality is in the cards for any of us at any price. "Antiaging claims in medicine are false advertising," he asserts. " An illusion. Our maximum life span has not changed by any plausible method known today." "In fact," he adds, "some of the most well-known treatments like HGH growth hormone have side effects, some quite serious. He agreed when I called them a profitable illusion.

But Dr. Moody recognized that we can "live longer within the boundaries of our life span," pointing to treatment for kidney and heart failure. But he calls these "incremental gains" with "diminishing or marginal returns." And that is where significant ethical issues lie, at the "ragged edge of technology"—a concept that Dr. Moody explained was first introduced by philosopher Daniel Callahan, and around which a great deal of attention and research money flows.

The more immediate ethical question is, who is entitled to this incremental technology? Dr. Moody commented, "There are no obvious answers. Perhaps money is best spent on 'intervention' promotion and prevention—in other words health maintenance."

I asked him whether he thought that those who did not voluntarily take good care of themselves when they could might be more severely rationed than others. "We all have it in our power to intervene in our own lives early, but we seem unmotivated. In the trade off between short- and long-term goals, the short-term goals always seem to win out." He pointed out that

(Continued)

Interview: Dr. Harry R. Moody (Continued)

this is so with money and savings as well as health. "We find it difficult to identify with our future self."

He felt that medical spending decisions might go toward cutting incremental technology (prolonging life for only short periods of time) rather than discriminating in preventive or curative healthcare. "Even prescription drugs that merely prolong a painful life might be in question."

But what about those who can pay, would they simply be able to choose to extend their lives and squash their pain? "After extending a decent minimum level of care, that's all our society can do. It becomes a matter of individual choice. And that choice may be different depending on finances." Dr. Moody gave the example of public transportation. "We all deserve good public transportation. But only those with wealth can get the convenience of a private jet." So it may be with top of the line medical care, as well.

Chapter SIXTEEN

Wealth Is Health—Life for Sale

I don't think I have to sell you on the idea that money makes a difference in your health. Not only do you want to afford the best care when you're ill, but you also want the best in preventative services. And the nexus between longevity and money goes much deeper than that. Financial security increases optimism, which in turn enhances successful aging. In today's world of medical cutbacks and atrophied government programs, money literally helps you fight for your life and those of your loved ones.

Ten percent of the budget of every American family goes to healthcare. But what we are paying for is "sick care" through health insurance, Social Security/Medicare, and private pay when we are ill. Very little in comparison goes toward well care, or even the new and trendy chronic care, a by-product of longevity. How are you about spending your healthcare dollars on prevention, exercise, nutrition, medical research (contribution to causes that affect your family), and efficient acute care insurance? What is your current healthcare budget? Divide the total into percentages for each member of the family. Is anybody getting shortchanged? I bet it's Dad.

(Take your exercise equipment and massage out of the luxury category, and put it into healthcare. Bodily maintenance is a new category of expenditure that saves money later on.) The list includes:

- Health insurance
- Long-term care insurance
- Noncovered prescriptions
- Noncovered doctors visits
- Colonoscopy and other diagnostic procedures
- Chiropractic
- Exercise
- Massage
- Nutritional foods/Nutritionist
- Mental health and counseling
- Dental care
- Eye care
- Vitamins and other supplements

How much goes to sick care? How much to well care? Are there any changes you would like to make?

No matter how you slice it, both individually and collectively, we simply do not have all the money we need to pay for every aspect of healthcare. Hard choices must be made. With the addition of advances in medical technology and biogerontology, there are monumental ethical issues on the horizon with regard to money and longevity, which will be played out in a worldwide arena. Your job, for yourself and your family, is to make sure you are a medical *have*, not a medical *have not*. To do this, you must carefully husband every healthcare benefit coming your way, and then make careful choices about where you will spend your out-of-pocket dollar.

A glaring example of medical haves and have-nots is designer

Everlasting Wealth

If an increase in longevity were our only goal, we would actually have a negative expenditure (we would save money) as the few verifiable longevity health habits are undereating, positive attitude, and emotional support.

drugs. Ask any senior, the side effects from their prescription drugs can be worse than the condition they take them to cure. How many of you spend a few hours a month or more on the telephone with an older relative or friend talking about the headaches, nausea, dizziness, or cramps caused by their medications?

In the future, you may not hear these complaints, at least from people with enough money to buy designer drugs. When I was the assistant general counsel of the Community Service Society I went on a campaign with the legendary Janet Sainer, one of the grand dames of senior rights who among other things created the pilot program that led to the Retired Senior Volunteer Program (RSVP), and Elinor Guggenheimer the then commissioner of the City of New York Department of Consumer Affairs, to be sure we could all buy generic drugs. We wanted everyone to have a choice between the brand name and the cheaper generics. But the truth is, everyone did not have a choice. Those with money could choose to save it; those without money could not choose to spend it.

Now we have come full circle. The cutting edge in pharmacology is the compounding of pills made especially for you. One that takes your allergies, your reactions, your other medications, your body clock, and your genetics into account so that you will suffer as few side effects as possible. Any of my women readers who know about the Prescriptives cosmetic line that compounds personal fragrances, powders, and foundation just for your skin will get the idea. A pill only for you to pop!

Imagine the cost. At the very least, medication selection would require allergy tests, food-drug sensitivity tests, and drug-drug sensitivity tests ("A Guide to Medication and Aging," Kathleen Cameron and Anne Richardson, www.asa.org). Sure you can get arthritis medicine, but wouldn't you rather have a pill meant for your biological temperament, and the money to pay for it?

What price do you put on a year of your life? Would you like someone else to decide? The May 6, 2003 edition of the *New York Times* (Science Section, page F5) published a chilling article by Dr. Sandep Jauhar, "Buying Time: Doctors Debate the Ethics of Care and Cost." Dr. Jauhar wrote of his 55-year-old patient who could barely walk a few steps without breathlessness because of heart valve failure. A biventricular pacemaker may prolong his life, but it would cost $20,000. There are more than 5 million heart failure patients in the United States. A half million are added each year. If even a small fraction got this device

Everlasting Wealth

On May 19, 2003, the U.S. Supreme Court ruled that the Maine Rx Program that used Medicaid coverage as leverage to negotiate a discount in prescription drugs from drug companies (or their products would not be covered by Medicaid) was legal. The argument was that the prescription drug savings would keep people off Medicaid and better serve the program.

it would cost billions, and for many would prolong life no more than eight months. Dr. Jauhar acknowledged, "Cardiologists are beginning to ask is this a sensible way to spend healthcare resources?"

He recounted a debate in his office among fellow cardiologists, one of whom posited the case of an older patient with mild dementia, who could not give consent to the type of defibrillator that Dick Chaney had implanted, at a cost of $30,000. Millions of Americans can qualify for such a device, but who will get one? The cardiologist wondered if he should push for it for his patient. "It makes sense to implant a device in the chest of a 50-year-old with a good life who is providing to society," the doctor said, "but what about a 70-year-old debilitated by heart failure and living in a nursing home? That patient might benefit the most," he added, "but would also have the least to offer to society in terms of productive years." Until policy makers get into the debate, doctors are forced to make individual judgments about life and death, "who should get a device and who should die without one."

In that same issue of the *New York Times*, an interview with Dr. Floyd Bloom, part of the team that uncovered a major drug used to treat depression, another big issue for those in advanced age, revealed the doctor's frustration with the way medical care is distributed. He suggested that healthcare should be tantamount to a public utility, with universal access, but private cost. In speaking of genome research and its effect on preventing Alzheimer's disease, he said, "My big fear is that the healthcare delivery system is in such crisis that we may not be able to translate the fruits of this revolution to everyday medical practices." Will you trust the government, the doctors, the insurance companies to determine if you will benefit from new technologies and discoveries?

It is my intention to both raise your consciousness about the debate to come, and to prepare you to transfer as much risk of longevity as you can through a combination of careful selection of medical insurance, long-term healthcare insurance, and private pay so that the only arbiter of your healthcare choices is you.

You control your aging and the money you have is part of that control. Genetics is not destiny. Dr. Thomas Perls of Boston University has followed 1,000 people who lived to be 100 or more. His seminal study revealed that genetics plays a much smaller role than thought. This is especially true in cases of heart disease and diabetes, which often can be controlled or prevented through exercise, diet, nonsmoking, and cholesterol and blood pressure management (*Consumer Reports* "On Health," Vol. 15, No. 2, February 2003).

A little prevention goes a long way. A University of California study tracked 7,000 males age 45 until they reached age 56, and concluded that those with four or fewer bad habits (smoking, excessive drinking, lack of exercise, high stress levels, poor diet) would increase their longevity by 11 years against those who displayed six or more unhealthy lifestyle habits. Even those whose habits are far less than perfect can impact their longevity with a little work. And while walking is free, personal trainers and weight equipment are not. Given our largely sedentary life, it would be great to have the wherewithal to make a personal trainer a line budget item that you could sustain all your life. (Yes, all your life. Weightlifting has been shown to build muscle mass in 90-year-olds.)

You Can Get Healthier with Age

I cannot count the times that grown men, and a few women, have sat at my desk and told me without hesitation, "If I have to go into a nursing home, just shoot me." Part of this attitude comes from equating all chronic illness with "going to a home." Right now, only 5 percent of the chronically ill are in nursing homes and that figure is declining. But part of this shoot-me-first attitude also comes from a misunderstanding over what health is like in extreme old age, and an unwillingness to pay for insurance that might prolong such a life. In effect, my protestors agree with the view that we will be disposable after 70. The truth is far from that, unless we make it so.

The National Endowment for Financial Education has labeled three phases of our overall health status. The first is the *go go phase*, during which we are active adulthoods with family, friends, and a full time or consuming job. This is the phase that has been extended by decades through the new longevity. The *slow-go phase* is one of independent living, but slowing down and probably fully retired. The *no-go phase* occurs when we are in need of physical assistance or have some cognitive impairment. This is this phase that we are just beginning to experience, and about which we are just now able to draw conclusions. What has emerged so far is that we gradually lose our ability to stay independent, and that the decline is by no means steady or irreversible. That is why the advent of continuing care retirement communities with different levels of care is catching on. It is also why residents experience a significant amount of movement among levels of care, including regaining strength after a fall or a stroke, and resuming a higher level of independence.

Researchers at Duke University have studied 41,947 people over the age of 65 in a series of surveys starting in 1982.[1] They found that three-quarters of them were functionally independent until age 95, and that although our actuarial age has increased by three years since the study began, the incidents of dependency by those over age 65 (cannot bath, dress, or feed themselves) declined by 25 percent. We are not only living longer, but more independently. In short, it is worth getting old.[2]

Healthy Longevity Is Cheap

To paraphrase Woody Allen, death is a big cost saver. But so is a healthy life. Those who live longer cost society less in the last few years of their life than those dying younger. And this also reflects on family expenses. The National Mortality Follow Back Survey and the National Medical Expenditure Survey tracked Medicare, co-pay, nursing home care costs at a skilled facility covered by Medicare, as well as the cost of covered and noncovered prescription drugs (in 1996 dollars) to calculate end-of-life health costs. The surveys revealed that *acute* care costs decrease as age at death increases. For example, acute care costs for the last year of life for those that die at age 65 is $31,181, and for those that die at age 70, $22,590, a 37 percent reduction. And it gets better. For those who die at age 75, the cost averages *down* to $37,000 in the last *two* years of life, and only $21,000 for those who die at age 95. At 101, the last-year expenditure is a mere $8,296.[3]

I had the privilege of speaking with Dr. James Lubitz, a renowned expert on end-of-life and health costs. Mark his words: "The additional years covered for the longer-lived person are the relatively healthy and low cost years substantially before the end of life." Healthier people live longer.[4]

Health and Money, Perfect Together

I know firsthand the power of independence in surviving an acute illness. When I was a small child, I witnessed a virtual parade of pitiable deaths. One by one, my mother's large family of siblings contracted various types of cancer and made our home a kind of hospice. They were financially broke and emotionally depressed, and completely dependent on the ministrations of my Aunt Rose, a registered nurse. Although I could not articulate it then, as a child I realized that their overwhelming feeling was one of resignation. "Death would come, the sooner the better." I know, of course, that not all acute illnesses have a happy ending no matter how perky your attitude. I don't buy that we are the authors of our own disease, or that we can always shrink tumors or repair a failed heart through mind control. I *am* convinced by the many studies that show how we survive and heal after a serious operation that we have more control over our survival rate than we imagine. Many of these studies show a clear relationship between wealth, in terms of security, a feeling of self-worth and status, not just the absolute bottom line of assets and liabilities. Whether societal or individual, health and money are no longer two separate topics, if they ever were.

Chapter SEVENTEEN

How Will You Pay
for Your Healthcare?

Cost Containment

Americans who wouldn't think of dropping a candy wrapper on the street think nothing of eating a fried hot dog, which eventually costs the rest of us $50,000 for their heart attack. Strong words, but it's time that personal health maintenance is recognized as a public issue. As a lawyer, it's my belief that your rights stop at my nose. I don't want anyone to tell me what to eat or when or if to exercise. But when the cost of healthcare becomes the number one financial issue of a nation, rules and regulations start to set in. Ask anyone in business. They know that they are better off policing themselves, instead of being at the mercy of a review board. If you think that it's impossible to have a health police in this country, just remember that littering is fined, as is parking in the wrong spot. Today, people are seeking millions in compensation from the fast food industry for even serving the stuff that makes us sick. How long before we are fined for eating it, as we are now for smoking, in off-limit areas?

All I am asking is give bran a chance. At a recent joint conference of the American Society on Aging and the National Council on Aging, Mary Ferron of Health and Economic Outlook and Mary Swanson of HealthCare Dimensions spoke of the Silver Sneakers Fitness Program,

---

Everlasting Wealth

"If I Knew Then What I Know Now. . . Dentistry

As you budget for preventive care, don't forget your teeth. Teeth are like refrigerators; they last for a long time, but eventually need to be replaced. The time often comes, just when you can least afford it, that you must plunk down several thousand dollars for implants, bridges, or dentures. Geriatric dentistry is a growing field, with almost no financial coverage from government programs. And private dental plans are costly. To see if you or a relative can get dental discounts through state programs, log on to www.benefitscheckup.com. For information on innovations in dental care for seniors, contact Oral Health Services for Older Adults, University of Minnesota School of Dentistry.

---

an exercise program that is Medicare covered under several health plans as part of the National Blueprint for Physical Activity Among Adults Age 50 and Over. Why not make your own blueprint and start it years before you're Medicare eligible?

I'm not expecting civic guilt to result in your taking your vitamins or flossing every day. I'm just giving you fair warning that your health habits may come under official scrutiny when the cost of preventable chronic disease becomes a national emergency. And remember, the insurance industry already asks lifestyle questions before they underwrite you.

Even more compelling (until you actually suffer from your bad habits) is that you live longer when you try to stay healthy. A Harvard study showed that is takes about 28 days to change a life habit. All I am asking is give bran a chance!

Work-Related Benefit, After Retirement

Ninety percent of our employee benefits packages are devoted to medical coverage. When you quit, retire or are excessed, you'll have to choose between exercising your conversion rights under the Continuation of Benefits Rights Act (COBRA) rules, and buying an independent policy. If you take new employment or accept early retirement, you'll want to make the best deal for new continued coverage.

If you work for a large company, your employer may have unique information to help you make health maintenance organization (HMO) and other plan choices. For example, GTE visits each of the 125 managed care facilities that are part of its plan. Marriott has formed a purchasing coalition with other large employers to rate HMOs. PepsiCo requires that their HMOs offer preventive care programs. US Air compares the treatment programs that their employees get with a standardized nationwide norm.

More and more companies are also offering long-term care group insurance with the federal government leading the way. Before you buy, compare the group program at work with a private policy. You may find that the group policy evaporates when you leave the job, and you are stuck with a higher premium or are disqualified by a preexisting condition. If you are an employer, offering such a policy goes far in attracting and retaining workers. Uncle Sam wants to help. A C corporation can take 100 percent of the premium as a business expense. Yet another reason to form a corporation even if you are its only employee.

Private Healthcare Coverage Insurance

Comparison shopping in the $1 trillion healthcare megasector is like shooting at a moving target. Costs, coverage, and delivery of service procedures change with such lightening speed that we are tempted to accept what's offered and hope to stay healthy. But your healthcare coverage is no place for surprises. Not only do prices vary widely, but the extent and quality of coverage can ultimately mean life and death to you or someone you love. You must ask yourself the following questions.

What's Covered?

Marketing brochures are far from adequate to determine the treatments and procedures covered. You'll need a sample contract or subscriber agreement. If you have coverage at work, ask your benefits manager for a copy. You'll usually get a handbook. If you're on your own, ask your insurance agent or contact the plan directly.

When comparing independent coverage, start with the list of treatments and procedures offered. Some to look for are: maternity, well-baby care, emergency room coverage, maximums on hospital stays per day and per year, hospice, private duty nursing, and short term rehabilitation. But don't stop there. Check out preventive services. Are annual physical exams covered? Massage? Diet aids? Physical therapy? Chiropractic? What about mental health and dental coverage?

You must understand the details of the coverage. For example, most policies will cover childbirth. But, some require you to leave the hospital within 24 hours. Others apply the 24-hour rule, but cover visiting nurse or in-home care. Still others allow the physician to decide on length of stay.

Attention to the details is particularly important in the following areas:

- *Emergency Room Care*. Care may be denied under some plans, if the primary care physician is not first notified. There are various definitions of emergency.

- *Off-Label Drugs*. Plans vary widely as to which drugs are FDA approved for limited use, but which studies show are curative of other disease. Doxil, for example, is an AIDS approved drug, which may be helpful in slowing down the spread of different cancers. If not covered, the cost is $2,700 every two weeks.

- *Special Treatments*. Infertility treatments, bone marrow transplants, and pacemakers are only three areas where life, death, and (birth) decisions may depend on the fine print.

- *Long-Term Healthcare Allowances*. The type of service, that is, cleaning and cooking, and the venue where the services will be performed, that is, nursing home or in-home vary with price.

- *Mental Healthcare*. Health maintenance organizations (HMOs) usually cover 20 visits to a psychotherapist. Fee for Service plans (FFS) often cap visit costs at $1,000 per year. But, the wide variances in definition of emotional and mental conditions make the coverage itself surefire under some policies and denied under others.

Before selecting, visualize your probable medical future. Are you a constant victim of sports injuries? Do you intend to have children or are those days past? Are there medical family histories making you prone to cancers, and so on?

Who Will Treat You and Your Family?

Fee-for-service (FFS), the most traditional (and expensive) plans allow you to select any physician, pay on your own, and receive a reimbursement according to a designated co-pay schedule. Usually, after the deductible is paid, the insurer will cover 80 percent of your costs. There are also yearly caps on the amount you must pay and lifetime ceilings on the amount the insurer must pay.

Recent varieties of FFS plans are closed and open panels. The *closed panel* type limits your choice to physicians who have agreed to a fee schedule negotiated with the plan. The *open panel* allows you free reign, as well as closed selection. But, if you choose an independent doctor, you must pay the doctor yourself, then seek reimbursement from the plan.

Health Maintenance Organizations

The goal of cost containment has spawned an alternative to the FFS system, *managed care*, most notably HMOs. Today, there are at least six models to choose from, varying mostly with your autonomy to choose a physician.

Staff Model. The doctors and other professionals are employees of the HMOs.

Group Model. Groups of medical professionals contract independently with the HMO. They continue to practice independently as well. So long as you stay within the group, there will be no out-of-pocket costs to you and no reimbursement paper work.

Point of Service (POS). You can use doctors outside of the network, but you must pay more, usually a 20 percent deductible, as well as a higher premium.

Preferred Provider Organization (PPO). You are encouraged to use members of a specified directory of physicians, although you may choose out-of-network services with a higher co-pay.

Dental Maintenance Organizations (DMO). All of the aforementioned variations are available for dental care.

What Will It Cost?

The cost depends on you. The amount of the deductible, the coverage and the scope of extra medical functions (dental, psychiatric, chiropractic), and the number of family members covered all make a difference. In judging costs, Beth Kobliner, author of *Get a Financial Life: Personal Finance for Your Twenties and Thirties* (Fireside Books, 1996), advises younger people to watch the deductible. A 30-year-old single woman would pay a premium of $184 per month to Blue Shield of California with a $200 deductible. With a $1,000 deductible the monthly fee goes down to $95. The HMOs usually do shine in the cost arena as they have no deductibles (which increased in FFSs by 59 percent from 1988 to 1993). Preventive care is often 100 percent covered (i.e., free cancer screening, yearly checkups, and well-baby care).

Will Treatment Be Withheld to Cut Costs?

With most HMOs and their variations you will be assigned a gate-keeper physician. He or she dictates your course of treatment, including whether and which specialists you see and which medication or special treatments you receive. Is the gatekeeper a health enhancing case manager or a barrier between you and recovery? The answer might be in how he or she is paid!

Whether the managed care gatekeeper will recommend an experimental treatment varies widely among HMOs. In most HMOs, a technology assessment panel or the medical director of the managed care program sets the quality, policy, and tone. Opinions and decisions among them vary widely. Even within the same company, one patient may be denied a treatment that is afforded to another.

Critics report that doctors who are too aggressive in prescribing expensive medication are asked to leave. Champions insist that cost containment shields the patient from numerous, unnecessary tests that are designed to protect the doctor from lawsuits, rather than help the patient.

Cost-cutting experiments abound, like the *withhold system* where money is withheld from the HMO if too many referrals or tests are ordered. Other companies give bonuses to doctors with low specialist referral rates. Still others give doctors a pool of money to spend on their patients. If there is money left over, the doctors get to keep it.

Everlasting Wealth

You Be the Watchdog The National Committee for Quality Assurance (NCQA) is a nonprofit Washington based organization, founded in 1990, to give objective evaluations of managed care programs. The NCQA uses 50 measures to evaluate plans, from routine offerings of Pap smears to number of board certified physicians empanelled. It has set up its own criteria for accreditation. It has reviewed about half of the nation's health plans and about one-third has received accreditation. Check out a plan by calling 202-955-3515, or log on to www.ncqa.org to see if it was audited and passed the NCQA review. While you're at it, ask for an accreditation status list of all the plans screened.

Plans may offer you a report card based on Healthplan Employer Data and Information Set (HEDIS), which is based on standardized performance tests developed by NCQA.

Another watchdog is the government. Medicaid, public health, consumer affairs, offices of the aging, and the U.S. Department of Health and Human Services may be of help in special situations.

Does this pit doctor against patient so that stingy treatment is doled out? Or, by encouraging prevention and avoiding excessive testing, do cost penalties actually keep members healthier?

Some important questions you'll need to ask the doctor is:

- *Access.* How long do you wait for an appointment? How long will you cool your heels in the waiting room? Is there telephone access to doctors?
- *Continuity of Caregiver.* Will you get the same professional or will your file float?
- *Coordination of Your Treatment.* How is case management conducted? Are there weekly meetings or memos?
- *Vacation Schedules.* What happens when your doctor takes a breather?

- *Disagreement Forum.* Where do you go to change an assigned doctor or request a different treatment program? Are such requests resisted or honored?

- *Preauthorizations.* Aside from emergency treatment, what other care requires authorization? How long does approval take?

Chapter EIGHTEEN

Medicare and Medicaid

Medicare is no panacea for the costs you will incur because of increased lifespan. Medicare is part of our Social Security system and was created in 1965 as an amendment to the Social Security Act of 1935. Medicare is available to all those over the age of 65 and to certain younger, disabled individuals. It is an *acute* care program and to some degree a preventive care program. It pays little toward chronic care and nothing toward unskilled chronic care. Nor does it pay for residence in adult homes or assisted living communities, or cover the cost of your prescription drugs.

My father-in-law, Marvin Bochner, is a Medicare counselor. He is part of a volunteer program of older Americans assisting other seniors to understand the system. When he discovered that I was writing this book he toted over a ton of information. It's all available to you by contacting www.medicare.gov.

A Quick Primer on Medicare and Medigap

Medicare with its limited resources is an illness, not a wellness, program. It pays for *medically necessary service*, for diagnosis and treatment. In 2000, Medicare paid 21 percent of the national spending on health services, financed 32 percent of the nation's hospital services, 22 percent of physician services, and accounted for 12 percent of the total federal budget. No wellness spending even comes close.

At present, the Medicare Hospital Insurance Fund, which pays for Part A (described later), is so-called safe (will not run out of money) until 2025. Medicare +C (managed care programs) has grown, but with spotty results. Many doctors have removed themselves from these plans, accepting only fee for services. However, under the Benefits Improvement and Protection Act of 1999, there are increased payments to doctors and some easing of paperwork, so attrition may slow.

Medicare has two parts, neither of which covers prescription drugs or chronic unskilled care.

1. *Part A*: covers hospitalization including the cost of a semiprivate room in a hospital including skilled nursing services, operating room, meals, x-rays and in hospital medications, home visits after a discharge, and hospice care. Eligibility is automatic once you reach age 65. If you take early Social Security benefits, you still must wait until age 65 for Medicare. It does not cover a private room, a private duty nurse (unless medically necessary), television or telephone or over 190 days of inpatient mental healthcare in a lifetime.

   - For a benefit period of 60 days consecutively the co-pay is over $840 per benefit period. After 61 days, the co-pay is $210 per day. After 91 days it's $420 dollars a day, and 100 percent after 150 days.

   - Many people think that Medicare pays for a long-term care, but they are wrong. Part A pays for 20 days in a skilled nursing home facility directly after a three-night hospital stay, and the difference between $105 a day (which you pay), and the cost of the stay after 21 days up to 100 days.

   - Medicare has no monthly coverage for people not in the Social Security system or their spouse. But, if you are not in the system you can buy in at a premium of $316 a month, if you have 30 to 39 credits, the tariff is reduced to $174 a month (2003 figures).

2. *Part B*: covers physicians, and outpatient services including labs and related services like the MRI, mammography, cancer screenings, scans, and certain preventive treatments. Part B is voluntary but 95 percent of all Part A recipients enroll.

- Premiums for Part B are $58.70 a month (which are deducted from your Social Security benefits). Apply within three months of the retirement date or by six months after, or there will be a 10 percent increase in premium for each elapsed 12-month period or part thereof. And just about all services have 20 percent co-pay, plus a $100 yearly deductible. Because of the deductible and co-pay, many people carry supplemental insurance or co-insurance. At age 65, you are eligible to buy a Medicare supplement policy called *Media* that covers the deductible, some treatments not covered by Medicare, prescription drugs, and international treatment; but not chronic or long-term care.

Credits are what you need to be eligible for Social Security, Medicare, Survivor's benefits, and Disability benefits. You get credits by working. Not every worker gets credits; for example, certain railroad and federal government workers are covered under different programs. But most people do. If you were born after 1929 you need 40 credits to collect full benefits. These are the building blocks of your secure future. How many do you get? That depends on your earnings and the amount of the credits awarded for them, which changes each year. Once you earn 40 credits you can work forever and still get no more. Before 1978 employers reported your earnings quarterly; now it's yearly. Under the formula for 2003 you get 1 credit for earning $890, and 4 credits (the maximum you can earn each year) for earning $3,560. What happens if you become disabled before you get the 40 credits? That depends on how old you are when you become disabled:

Age	The Amount of Credits You Need to Get Benefits
31–42	20
44	22
46	24
48	26
50	28
52	30
54	32

Some people take a Medicare alternative called *Medicare + Choice*. These are either HMOs or fee-for-service plans, as discussed in the previous chapter, and are not available everywhere in the country. You enroll in these plans and disenroll at specific times of the year. Call 1-800-Medicare for details. Ask the questions listed in the previous chapter and remember that the HMO will likely have a gatekeeper, a doctor who must refer you to a specialist. Be prepared to be your own advocate or the advocate for an older parent. Unfortunately, this is a squeaky wheel system, where a new type of professional, which we will discuss later on, the geriatric care manager, can make a difference.

As you can see, Medicare is far from an all-inclusive program. Some experts, like Sharon Burns and Raymond Forgue, in their book, *How to Care for Your Parents' Money While Caring for Your Parents* (McGraw-Hill, 2003), say that it covers only half of an elder's medical costs.

Medigap to Fill in the Gaps

Medigap policies cover co-pays and go beyond the benefit period. And some plans cover prescription drugs and foreign country emergency care abroad. Medigap offers 10 plans, A through J, as mandated by law. You can enroll within six months of applying for Medicare B with no medical underwriting or consideration of preexisting conditions. You can compare Medigap policies on www.weissratings.com. Dental visits, glasses, and hearing aids are generally not included and require a separate policy or a discount card.

Medicare and Longevity

Medicare pays part of some preventive and diagnostic services that aid our longevity. For example, it pays for 80 percent of approved mammogram screenings yearly and Pap smears every three years unless you are designated to be at-risk. Men can get yearly prostate screenings. And we all can get bone density measurements.

To give you an idea of the complexity and scope of Medicare coverage, let's focus on a unique longevity tool, the motorized scooter. You can see daily infomercials on TV touting the transformed lives of various seniors as they take excursions with their grandchildren, or play chess in the park. Presumably, these experiences were

Everlasting Wealth

Why Do Medigap Policies with the Same Benefits Have Different Costs?

Attained age policies prices start lower but go up as you age. Review the costs every five years to see what you are in for.

Issue age policies costs start out more expensive and stay consistent. Of course, for the predictable longevity budget I recommend issue age, especially since this is a policy you want to keep all your life.

Community rated policies are the same as issue age policies but pricing depends on geographic area and risk assumptions are different. Shop around. And don't stop shopping. Review rates every year or so. In most states, you will not be penalized for any preexisting conditions and you can change companies frequently for better pricing. But *never* change until you are sure that you cannot be turned down.

closed to them before this remarkable piece of equipment came their way. At the end of the infomercial a voice tells you that this magic carpet may be paid for under Medicare.

Now, here's the scoop. If the scooter comes under the category of Durable Medical Equipment (DME), which is similar to medical supplies, prosthetics to replace limbs, and braces to support body parts, the Medicare statement is true—to a limited extent. But beware, scooters and other advanced equipment are not covered unless you need them for medical, not lifestyle, reasons.

Medicare pays for the scooter if *you cannot walk in the house, not just at the mall.* It all starts with your doctor's diagnosis and prognosis. He or she must order the DME and issue a *certificate of medical necessity.* And there is no payment for upgrades without supplementary physician orders. Rent and repairs for rentals may be capped, and if you do rent, you must usually buy the DME after a certain period of time and pay for noncertified upgrades within nine months of purchase. Even then, only up to 80 percent is covered if from a Medicaid-certified supplier that takes Medicare assignment.

Whew! The point is simple. You make a big mistake if you expect that living to age 65 and becoming Medicare-eligible takes you off the hook for medical expenses. Lifestyle enhancers from minioxygen tanks to designer grab bars are private-pay or part-private pay items. As we improve technology, more and more items go off the list, as coverage costs would skyrocket.

The Geriatric Care Manager—A New Profession, a New Cost

Recently, two of my best friends lost a parent. One's mother died and the other one's father died, within three weeks of each other. I can't help but compare the difference in healthcare that each parent received, and the effect it had on his or her family.

In one case, my friend's Mom lived out the last several years of her life in a nursing home, not far from her daughter and grandchildren. They saw each other on a regular basis. And I saw her, too, on holidays and at her granddaughter's bat mitzvah. She died at age 89 of complications caused by pneumonia, with her family standing at her bedside with ample time to say goodbye.

My other friend's father lived in Florida. For many years he was ailing with loss of blood, stomach pains, and various symptoms that seemed to elude diagnosis. A few days before he died, his new doctor sent him to the hospital for observation due to an irregular heartbeat and edema of the legs. He seemed to improve and there was talk of discharge, although still no diagnosis. On the fourth day, my friend got a call from her brother, "Dad died." The presenting cause was fluid in the lungs. He was 88 years old. But many questions remain, not the least of which was the sudden turn of events, which left my friend heartbroken at not being there at the end.

The importance of a geriatric care manager (GCM) cannot be overemphasized, especially if parents (or you some day) will live far away from family. Geriatric care managers may be social workers, nurses, psychotherapists, or social psychologists by background who manage the care of older people or the disabled through their life transitions. They put emphasis on family unity, cooperation, and the maximization of life options. They may play an advocacy role in court or with facilities and government agencies regarding entitlements. When elders are far away from family, GCMs act as surrogates for the family with doctors and hospitals. Typically, they will see a

Interview: Kathleen Driscoll and Doreen Spelbrink
Elder Care Services—How They Can Help

I interviewed Kathleen Driscoll and Doreen Spelbrink who are the vice presidents of Seniorbridge Family, a growing network of geriatric care and eldercare service in at least eight states. They recounted a situation when a client had a minor stroke and the assisted living facility insisted that she be moved to a permanent higher level of care. By advocacy and monitoring, her GCM was able to keep her out of the permanent "new level," and in the more independent part of the facility. The aphasia improved and all were satisfied.

"The effort to stay independent is assisted by GCM in other ways," says Kathleen. "GCMs can help refit your condo, offer a bill paying service, or help you cope with a spouse's death. We are part of the growing recognition of an integrated model of care."

client every other week to check out their skin tone, frame of mind, robustness, and level of medication management, and generally review their ability to thrive.

If you or a loved one is residing in a continuing care facility, the GCM may help you stay at a lower level of care within the facility, and therefore, keep you at your highest level of independence.

Your GCM is on private pay. Just like your accountant, CPA, or attorney, he or she charges by the hour. Your best referral sources are from attorneys, hospitals, doctors, discharge planners, CPAs, religious leaders, and general word of mouth. Look for a professional that is a Certified Care Manager (CCM or CMC), and is a member of the National Association of Professional Geriatric Care Managers.

Many long-term care insurance polices offer a case coordinator after a claim is made. These may be gatekeepers to keep down the costs of care, or they may serve a similar function to the GCM. Take nothing for granted. Before you buy, ask your agent exactly what the service offers, where the coordinator is located, and whether they actually see the claimant periodically.

Interview: Judith Sexton

Judith Sexton is head of the Alzheimer's program at Home Instead Senior Care, a nonmedical home care service, with most of their clients over the age of 65. "Home Instead Senior Care," says Judith, "is dedicated to providing at-home services through franchising operations in 45 states and abroad. After 14 months of training, including Alzheimer's sensitivity training and home safety, caregivers provide services like house keeping, bill paying, escort and all kinds of other services." (Check out their website at www.homeinstead.com.) They are often housewives, church and hospital volunteers. The franchises who employ and manage the caregivers meld a calling with the opportunity to make money and build a business.

Services like Seniorbridge Family or Home Instead are not covered by Medicare. For those that cannot afford private pay the alternative is *informal care*, a fancy phrase for you.

Unpaid caregivers account for 57 percent of all home care given to adults over the age of 65. When compared to the 36 percent who are paid, it is clear that the majority of families are seeing to the care of their older members. Without compensation the drain on personal time must never be dismissed.

Medicaid—Not a Free Ride for Those Who Fail to Plan

Medicaid is a means-tested program for the poor and medically needy. You must be both. Although it is a federal program, the eligibility and extent of the programs varies from state to state. Medicaid is not a backup plan for middle- and upper-middle class people who have failed to plan. I admit that as an elder law attorney and one of the founders of The National Academy of Elder Law Attorneys (NAELA, www.naela.org), I participated in finding the strategies that permitted clients to transfer assets and qualify for Medicaid. It was my job. But through the years things have changed and so has the attitude and responsibility of the elder law bar. Recently, the New York State Bar Association embraced long-term care insurance as an important method of paying for chronic care and provided guidance to practitioners on how to help clients select a policy. A cogent statement at the January 2003 New York State Bar Association's Elder Law Committee Annual meeting handbook makes the point: "Long-term care always pays for more care than Medicaid. It pays for nursing home care, assisted living and home care. Medicaid pays for a nursing home, does not pay for assisted living, never seems to pay for adequate home care (except in limited circumstances). Long-term care insurance pays to keep you out of a nursing home, while the Medicaid bias seems to push you in."

If you want to fully enjoy your longevity, here's why Medicaid planning should not be your first line of defense:

1. You can keep very little of your income and assets. Here's an example of the present Medicaid eligibility requirements in New York State. If you live in the community (age in place, a NORC) your monthly income cannot exceed $642 plus $20 per month if over age 65, and you are blind or disabled. Your total assets cannot exceed $3,850 plus a burial amount which is unlimited (so long as there is an irrevocable burial fund agreement with a funeral home), plus your home and car. If you are institutionalized there is no allowance for a home or car. If you are married with a spouse living at home, you may have joint assets up to $90,660 and the home. These figures are a moving target and differ from time to time and state to state.

Everlasting Wealth

Medicaid Is Local!   Even though Medicaid is a national program, its rules are highly controlled by the state in which you live, and its implementation may be county by county. For example, some states look at your assets and also cap your income. This means that if you have over their designated amount you are not Medicaid eligible. Other states will extend eligibility to you, but require that you contribute your income first, before they pay the difference in the cost of care. Always seek local elder law help, and do not compare your situation with that of others, one small difference in their fact pattern may make all the difference in the way the law operates.

2. You cannot simply transfer assets to a child or anyone else, because of the "look back formula." *Medicaid look back* means that any assets available to you that you transferred to any other person or entity in the 36 months before you applied for Medicaid (60 months if transferred to a trust) is totaled. That figure is divided by the monthly cost of a nursing home in your state or region as published by the Department of Social Services (DSS). The mathematical result is the number of months you are not eligible for Medicaid. For example, if you apply on January 1, 2003, any assets you transferred on or after December 31, 2000 will be totaled. Let's say that's $100,000. If, as in New York, the DSS monthly nursing home cost figure is $7,500, divide $100,000 by that number. The result, $(13\frac{1}{2})$, is the number of months you must be on private pay before you are Medicaid eligible.

The federal government has made transfer of assets just to claim Medicaid benefits illegal. First, they tried to dissuade clients with the "granny goes to jail law," an unenforceable technique. Then they simply made it illegal for lawyers to manipulate clients' assets to help them become eligible. The message is clear: Medicaid is a poverty program, not a back-up plan for middle- and upper-middle class Americans who fail to plan.

The problem is that Medicaid eligibility sounds very attractive. It pays for unskilled chronic care help in nursing homes and at home in a few states, as well as prescription drugs, where Medicare does not.

People who do not make themselves Medicaid eligible by transferring assets may feel like chumps, the way folks who pay full fare for an airline ticket feel nowadays. And those who know the system may still render themselves eligible, while those who don't cannot. "Financially sophisticated people who are accustomed to dealing with attorneys, accountants, and financial planners can find ways to protect their assets and still qualify for Medicaid."[1] One such sophisticated technique is the use of the immediate annuity in Medicaid planning.

Immediate annuities, discussed in Part V as a premier strategy to be sure that your money line is as long as your lifeline, is also used to gain Medicaid eligibility and still preserve some assets. Tony Webb, economist and annuity expert whose work we review in Part V, cites an 85-year-old woman with an actuarial life expectancy of six years. She becomes ill and wants to qualify for Medicaid to cover nursing home costs, but has assets of $100,000. If she buys an immediate annuity that lasts at least five years (called a *5-year certain*), she can structure it so that she receives monthly payments of $490 *plus* a lump sum balloon payment of \$95,000 at the end of the fifth year. By naming her daughter as the beneficiary of the term certain annuity and the balloon payment, if the woman dies in less than five years, she will have sheltered for her daughter the remainder of the monthly payments and the balloon lump sum. Yet, she will be Medicaid eligible from the moment of the transfer.

Interview: Howard Krooks

Howard Krooks, partner at Littman Krooks Limited Liability Partnership (LLP), is chair of the Public Relations Committee of the NAELA, chair of the Elder Law Section of the New York State Bar Association, and a lecturer at NYU in asset protection.

I asked him how he proceeds in a typical case where a family member, other than a spouse, comes in to plan for a chronically ill senior. "When children or other relatives do planning with a senior," says Harold, "I have a definite protocol. I immediately check whether there is a Power of Attorney and healthcare proxies. Then I assess with the family where the senior should go. The facility selection may require an assessment by a geriatric care manager. I then see where the person may be 'medically eligible' for residence. Finally, we plan monetarily. But remember, home healthcare is not available in most states even for those eligible for Medicaid. So we in New York have more care options for people on Medicaid."

I asked him about a technique through which transferring assets to an immediate annuity allows you to be eligible for Medicaid because the transferred sums are not counted in the look back period. "That's very true," he replied. "But the annuity, which may be privately created between family members or bought from an insurance company, must be actuarially sound. That means it must pay income to the person who made the transfer for their life or for a reasonable period consistent with their life expectancy."

I asked Howard how using an annuity to convert assets into monthly income might work in states where too much monthly income could keep you off Medicaid. "If too large a sum is transferred, the cash flow could keep you from qualifying. But in many income-sensitive states a Miller trust becomes the actual owner of the income. And eligibility is possible."

The message is clear. If Medicaid is your only alternative you *must* get specialized help. And that help is clearly out there from the best of the elder law practitioners. But remember that you are aspiring to coverage from a poverty program, with limitations on your freedom to choose.

3. You cannot simply transfer assets to a spouse because the computations are joint, even if only one of you applies for Medicaid. The well spouse keeps about half the assets and may stay in the home. But the other half of the assets is earmarked for spend down before Medicaid kicks in. As usual there is a complicated formula. First, the total assets are calculated and a yearly minimum amount is set based on the Consumer Price Index (CPI), this year it is $18,132. If joint assets or assets in either spouse's name exceeds twice the minimum, the well spouse can keep 50 percent, up to a total of $90,660. Unless they make a *spousal refusal*. New York, Florida, and Illinois may be the only states where spousal refusal makes a significant difference; in most states it's not an option, as it would not be in cases of nonspousal transfers.

Interview: Daniel Fish
Spousal Refusal

Daniel Fish, senior partner with Freedman and Fish in New York City, past president of the NAELA, and current officer of the Elder Law Committee of the New York State Bar Association, described his typical case. He wanted to dispel the "myth of the Medicaid millionaire." Bear in mind that Dan provided real numbers for New York, one of the highest cost, highest asset areas of the country.

"My typical clients are a husband and wife. Generally, she has already been taking care of him for four or more years and is exhausted. No, beyond exhausted. Her health is failing and neither has long-term care insurance.

"Generally I get a call from the hospital. The husband has a hip fracture and five days have passed and they are about to discharge him. But, he can't return home. Someone told them that they must spend all their assets, and she is crying.

(Continued)

Interview: Daniel Fish
Spousal Refusal (Continued)

"Here's how I help. First, I have a thorough consultation, which takes me no more than one hour. We make a plan. I always hope they walk in with existing powers of attorney and healthcare proxies. We discuss the family and the alternative of moving to a less expensive area. I give them options. My work is all about options; as with a surgeon, people want options, they make the choice. If they choose Medicaid, I transfer their assets to her entirely. She makes a "spousal refusal to contribute income or resources." From then on, the husband is treated as an individual to determine eligibility."

"But what about the look back period? Don't the Medicaid authorities question the transfer?" I asked.

"They can," says Dan, "but it's rare. As it's rare for them to go after assets after the recipient dies."

"So why doesn't everyone take a shot at Medicaid?" I wondered.

"In fact, Medicaid is a last resort for most. Medicaid really does put you on the dole. Remember, New York uses 90 percent of all the federal home healthcare funds available under Medicaid. Most other states have no home healthcare program and won't. Medicaid is for nursing homes in most states."

Dan, again, reminded me that enforcement also varies from state to state. And his experience may not be that of practitioners nationwide.

Recovery from Your Estate

When the well spouse dies, if he or she has made no transfers, Medicaid is technically able to recover some of its costs from the estate. Aggressiveness in collection varies from state to state. At present, a simple planning tool can protect all assets. The law permits recovery *only* against assets that will go through probate. By using a revocable trust or even joint names on accounts, there are no assets to be probated through a will. Medicaid has no probatable assets to collect against. In fact, because of the privacy of the revocable trust, it will not have notice of the death of the spouse through court records. So even in states where probate goes smoothly, it may be important for you to create a revocable trust instead of a will to pass assets onto your heirs, if one or both of you might be Medicaid eligible. It is this nexus between elder law and estate planning that makes most elder law attorneys expert in estate distribution.

Chapter NINETEEN

Nursing Home Costs

If you are currently considering a nursing home for yourself or a loved one, I want you to know what you'll encounter. The nursing home's administrative officer will look for a valid *payer source*, prior to admission. This can mean private pay, long-term care insurance, the family (if they sign), or the government. Medicare covers only the first 20 days after entry, and then only directly from a hospital, and then, only so long as skilled care is needed. From days 21 to 100 you'll be required to chip in $105 a day. Medicare will pay the rest so long as skilled care is needed. You may have supplemental, Medigap, or secondary insurance that fills the gap. Within that time there is some opportunity to plan for Medicaid eligibility, but you'll likely be on private pay for many months.

Overall costs are taken up with the admissions officer of each facility, which of course differ by facility and location. Make no mistake; there is a world of difference between high-end and low-end facilities. Life insurance agents with whom I work in New Jersey go out to visit facilities at all levels throughout the state. They meet to share their war stories. I visited with them, and as I listened, I became more convinced than ever that money and health couldn't be separated. "They have chandeliers like you never saw. Gorgeous." Offered one agent, who felt personally better after visits to a high-end establishment. "I couldn't stand the smell; I dreamt about it," said another assigned to report on a low-end facility. All were within government standards.

Adam Parton, director of Summit Ridge, which is one of many nursing homes in the Genesis Network in New Jersey, shares these cost figures:

- Medicaid certified rooms—$252 a day ($168 a day nationwide)
- Alcoeur—$268 (special Alzheimer's services)
- Noncertified room—$247
- Private noncertified room—$268 ($127 in the South)

He says the three biggest mistakes that families make with regard to long-term care and nursing homes are:

1. Fail to plan for the transfer.
2. Deny it will happen to you.
3. Have no Power of Attorney or healthcare directive (see Appendix C to fix that).

When a family member needs a nursing home, make common sense inquiries (i.e., taste the food, look around, and get referrals from geriatric care managers). Also:

- Ask for the Department of Health Annual Survey of the facility.
- Make a surprise visit.
- Interview residents asking, "How do you like it here?" (And look at them when you speak to them.)
- Ask which insurance companies work with the facility, and ask to see the contract and the audit used to recredentalize the facility.
- Ask if the facility does customer satisfaction surveys, and if they have a customer satisfaction team. If so, read the surveys and talk to team members.
- Compare the costs and care of a nursing home with an assisted living facility.

The Personal Needs Allowance

Those on Medicaid are allowed $50.00 a month to cover their personal needs. If you are virtually penniless, Supplementary Security Income (SSI) will give you the funds. If you are on private pay, there is of course no limit beyond your own means. Personal needs allowance (PNA) accounts can be established at a bank, but cannot exceed $2,000. If it builds beyond that limit, your Medicaid is cut off and you must reapply. Typically, the nursing home informs the resident when the account grows within $200 of the limit. If you are unable to manage your account, a family member can apply to be your Social Security representative payee, if there is no power of attorney. The PNA may come from your Social Security or money contributed by the family.

Will There Be Nursing Homes in the Decades to Come?

Perhaps not as we understand them today. At current usage rates, there will be 3 million Americans in nursing homes in 2030. According to the American Nurses Association (ANA), "preventing premature institutionalization is a major public health goal." For many, quality of life is better outside a nursing home and in the community. The ANA postulates the development of *light care facilities*, the new phrase for chronic as opposed to acute care. The federal government agrees. Josefina G. Carbonella, assistant secretary for the aging (U.S. Department of Health and Human Services), asserted that there is a federal initiative to move people out of nursing homes and into more independent facilities wherever possible.

Nursing homes are expensive to manage. In 2002, seven of the 10 top nursing home chains went bankrupt even though they were still operating. Owners complain that government (RUG) Rates are too low, causing them to skimp on care or go under. A recent reform requires the itemization of expenditures. There are now 22 allowed categories of expenditures according to level of care needed. If you want an eyeful of the government's struggle, visit the U.S. Department of Health and Human Services at www.hhs.gov./news.

But despite the expense, nursing homes can be the best alternative and a godsend to beleaguered relatives. And Medicaid is more liberal in covering nursing home expenses for those who are eligible than in covering assisted living or care in a continuing care commu-

---

Everlasting Wealth
Private Care Is Available, But Monitor the Situation

If you hire an aid to assist you in any type of facility, whether an assisted living community or a nursing home so that the resident can get specialized personal services like reading, answering letters, and so on, make sure the staff does not think that the assistant has been hired to take over their job, thereby innocently or deliberately slacking off. And remember, you are liable for any damage they may do to another resident. This tip is from Friends of the Institutionalized Elderly (FRIA).

---

nity. Moreover, nursing homes provide the highest level of care for those who need it.

Alan Parton, the director of Summit Ridge Center, a top-ranked skilled nursing facility in West Orange, New Jersey, whom you read about earlier, runs a deficiency-free home. He points out that a nursing home is not just longevity housing. It must provide a very high level of care to residents, 24 hours a day, seven days a week. There is a Registered Nurse in-house at all times, as well as other nurses. Rates cannot be compared to other facilities that offer lower levels of care. To conclude that there will be no nursing homes in our future is to be unrealistic. What we can hope for is to be able to afford a state-of-the-art facility for our loved ones and ourselves.

Chapter TWENTY

Long-Term Care Policies— Choice Not Chance

'll put my cards on the table. I am a long-time advocate of long-term care insurance. I can't imagine how people cope with both the emotional and financial strain of a chronic illness like Alzheimer's or Parkinson's disease without financial help. I know many adult children who have tried in vain to care for their parents by themselves. They either dissipate all the elder's assets until Medicaid is available, or meet a tad too late with an elder law attorney who makes the best of a bad situation.

Despite statistics from many sources, and not just the insurance industry, one in two of us will have occasion to make a long-term care claim. Are you ready to take a chance on which of the two you will be?

In "Shoot Me First," an article I wrote for *New Jersey Commerce and Industry*, I told the story of the best businessman I had ever met. He had every type of insurance from key man to yacht coverage. He kept his employees happy with split dollar, and employee whole life riders. He could be the poster boy for the insurance industry. I asked him why he didn't have long-term care insurance. "Well," he replied, "If I must go into a nursing home, let them shoot me first."

Long-term care insurance has not yet shaken the nursing home stigma. This is off the mark. Today's seniors are more likely to make a claim for the purpose of paying for a caretaker and living at home than going into a nursing home. This will be even more the case when boomers make a claim, and more so, yet, when Gen Xers and those younger do so. More and more, the coverage will be for a new pattern of living, like assisted or continuing care, for prostheses, and for medication management, and less for nursing home stays.

Also, an AARP study showed that people over age 45 think that Medicare pays for long-term care, and only 15 percent could estimate the cost of care in their area. The average national cost is $55,848 to $120,000 a year for residence at a nursing home; $1,500 to $3,000 a month in an assisted living community, and $477 a day for at-home care.

And the cost to you of ill health may be due to someone else's chronic condition. It comes as a shock when working women must abort their careers in their prime to care for mom or dad, or both. Eighty percent of caregivers are women.

So what will your parents' illnesses cost you in retirement savings for yourself? A 1997 Merrill Lynch study revealed that of the 62 percent who lose work time, the average loss of Social Security benefits is $25,494, and $67,202 in pension accumulation. What's more, the bell may ring just when you are accumulating your retirement nest egg. In the Merrill study, 40 percent reported that caregiving resulted in an inability to advance in their jobs, 20 percent turned down an opportunity to advance, and 30 percent had no time to increase their skills or education.[1]

Deny as we may, one in four families are currently caring for a person over age 50, of these, 60 percent also work outside the home. Caregiving profoundly affects the caregiver's health and work. The National Committee to Preserve Social Security and Medicare found that 27 percent of caretakers they surveyed report more headaches, 24 percent more stomach disorders, 41 percent more back pain, 51 percent more sleeplessness, and 61 percent more depression than they experienced before the caregiving began. Caregivers are three times more likely to use prescription drugs than those in their same general age group.[2]

When Is the Optimal Time to Buy?

Insurers report that long-term care policies are being purchased more and more by people between the ages of 45 and 55. When long-term care insurance is offered at work the average age of applicants is 43.[3] I

My Mom Doesn't Need Long-Term Care Insurance. I'll Take Care of Her

Many boomers cannot fathom the generations of missed inheritance that one long chronic illness can cause. One healthy, active 84-year-old told me that she would be insurable for another few months, as many companies cut off availability at age 85. But her baby boom daughter talked her out of spending $10,000 a year for lifetime coverage. My senior friend is extremely wealthy, but hated the notion of spending her grandchildren's inheritance if she became dependent, especially when the premium was not only affordable to her, but yielded a small tax deduction. "Why," she asked me, "is my daughter so against the insurance?" One answer is that we have trouble admitting that our parents will grow old, and certainly a policy that provides for it represents an acknowledgment of their aging.

But this resistance comes at a high price. Few of us have really thought through all the myriad costs and consequences of caring for an elder. In this case, I suspect the daughter planned to hire someone for her mom if the worst happened. Maybe she figured $15 to $40 an hour. Maybe this seemed doable. But did she figure the tax?

She'll pay Federal Insurance Contributions Act (FICA) for anyone who earns over $1,400 a year, and she will be required to withhold 7.65 percent of the employee's salary (that's 15.3 percent to the IRS). And another 0.08 percent on $1,000 to $7,000 will go for Federal Unemployment Tax Act (FUTA) (unemployment coverage).

believe it's because we see what is happening to our parents and we want it different for ourselves. So when do I think is the optimal time to buy? As soon after age 45 as you have the cash flow. If your budget is tight, choose a lower daily benefit with a compound inflation feature that ratchets up the benefit on each anniversary year. For those over age 50, if you must economize do so with a shorter benefit period (typically you choose from three years, six years, and lifetime), and a higher daily benefit. To accommodate buyers with a small budget some companies offer a policy that allows you to periodically increase the daily benefit according to current inflation costs. This makes the policy cheaper at first and more expensive as you age. I like the steady predictable rates of compound inflation. Others prefer that you avoid prepaying for inflation. We all agree that the decision is individual in each case.

One interesting possibility for those in their peak earning years in their early 50s is to consider a 10-year pay policy. You'll increase costs about double but you'll have a fully paid up policy by age 60. The counterargument is that most policies are immediately paid up when you make a claim. So if you had an early need you would not have to pay any longer.

If mom and dad do not have the budget for a long-term care policy, siblings can join together to insure their parents and protect their own health and inheritance. If siblings buy a policy for mom and/or dad they can share in the tax deduction available to their parents. The deductions are based on a sliding scale depending on age. Adult children who subsidize the policy get to take the higher senior deduction not the one applicable to their ages.

Moreover, parents with assets can help their baby boom children buy a policy and show no favoritism among siblings. A handy strategy is the *family bank*, a trust with a clause that allows the children to borrow out dollars and pay premiums that cover several policies. The loans can be forgiven at the discretion of the trustees, which may be family members.

Long-Term Care Insurance

How to "Build" a Policy

The best policies are those issued by the strongest companies. Watch out for companies that have firewall protection—the company cannot tap reserves and premiums from other policies if long-term care claims exceed their estimates. In that case, they will have to raise money to pay claims. Companies can raise premiums provided that they do so across the board and with the permission of the state department of insurance. Florida has allowed several rate hikes. Don't let the rate hike specter stop you, but do choose a company that is a tough underwriter, charges enough, and has a history of substantial reserves and a stellar record of claims paid. The earlier you buy the better.

Look at company ratings and see if they have been downgraded recently. A major choice you will have to make is whether to buy a *reimbursement* or an *indemnity policy*. The latter will reimburse your provider and operate much as health insurance does. The indemnity policy will pay you the daily benefit you select by sending a check to you each month. For freedom of choice, indemnity sounds best. But, it has its drawbacks.

Claimants receive a large monthly, tax-free check. The average policy in the Northeast covers $200 a day. It's tempting to spend the $6,000 tax-free dollars from your indemnity policy per month on care without realizing that there is a lifetime cap on the kitty. And beware, if you are under custodial care that check will come to a family member or other legal representative. Let's hope they are spending it for your benefit. If you choose indemnity, make sure your company has a Tiffany stamp.

By contrast, the reimbursement policy pools all your total coverage and saves the amount you do not claim to extend beyond the number of years of coverage you have purchased. For example, if you bought a three-year $200 a day policy you have a pool of $216,000 total. For every day on claim that you spend under $200, the rest remains in your pool. You may still be covered in the fourth or fifth year after making a claim even if you bought three years of coverage. With indemnity the total check comes to you. If you spend less you must manage the unspent amount or it will not be there if you need it.

How to Make a Claim

Once you need help with at least two of six so-called activities of daily living (ADLs) such as dressing, bathing, feeding, transferring (moving), toileting, continence, or have any cognitive impairment such as dementia or Alzheimer's disease, you may make a claim. Don't take a policy that does not count inability to bathe as an ADL, because it is usually the first to be needed.

Usually situational depression is not included as a cognitive impairment, nor is schizophrenia. A test to determine orientation similar to those given by neurologists is imposed where there is no other diagnosis.

Length of Coverage Considerations

These have to do with age and genetics. A person under age 70 should consider lifetime coverage if it is affordable. Today, the average length of claim ranges around three years, and is the shortest period many companies offer (some offer a year). A compromise of six years can work well if you are prepared to pay if you need care for longer.

Amount of Daily Coverage

The daily coverage you choose will depend on where you intend to age. Each state has different costs, which parallel the cost of living and real estate in the locale. There are different policy limits in different states (i.e., the Northeastern policies have higher available limits than in most other areas). Today, $150 is a typical minimum buy and $350 a typical maximum buy. But the coverage is easily changed through the all-important inflation factor. There are four approaches:

    1. No inflation feature (not recommended).

    2. A simple inflation rate of 5 percent a year. The daily benefit increases by 5 percent each year of the original benefit. A $150 daily benefit would increase by $7.50 each year.

    3. Compound 5 percent inflation factor would increase the daily benefit based on the new higher rate each year. For example, the 5 percent would be calculated on $150 the first year, $157.50 the second year, and so on.

    4. Some policies allow you to skip the inflation feature and buy a larger daily benefit every few years and pay premiums as if you were the age at original issue.

Covered Facilities

You'll want a policy that pays for home care, assisted living, continuing care, hospice, and adult day care. Durable medical equipment should also be covered and home renovation at least up to $10,000.

Elimination or Waiting Period

Usually, 20, 30, 90, or 180 days is the time that you must self-pay before benefits are extended. The longer you wait, the lower the premium. Medicare pays an average of 28 days of acute services if you spend at least three nights in a hospital immediately before getting the services. But some policies do not count the Medicare payments to calculate your waiting period. Check it out. Others make waiting periods cumulative if you make several claims (short recoveries, such as after a stroke). Others begin counting all over again.

Waiver of Premium

You will no longer have to pay premiums if you make a claim. But even here there are differences as some policies waive premiums automatically upon making a claim while others require that policies be in effect for a number of years before the claim is made to grant waiver.

Spousal Discounts and Other Perks

To capture the business of both spouses, many companies offer these incentives:

- *Premium waivers*. Both spouses may have premiums waived if one is eligible for a waiver of premium.
- *Discounts*. A discount of 10 percent to 25 percent for two policies. Some companies give the discount even if one spouse is rejected for the insurance.
- *Double Credit*. Each day that counts for your spouse's waiting period also counts for yours.

Jackson, age 60, was diagnosed with prostate cancer last year. His wife, five years his junior, hoped that they could both get insurance. But no company would issue a policy until he was two and a half years treatment free. Did that mean there was no spousal discount? Not entirely. One company offered a 25 percent discount if they both applied, even if he were turned down. (Not recommended.) Another offered her a 10 percent discount just because she had a spouse in the household—a nice and unexpected perk. The moral is shop or use an agent that specializes.

- *Transfer of benefits or survivorship benefit feature.* If policies were in effect for a period of years differing with each company and one spouse dies, the survivor's policy is paid up for the remainder of their life.

- *Shared benefit pools.* These occur when you and your spouse buy identical policies.

- *Informal Caregiver Training.* Your loved one goes to caretaker class.

- *Restoration of Benefits.* If you have paid for a period of years, make a claim and then do not need the care, some of the unused benefits are restored.

- *Same-Sex Couples.* The same premium discounts are available from some companies as for spouses. Some states permit this for family members as well.

- *Linked Benefit.* Your premium is converted to a death benefit if you never make a long-term care claim. This type of policy is not approved in many states, and is popular in the West. The Northeastern regulatory agencies are concerned with the ability to pay claims and require a large reserve.

- *Portability.* A portion of your coverage can be worldwide either for a specific period of time, usually six years, or up to a specific sum, usually 100 times the daily benefit. After this time you must repatriate to get the remainder of your benefits.

- *Respite Care.* A temporary caretaker comes in to give your regular caretaker a vacation.

- *Nonlapse.* If you lapse a policy, you get a paid-up benefit. In most cases the policy must be in effect for a few years, and the paid-up period is equal to the premiums you have paid.

- *Care Coordinator.* Many companies will pay for informal care by a spouse if you have a care coordinator assigned by them. Be sure they are not just cost containment watchdogs, but are there to improve your comfort and level of care. Ask where the coordinators are located, their exact function, and if they see the patient.

- *Bed Hold.* Your bed will be held for at least 30 days if you leave a facility.

- *Alternative Plan of Care.* Special flexibility if you need unique services. This is where home renovation may come in.

Taxing Questions

All reimbursements for actual expenses are 100 percent nontaxable. Up to $175 per day is nontaxable for unallocated per diem reimbursements (indemnity policy). If your policy is *tax qualified* and you itemize deductions, you can deduct a portion of premiums as part of your medical expense deduction.

Age under 40= $200.00

Age 41 to 50= $375.00

Age 51 to 60= $750.00

Age 61 to 70= $2,000.00

Age 71+= $2,500.00.

There is disagreement among insurance professionals as to whether it's worth buying a tax-qualified policy. According to the present law, before benefits are payable under a qualified plan you must be certified as chronically ill for a condition that must last for at least 90 days. In addition, benefits cannot start unless the insured is certified as unable to perform at least two of the activities specified on the government's list of daily activities. And, the deduction may be very small in proportion to the premiums. Medical expense deductions cannot be claimed unless medical expenses exceed 7.5 percent of your adjusted gross income. And even then, only for the amount that actually exceeds that amount. This means that a taxpayer with income of $100,000 may only deduct medical expenses greater than $7,500.

THE HEALTH CHALLENGE THINK AND DO LIST

Make your health prevention wish list. Change habits slowly but thoroughly. Remember the 28-day rule (it takes 28 days to change a habit):

Smoking

Diet

Exercise

Stress

Improve any of the big four above and make a lifetime of difference. Write up your own plan.

Check out your health benefits at work, and take advantage of any preventive care they offer (e.g., teeth cleaning, massage, eye exam, mammography, and colonoscopy).

Check out organizations to which you belong to see what group health benefits they might offer.

If you have responsibility for loved ones' health, do the same for them, and consider a geriatric care manager if you need help.

Meet with an insurance professional to scope out the provision of a long-term care policy. Visit www.wealth102.com for guidance.

Meet with an elder law attorney if you or a relative needs to apply for government entitlements such as Medicaid.

Visit www.benefitscheckup.com for the entitlements offered by your state.

Part FIVE

Longevity and Your Money Life

Everlasting Wealth

It seems to me that a book like this, subtitled *Achieving Everlasting Wealth*, must ask the threshold question, "What do we really mean by wealth? What is enough?" And perhaps, most challenging, "Why does enough, no matter what the dollar figure, seem always to be more than what we have, at the moment?"

Polly LaBarre, in an article entitled "How to Lead a Rich Life" (*Fast Company*, March 2003), cites the Easterlin Paradox (named for Richard Easterlin, the economic historian)—"the more we have the more we not only want, but also the more we think we 'need and deserve.'" You probably figured that out by looking at your shoe closet or your neighbor's new kitchen. As we achieve greater monetary wealth, we set the bar a little higher, especially if those around us have more. And what can we expect? If we supersize our needs, our cup seems no more than half full, no matter how full that cup may be. Couple our overblown view of enough with the recent bear market, in stocks, and we have a growing fear that our money line will not keep up with our lifeline, that our wealth will disappear long before we do, and that we will never get the rewards we deserve.

This is a terrible fear and it can lead to a very sad and deprived advanced age no matter how much our bank account says we have.

Baby boomers see this in their own parents, already, and it upsets them. Comedian Mal Z Lawrence has made a masterfully funny routine out of seniors taking food "for later" and bringing plastic bags to the buffet. How sure are we that that won't be us? Can we dismiss this as depression mentality that will end with the Greatest Generation? Or is this part of the same distortion of what it takes to get by, and a willingness to eat at 4:00 P.M. to catch the early bird special, because of a misguided belief that even a great deal isn't enough.

I know this sounds preachy, but I am speaking of myself, as well as millions of others. According to the 2003 Employee Benefits Research Institute's *Thirteenth Annual Retirement Confidence Survey*:

- Sixteen percent of those surveyed were "not at all confident" of having enough money to live comfortably.

- Only 33 percent as compared to 38 percent in prior surveys were "very confident" that they could cover basic expenses.

- Twenty-four percent of those over age 45 had decided to postpone their retirement in order to increase their financial security.

Why do so many educated hardworking people feel financially troubled, in the richest country, not only on earth, but also in all of human history? One way or another I've struggled with this issue personally all of my adult life. No matter what my actual bottom line, whether fat or lean, I never feel completely secure about money. And I know I'm not alone. What is security? What is financial success? Why do we never feel that we get it right? And how might our growing longevity affect and be affected by the answers to these questions?

For most of us, the future requires some form of downscaling and downsizing. My goal is that we do this not just wisely, but with *joy*, a word rarely used in the same sentence with money.

Now that we are given the gift of longer life, will we be able to break the cycle of more money means more spending? It depends on whether we can redefine wealth to mean something deeper than the bottom line. We get a hint of how to go about this from the work of Andrew J. Oswald, professor of economics at the University of Warwick in England.[1] He has studied longevity and status (which for many of us, if we are honest, is synonymous with having money) as status correlates with life expectancy. Oswald found that the more senior people are when they retire, the longer their life expectancy. Accordingly, Polly LaBarre tells us that status has an even bigger effect on lifespan than does smoking. She offers, too, the delicious fact that a study by two economists revealed that Academy Award winners live at least three years longer than mere nominees.[2]

And so we are compelled to ask, "Can we redefine wealth to be synonymous with the state of joy, and freedom we can achieve? Can we gain satisfaction and status that enhances longevity from cultivating these inner qualities instead of through more acquisitions and admiration based on what we have rather than who we are?" I think we can and will. The tide has already turned, although subtly.

There has been a quiet evolution in what we mean by *everlasting wealth*, and in what we value and prize. It has started with our concept of what we want in monetary wealth in the age of longevity. We seek more than paper profits, or to be a millionaire. We seek wealth that sets us free, not the type that drives us for meaningless more. Wealth that's easy on the spirit—on automatic pilot, reliable and guaranteed; the wealth you use to enhance self-fulfillment, make bold decisions, stay independent, enjoy lifelong self-reliance, and neotiny.

Radical as it may seem, wealth, itself, is not a life achievement. And to the extent that we believe it is, we diminish our chances of becoming wealthy by any definition. Thomas J. Stanley and William D. Danko, in *The Millionaire Next Door*,[3] tells us that there are more than 5 million households of millionaires in this country. That figure surprises and impresses many. But I ask, "Why so few?" At $2,000 a year savings in an IRA, at 5 percent return, starting at age 25, anyone can retire at age 65 with a nest egg of $241,600.

We have already seen that longevity has affected our taste in housing, our behavior toward our health, and our career goals. And we have seen that changes in us have generated changes in government policy, business focus, and delivery of services. Money and investing is not an exception. There is a changing trend toward safety and conservatism that I believe would have occurred even without the cold bath of the past bad market and the agony of September 11th. There is a demand for disclosure that is understandable to the investor, and investments with measurable results. In short, we want to put back the security in securities. Longevity planning requires investments that yield income streams that will last a lifetime and beyond, coupled with our own commitment to choose a sustainable lifestyle.

The prospect of many extra decades to do good works, to enjoy ourselves, to relate more meaningfully to our family, motivates us to get rid of debt, avoid overspending and the pursuit of money for its own sake. We want peace, financial simplicity, and life experience, not disposable junk. To me this is a sign that we are a population growing both older and wiser. LaBarre writes of what she calls the "new influencials," people with middle-class wealth living first-class lives. They volunteer at every age, spend true quality family time, and have loyal friends.[4] In the mix is financial security; not for its own sake, but to support the fine handcrafted life they and we want to lead.

Your money line deserves to be as long as your lifeline. All financial planning is about funding your future and managing your risk. It is a wonderful endeavor, but it is meant to be a facilitator not a dictator. In great design, form follows function. If we need a chair, we design something to sit on. We do not design any old thing then find ways to sit comfortably, if we can.

But that is exactly how we design our money future. We see how much wealth we can accumulate, then tailor our desires to fit the sum. This might work, but we rarely carry out even our puniest plans. We are so frightened of the future that we rein it in with both hands. Then we lament when we get a surprise like forced retirement, a downturn in our stock option values, a divorce that splits our assets, uncovered medical expenses, or just a big dental bill.

Do you want to live backwards? Or are you willing to express your hopes and dreams for tomorrow without your internal money police censoring them? Your future will be as rewarding and liberating as you hope, if your life is rewarding and liberating right now. There is no magic fairy that makes everything different when you retire and walk out your office door. Sustaining self-fulfillment over three extra decades is no slam-dunk. There is nothing to guarantee it, not money, not health (these are just tools), only your own willingness to take on the future.

> When money is a prerequisite for the rewards of retirement, you have a monumental and unpredictable barrier to everything you seek for your future.

Why narrow our lives to what fits into our projected means, instead of tailoring the means so they fit the life we desire?

It's natural to believe that money is the major barrier to creating the future we want. Think again. Many unions give their workers free access to retirement planners. The workers have Social Security, a guaranteed pension, and for the most part, have lived well on their income all their adult lives. Their retirement package often exceeds their salary. Yet, they cannot craft their retirement. Many waited to make their plans because, "I wanted to see how much money I would have." Many have found their dreams so dusty and abandoned that they need counseling to recreate a vision.

Chapter TWENTY-ONE

Living the Handcrafted Life

Finding David

The legend goes that when Michelangelo was asked how he sculpted David he replied that he took a mountain of marble and cut away everything that wasn't David. To live the life we desire throughout our longevity requires only that we find ourselves within the mountain of marble in which we hide. We are already there in whole. When my Aunt Rose, the registered nurse was at death's door, she offered her food to her fellow patients. Her role was to be a caretaker. When a terminally ill client of mine, one of the wealthiest women in the America, turned her home into a hospice I visited her in order to make changes in her will. She requested that I help move around her Rembrandts. She was one of the world's greatest collectors and endowed an entire wing of the Metropolitan Museum of Art. Neither age nor illness had changed either of these women in any fundamental way. In fact, their enduring passions had heightened. Longevity does not provide us with a greater opportunity for change. On the contrary, it distills what we always were to a deeper essence. To lead a handcrafted life we do not need to recreate ourselves, only our life situation so we can be free to be ourselves.

Money Is a Tool of the Handcrafted Life

Part of what must be cut away to emerge into the life we want to lead is not a mountain of marble but a mountain of debt, obligation, and outmoded spending. Money is an efficient life tool. It ought to be used that way, not as a substitute for success.

On my way home from speaking at a gathering of 10,000 seniors attending the annual Age in Action Festival at Flushing Meadow Park in Queens, New York, I had occasion to meet a 58-year-old out-of-work IT specialist. He was having a bad time finding work in his field after his entire department was closed down. Yes, he was upset and worried, but he was also very excited. His belt tightening had forced him to chip it all away until only "David" was left. He was surprised at how little a $55,000 car or an Armani suit meant to him anymore. We chatted all the way home on the subway and wondered if anyone would really believe us when we told them how little the material life had come to mean to high spenders like us.

It had taken bad financial blows to force both of us to make a change. But once we changed, we found deeply worthwhile things to pursue. He coached neighborhood basketball ("during his usual shopping time," he quipped). At the end of our conversation, he confided that he had decided to get married and to take a teaching job in Virginia. He would go from Manhattan executive man-about-town, to married guy with high school students and a lawn. He couldn't wait.

Make a Budget

One of the best things you can do to get in touch with yourself is to make a budget. I know you don't want to hear that. I certainly didn't enjoy writing it, but it's true. A budget shows you where you stand with respect to your cash flow, but more importantly it is a reflection of how you live your life, whether you like where you're at, what you'd rather be spending it on, and how to make a change. Maybe that's why it's so difficult for most of us to make a budget, let alone stick to one. We spend our money on past debts or on needless or foolish items and it makes us feel regretful. The things we really do want we call luxuries and feel guilty to get, or overdo them, or talk ourselves out of them.

A good budget is not a straight jacket for your soul. It's a blueprint for your rewards. A budget helps you check your internal wardrobe to see if you have put on someone else's clothes. My fa-

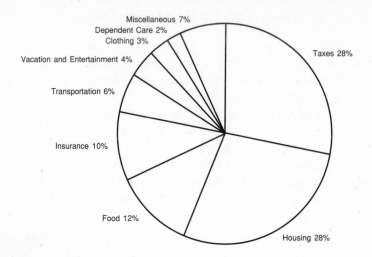

Figure 21.1   Make a Budget

vorite budget device is a pie chart with expenditures expressed in percentages. This takes the focus away from how many dollars we spend, and places it on the percent of income we devote to housing, entertainment, food, education, transportation, and healthcare. Make your pie chart budget using a simple pencil and paper—remember those? Figure 21.1 is an example.

Do your percentages break down to what pleases you? On what will you spend less? On what more? How do your family members fare? Is any child getting shortchanged? What do you plan to be that will make a difference? I did not say *what do you plan to do* that will make a difference. What do you plan *to be*? Will you be someone committed to living the life you love? If so, a balanced budget will follow. There are no other rules. Write down your plan, and keep it in mind, always.

Disposable Income Is What Sculpts the Handcrafted Life

All income is disposable until you tie it up and relegate its use toward a necessity. As the song goes, "Necessity is the maximum thing a minimum thing can be."[1] The sooner you can unbind your money from necessities, the freer you are to live the handcrafted life. For most of us there are three major expenses that stand in our way:

1. Housing
2. Children
3. Debt

Probably in reverse order.

In fact, all of these are discretionary, but we have turned them into necessities. If you are committed to do so, you can create an exit plan for all three. If you plan to age in place, make extra mortgage payments and get rid of the debt by a prescribed date. It's OK if that date is several years from now just as long it's slated to disappear. If you sell and down-scale at retirement, consider a mortgage-free home, or carry only a very small mortgage. The only reason to have a substantial mortgage after downscaling is to use the cash to pay for income-producing property.

The Myth of Shortage

Three times in my life I have suffered devastating financial blows. Three times they resulted in a new freedom and a fresh appreciation of what is important. We all know people whose illness or deep loss has propelled them into being inspirations for us all, like Christopher Reeve. I'm not one of them, which may be why my experience is instructive, just because it is so ordinary and so am I.

My father died suddenly when I was 11, leaving my Mom and me completely high and dry. My Mom slowly built a life for us, but the experience left me with a hungry ambition and a need to prove myself by the acquisition of things. By the time I was in my thirties I was a millionaire, with several homes and lots more. I did it purely by working hard and building one of the first women-run law practices in New York.

But I hated it. I loved radio, and my two-hour-a-day WMCA money show meant more to me than my law practice. I took a ridiculous chance and failed. I became a real estate developer mostly to make enough money to stop practicing law and start full-time broadcasting. It was a disaster. And when I was smack up against bankruptcy, I made two life-changing decisions. The first was to pay all the debts, although my partners both disappeared on me. The other was to quit law and broadcast full-time.

(Continued)

The Myth of Shortage *(Continued)*

Just as much as a great deal of money might have set me free, no money at all surely did. If I wasn't about to be rich, I might as well be happy. I was amazed at how easy it was to give up mega spending when I loved the work I was doing.

After about two years of paying back debts and scrimping in my personal life, I decided to meet my listeners' demands for a newsletter that would help them invest better. My motto was, "I have a lot of rich friends, and I would like to make you one of them." I can remember the first $39 check that came in from a listener. Then another, then another. The Wealthbuilder letter has been in circulation since 1994, and is now an e-letter.

And I became rich again. At one time we had 15,000 subscribers at a price of $69 a year. You do the math.

But I never returned to my bad spending habits. On the contrary, I wanted much less, and had much less to prove. There was something missing, though. I wasn't sure what. I wrote a novel that was dreadful. I thought about real estate again. I was doing well, but I felt a little lost.

Then the third blow came. I decided to start my own radio network after one of my radio sponsors was revealed to be a swindler. I was so uncomfortable with the situation that I left my 50,000-watt station and invested in a five-station money show. All went well until the core station sold to ESPN, an all-sports channel, and out I went.

Now what?

I had lost not only my income and my broadcasting career, but also the marketing outlet for my newsletter. By this time my husband was also my publisher, so he was out of work, too. All around me I felt shortage: shortage of money, shortage of opportunity, shortage of hope.

From that ancient, overworked Chinese adage that crisis and opportunity are the same word, I found abundance from shortage. For years I had neglected one of the most sustaining pleasures of my life—traveling. And because I knew money would be short, I started to travel write and tooled a new career in the remarkable field of adventure and hospitality writing. Did I make a ton of money? No. Do I love it? Yes.

The Myth of Shortage *(Continued)*

But more happened. I worked within myself, and with the incredible Dan Chayefsky, my life coach whom I met through Landmark Education. I still can't say why, but I came up with a true mission—that all of us have a wonderful old age. From that came my present life's work. One direct result is this book, another is speaking engagements, another is a nonprofit organization dedicated to assuring all of us enough money to live the life we love for as long as we are here on earth.

The three "crucibles" (see Anita's foreword) I experienced gave me more freedom than money ever would. Yet they taught me that money is available even when we make monumental mistakes. And even when you must live on less, your success can be measured so much more inspirationally than in dollars and cents. That's how I know you can downscale, quit a job you hate, and do anything you please, and still keep up your responsibility to your family and community. Contribution is not costly. It comes from what you are being, not from what you are paying.

That's my story.

You can unbind yourself from the dependency of children, but this can be much more difficult. Or fortunately, you may not have to make any drastic moves at all. Perhaps your assets and cash flow give you access to full tuition and a nice car at graduation. If not, take heart. I am not one to believe that money corrupts children or makes them lazy; I have seen no correlation whatsoever between family money and success in life.

If you have to spend less on children, perhaps these thoughts will help:

1. *Tell the truth.* When there are money issues children make things worse than they are, unless they know the facts.
2. *The truth strengthens and instructs.* When it comes to money the truth does not hurt, unless you make them or yourself wrong.

3. *Get creative.* Some "stuff" is important to kids—they want to fit in. There's nothing wrong with borrowing, making, or renting where possible. Learning to save for larger items doesn't hurt either. My favorite is waiting to see if the need lasts.

I have watched my two children, who are ten years apart, grow up in very different financial environments at home. We have much less as my daughter is growing up, and we must balance her immediate needs against our future independence. Frankly, I think Rose is much happier and more comfortable about money. She seems less attached to the material, and happier and more pleased with the things she has. Maybe it's just my guilty way to feel better about saying no. But, I don't think so.

Where Have You Committed Your Dollars That Do Not Pay You Back in Fulfillment?

For most of us, the answer is present debt service for past purchases. Nothing is as easy as making an exit plan to get out of debt. Every credit card company will put you on a special arrangement, just for the asking. If you need help, choose a responsible group like Consumer Credit Counseling (www.cccs.org), to create your debt exit plan. And for heaven's sake sell something. Turn some of that stuff into cash and use it pay down debt.

What Overspending Really Is

A quarter of a century ago, in his book *The Pursuit of Loneliness*,[2] Philip Slater wrote, "It isn't money that runs our economy, but vanity." We are now that much older; it's time we learned that overspending means spending on anything to impress others, to give us the illusion of success, to deny our vulnerability. The Merrill Lynch Baby Boom Retirement Index estimates that baby boomers save at one-third of the rate needed to provide themselves with a secure retirement.

What are you spending your money on that doesn't matter to you? What are you supporting just to look good to others? Write them down and then get rid of the expenditure.

The Longevity Spending Bell Curve

You will likely spend less after you retire, barring a health crisis (or a new 20-year old girlfriend). After all, your mortgage may be lower or paid off, major work-related expenses are gone, the kids are independent (we hope), debts may be repaid, and you'll get some senior discounts for travel and entertainment.

Eventually, you will encounter some increased expenses. You will want to enjoy the type of leisure that excites you, and contribute to adult children and grandchildren. And you may want to go back to school. All this without the benefit of company perks and write offs.

As you begin to get into your 80s, expenses may continue to increase. One of my favorite longevity budget items is a pet. A Skidmore College study by Jesse Bank and Cay Anderson-Hanley measured improvement in blood pressure and memory for those with and without pets. They concluded that pets helped subjects maintain a higher quality of life and that the effect was most beneficial for those with lower cognitive function.[3] Although they worked with a small sample of prior pet owners, we all may want to consider pet ownership as an added expense.

As long as you have provided for chronic care, along about 90 years of age expenses begin to decline again. The declining expense curve looks something like Figure 21.2.

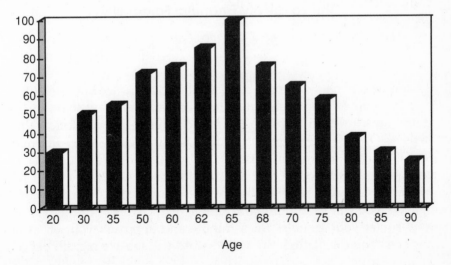

Figure 21.2 Declining Expense Curve

Everlasting Wealth
Drugs—Are You Spending for Your Life?

The $1 trillion healthcare industry comprises 10 percent of the average family budget, 22 percent for those over the age of 65. When professional certified financial planners work the numbers they are likely to project only 3 percent as the inflation rate. But the prescription drug inflation rate has been 6.3 percent in the past several years, and it is rising. According to the Congressional Budget Office, the "average out-of-pocket costs rose from $813 in 2000, to $1,051 in 2002, a 29 percent increase in two years."[4] Prescription drug costs are either entirely out-of-pocket, through an insurance program, from Medicaid if you are impoverished, but not from Medicare. Present planning is essential. This includes prevention and private plans. Twenty-seven states offer means tested drug programs. Check out www.benefits checkup.org. for this information. You can buy drug discount cards (some are available only if you are not eligible for any other program).

The Longevity Financial Forecast

I have all the money I need, provided I die by 4:00 o'clock.
—Henny Youngman

By now, you're ready to make a financial forecast to see how well prepared you are for your longevity. These are relatively easy steps. I will show you a low-tech way to perform each. But before you follow the steps, ask yourself if there is anything nonfinancial getting in your way. If you and your spouse disagree on goals, if you are afraid to face your present situation, if you are still unsure of where you want to live, or if you are threatened by possible changes like divorce or loss of a job, you will resist doing this simple math. Work it through anyway. Forget your troubles for a minute and approach yourself as a business. The calculations are painless and will make a big difference in your future.

Everlasting Wealth

Because the calculation of just the right number to ensure everlasting wealth to age 102 and beyond is a complex factor of income, expense, return, inflation, and time, the best way to determine that amount is electronically, either online or with a fancy financial calculator. Visit us at www.wealth102.com for online help.

Step 1. How Much Income Do You Need?
Finding the *Enough Number*

Put simply, the *enough number* is the amount that you require to meet your yearly expenses. The old rule of thumb is to shoot for 75 percent of your gross income, before retirement as your postretirement income target. A study by the Georgia State University and Aon Consulting 2001 for employees earning $30,000 to 90,000 revealed that the old rule comes pretty close.[5] So, you can use that 75 percent figure. Or, you can do a quick budget. Add the following amounts (make sure that you use a yearly basis for all):

Quick Fix Longevity Expense Sheet

Housing	_____
Taxes	_____
Transportation	_____
Insurance	_____
Food	_____
Entertainment	_____
Dependent care	_____
Miscellaneous	_____
Total (your *enough number*)	_____

In order to make *even more* sensible decisions about work, housing, healthcare, and investing, make a more detailed list. Determine both your present expenses and your anticipated expenses at retirement, and see if the difference comes close to the 75 percent rule.

Your best, and more important, your most candid recordkeeping is essential. You should list every expense you can reasonably anticipate, make sure that all of them use the same basis (that is, yearly, monthly weekly, and so on), and add them up. Or, you can use financial software like Quicken or Microsoft Money that will anticipate many variables of which you did not think.

Which *enough number* did you choose? Whether it is the 75 percent of income or the budgeted number, write it down (make sure it is yearly).

Enough number   _____

Step 2. How Much Retirement Income Do You Already Have, Guaranteed? Finding the Replacement Ratio and Shortfall

The *replacement ratio* is the calculation used to determine the source and amount of income that will replace the income that you will no longer be earning from work. To calculate it, first list everything you have secured that will give you a guaranteed, lifetime income. This usually is limited to Social Security, defined benefit plans and any charitable or immediate annuities you own. Most defined benefit plans are designed to replace 40 to 60 percent of the last three to five years of salary. Usually, you must have given 25 years of service to get the maximum benefit. Your defined benefit plan may be integrated with Social Security, that is, reduced by the amount you will receive to a certain degree.

The total yearly income from your replacement ratio assets is the floor or base on which you will live that can never run out, no matter how long you live. Fill out the information:

Total Annual Income that Will Last as Long as I Do:

Social Security	_____
Defined benefit plan	_____
Immediate annuity	_____
Mortgages? Loans payable to you	_____
Trust fund, business buy out, and so on	_____
Total (your *everlasting income*)	_____

This is your *everlasting income*. The money coming in that will always come in, forever, until you die.

Next, determine the percentage that this figure is of the total amount needed to cover your basic enough number. Calculate this by dividing the enough number by the everlasting income number.

$$\frac{\text{Enough number}}{\text{Everlasting income}} \quad \text{Equals} \quad \text{Replacement Ratio}$$

Although crude, this figure gives you a good view of how much you need to focus on other assets and income stream development. For example, those with a defined benefit plan based on 80 percent of their last two years average salary have an 80 percent replacement ratio. Not bad. Aside from Social Security, guess what my replacement ratio is. Zero percent. And so it is for anyone who owns his or her own business, freelances, or has a job with no guaranteed defined benefit plan.

Your replacement ratio is: _____

You must also calculate your income shortfall. This is the amount by which your enough number exceeds your everlasting income on a yearly basis.

Enough number _____
Minus everlasting income   − _____
Equals yearly income shortfall   _____

But even if your replacement ratio is very healthy and your shortfall small, you must go on to Step 3.

Step 3. Functional Inflation

Even for the best cradle-to-grave corporate program the specter of inflation can ruin the replacement ratio. Here's the rub. At 4 percent a year inflation your buying power halves every 18 years. So at age 65 you may be sitting pretty with a pension and Social Security that replaced 75 to 100 percent of your income. But by the time you're 80 that pension buys half of what it did at retirement. That would be fine if you died. But you won't. You will live on. And, by the time you are age 95, you will be living on a quarter of the buying power you enjoyed at retirement. If you are typical of today's seniors you have invested your savings on low-paying interest rates for their safety. And you are safely going broke.

There is of course the issue of whether inflation is really such a big problem. After all haven't we just lived through years of deflationary times? Yes and no. According to the Bureau of Labor Statistics, between 1976 and 2000, inflation averaged 4.7 percent. It was 1.6 percent in 2001 and 2.4 percent in 2002. Between 1991 and 2000, the average was only 2.7 percent. But, inflation has been 6.3 percent for prescription drugs, and runaway for healthcare.

You are not a statistic. Use inflation figures that are relevant to your life. I call this *functional inflation*, the way that pricing function affects you, day to day, in your real life. In figuring your functional inflation, you should take into account and weigh those areas of expenditure that truly affect you. The Consumer Price Index (CPI), the government's inflation figure, takes everything into account. It is made up of eight categories of expenditures monitored by the U.S. Department of Labor Bureau of Labor Statistics. They are:

Food and beverages

Housing

Apparel

Transportation

Medical care

Recreation

Education and communication

Other goods and services

An Example of *Functional Inflation*

From 1980 to 1995, postage stamps rose in cost 113 percent, from 15 cents to 32 cents, and now 37 cents. This matters to you if you write a lot of letters, or mail a newsletter every month as I do. It means nothing to my eleven-year-old who communicates by e-mail.

Do these increases mean anything to you?

- Paperback books were $3.25 to $5.95 in 1980, $7.00 to $9.00 in 1995, an 83 percent increase.
- *Wall Street Journal*, a 150 percent increase.
- New car, an increase of 159 percent.

If your lifestyle is fairly average with regard to the impact of inflation, use the 4 percent factor for the calculations to come. Otherwise, tailor it to what you have experienced. (For the illustrations and charts in this chapter, we are using 4 percent.)

What inflation rate is the one with which you will work? _____

Everlasting Wealth

Gold Could Be the Jewel in the Crown of Your Longevity
Inflation has a very serious impact on buying power, but so does the value of the dollar in comparison to foreign currency. So much of what we buy is manufactured offshore, that CNN FN did a power lunch spot on the few U.S. companies that do manufacture chips. The reporters found it miraculous that anything with a chip or an electronic device could be made here.

One investment that has traditionally done a yeoman job in keeping up with inflation and currency fluctuations is gold. It also helps when the dollar is devalued. (Not gold mine stocks, or mutual funds, they are a growth investment or a speculation. I write of the actual bullion that has a spot price quoted every day.)

Gold, along with platinum, silver, and palladium, is a favorite of conservative investors all over the world, but not as much in the United States. Get acquainted with gold as an inflation fighter. Glen Kirsch, vice president of Asset Strategies International and Michael Checken, president, have made many contributions to my *Wealthbuilder* newsletter through the years about this. They have statistics on how an ounce of gold bought a good suit in 1920, and can still buy one today, even though the price is 14 times more. Glen points out that even fewer ounces of gold can buy a midpriced car today compared to what was required in 1965.[6]

Sometimes gold can be difficult to buy and hard to store safely. Soon bullion itself will be traded on the stock exchange (not gold mining companies but the very metal). And right now a special program—The Perth Mint Certificate—is available to simplify gold buying.

Step 4. The Present Value of the Yearly Income Shortfall

It is now time in the calculation process to factor in time, rate of return, and inflation to determine how much in total assets you will have to have on hand at retirement in order to generate income, forever, which, when added to your everlasting income, will give you everlasting wealth.

In making this calculation, we need to assume a rate of return. I will choose a modest rate of 5 percent. In my book *Making Up for Lost Time* (Morrow, 1994), I used a more aggressive rate of 10 percent. Times have changed. I truly believe that using this conservative, yet realistic rate will, in the long run, prove correct.

Table 21.1 shows how much actual wealth you will need at retirement to generate the yearly income shortfall for the rest of your life, no matter how long it lasts. To use the chart, find your yearly income shortfall on the right-hand side and match it with the column that represents the number of years you have until retirement. The resulting figure is the gross amount needed at retirement to generate the income shortfall, forever. For example, if your yearly income shortfall is $5,000 and you are 15 years from retirement, you will, with inflation and rate of return taken into account, need $312,925 in assets at retirement. If your years to retirement or your shortfall are not on Table 21.1, you can extrapolate the number using the nearest values.

The assets needed at retirement to
meet your yearly income shortfall are: _____

Table 21.1 Asset Needs for Retirement

Yearly Income Shortfall	Asset Needs at Retirement to Meet Yearly Income Shortfall					
	Years to Retirement					
	5	10	15	20	25	30
$5,000	$211,400	$257,200	$312,925	$380,721	$463,205	$563,560
$10,000	$422,800	$514,400	$625,850	$761,442	$926,410	$1,127,120
$20,000	$845,000	$1,028,800	$1,251,700	$1,522,884	$1,852,820	$2,254,240
$50,000	$2,114,000	$2,572,000	$3,129,250	$3,807,210	$4,632,050	$5,635,600

Step 5. Present Assets Available at Retirement

The asset needs determined in Step 3 may seem intimidating. But do not despair. The calculations are not complete. You must now determine the probable value at the time of your retirement of your present savings, investments, and assets. So now we will see how much of your present assets will grow to make up part of the shortfall. To do this, add the following:

The present market value of your stocks, bonds, and other non401(k), IRA assets _____

plus

The present value of the equity in your home if you plan to downscale

_____

plus

Other (inheritance?) _____

       Total investment assets:_____

Everlasting Wealth

David May Have an Inheritance What about inheritances from parents? In gross numbers, $3 trillion is supposed to change hands through inheritance in the next five years. But the value of the family home skews the statistic. About 70 percent of the elderly's assets are represented by home ownership. If an inheritance is in your future, protect it.

1. Make sure your parents have the long-term care insurance they need to avoid spend down.
2. Help them with tax planning.
3. Be watchful for signs of financial concern like debt, financial disorganization, and excessive worry.

Step 6. The Retirement Value of the Present Total Investment Assets

Now we will see how much your present nest egg will grow by your retirement date. To do this, we will factor in the same 5 percent growth rate that we used earlier and stretch that over the time period between the present and the time of retirement. The resulting number will be the retirement value of your present assets, the amount by which we will reduce your retirement investment needs to get to your true shortfall.

Use Table 21.2 in the same manner that we employed with the previous table. Find the value of your present investment assets (extrapolating, again, where needed) and follow it across to the number of years to your retirement.

Your at-retirement value of your present assets is: _____

Step 7. The Actual Retirement Asset Shortfall

This is a simple step. We will subtract the at-retirement value of your present investment assets determined in the Step 6 from the assets needed at retirement calculated in Step 4. This will get us the actual retirement asset shortfall.

Assets needed at retirement (Step 4)   _____
Minus at-retirement value of present assets (Step 6) – _____
Equals actual assets needed at retirement   = _____

Did you come up with zero or a negative number? Then congratulations. You have enough present assets to generate everlasting wealth. If not, go on to Step 8.

Table 21.2   The At-Retirement Value of Present Assets

Present Value of Assets	Years to Retirement					
	5	10	15	20	25	30
$50,000	$63,814	$81,445	$103,945	$132,665	$169,318	$216,097
$100,000	$127,628	$162,890	$207,890	$265,330	$338,636	$432,194
$250,000	$319,070	$407,225	$519,725	$663,325	$846,590	$1,080,485
$500,000	$638,140	$814,450	$1,039,450	$1,326,650	$1,693,180	$2,160,970
$1,000,000	$1,276,280	$1,628,900	$2,078,900	$2,653,300	$3,386,360	$4,321,940

Table 21.3 Amount to Add to Investments Annually for Everlasting Wealth

Actual Investment Shortfall	Years to Retirement					
	5	10	15	20	25	30
$25,000	$4,424	$1,944	$1,133	$740	$512	$368
$50,000	$8,848	$3,888	$2,266	$1,480	$1,024	$736
$100,000	$17,696	$7,776	$4,532	$2,960	$2,048	$1,472
$250,000	$44,240	$19,440	$11,330	$7,400	$5,120	$3,680
$500,000	$88,480	$77,760	$45,320	$29,600	$20,480	$14,720
$1,000,000	$176,960	$77,760	$45,320	$29,600	$20,480	$14,720
$2,000,000	$353,920	$155,520	$90,640	$59,200	$40,960	$29,440

Step 8. How Much Is Needed for Investment Each Year from Now On?

The amount of your actual assets needed at retirement, determined in Step 6, can be obtained. All that is required is the discipline and strength to put the amount aside, every year, from now until the time you retire. It remains, then, to determine how much you must put aside. Table 21.3 does that. By now it should be familiar. Just find the actual assets needed at retirement that you calculated in Step 7 and read across to the years to retirement. The dollar figure you find is the amount that you need to add to your investments each year from now until you retire.

This is it. Write down the number you got from this table. That is your goal for each year from now until your retirement. Add it to your present investments and voila. Everlasting wealth. How did you do? How will you rearrange your budget to make your new savings goal? What if you cannot save that much?

Chapter TWENTY-TWO

Preserving Your Future
If You Do Not Have Enough

L et's get to the crux of the problem. If you live long enough it may be impossible for you to live well if you have not saved enough or invested successfully. Unless you have millions, or live like a church mouse, *you may truly go broke at 102.* A $50,000 lifestyle is modest for two people in any metropolitan area. To safely derive that income after taxes you need a nest egg of at least $1.07 million, at 5.6 percent. (Historically, interest rates have yielded 5.6 percent on average over the past 50 years.) And that is pretax.

If you find yourself short there are three things you need do. First, resolve to spend principle if you need to, in a strategic and organized way. Second, accept that stocks in your portfolio are absolutely necessary to sustain growth and make your nest egg last as long as possible. Third, stop doing what you are doing and do something new. It could be a side business or a hobby turned into a small venture to bring in more cash flow. It could be extra consulting work. But, my number one choice is that you consider income-producing real estate, which creates a cash cow for the rest of your life. See www.wealth102 for guidance on finding bank financing.

Spending Principle, the Final Taboo

It's hard to spend principle when you stop working. Few of us do. We are more likely to do without. When we do dip in we see it as a

Libby Monroe, Hair Salon Owner and Real Estate Mogul

Libby is miffed. She didn't have time to get to the latest real estate seminar in her area. "I like real estate," she said, while preparing my hair for my next TV appearance. I was curious. Libby is a beautiful blonde and owner of the Chelsea Set, in my sister town of Maplewood, New Jersey. What always charms all of us is her Scottish accent, which she has never lost. But real estate? That came as a surprise. "What kind?" I asked. And the story came out. With only $300 in her pocket Libby came to the United States and was soon married. The marriage failed but she got the house. It was too big for a single mom with very little money. Her decision was to sell and buy a two-family home, and live in the smallest apartment. That was the beginning. She owns several, plans to buy more, and has already sold a few at a profit. She is far from a full-time real estate manager, and has no trouble owning a few properties while running her salon and her present (and happy) marriage. As Libby puts it, "If I could come here knowing nothing and do this, why not you?"

failure and approach it with fear. "I get night sweats," says an 80-year-old woman with almost a million dollars in the bank. She worries because she is spending some of the principle. She becomes distraught and ill. Her problems are not about money; by any standards she is rich. Her problem is that her expectation is to never dip into principle no matter how long she lives. And when there truly is very little in the kitty, random dipping can create enough stress to threaten your immune system.

How Long Will Your Money Last?

It's easy to calculate how long a lump sum of money will last if you assume a growth rate and a rate of withdrawal. If you enjoy these exercises visit www.retireearlyhomepage.com and buy the report *How Much Can You Safely Withdraw from Your Retirement Portfolio?*, by John P. Greaney (April 1, 2001) and have a ball.

Here's a particularly well-thought out answer to the question, how long will my money last? (See Table 22.1.)

The American Council of Life Insurers calculated the results of three different strategies for a 65-year-old with $100,000 and a desire to conservatively invest. You'll see the problem right away.

1. *Self Annuitization.* If you invest $100,000 at 5 percent and take out $9,420 every year, your nest egg would last 14 years.

2. *Long Life Strategy.* If you decide to make your nest egg last to age 100 and you are 65, investing the $100,000 at 5 percent, would give you $5,756 to spend each year.

3. *Life Expectancy Strategy.* If you built in an actuarial table and took distributions accordingly, until age 85, you would take out much more in the first 15 years of your life, than in the last five years.

If you are willing to use principle, and set up an organized spend down program you will need to maximize the time span by investing in stocks. Recent studies have investigated the optimal allocation of a longevity portfolio. Trinity College investigated different allocations to see how a nest egg would last through a hypothetical 30-year retirement period. Researchers postulated a person withdrawing 6 percent of their retirement nest egg every year. They concluded that there was a 72 percent chance of success that the money would last through the period if it was invested all in bonds, a 90 percent chance if it was invested all in stocks, and a 95 percent chance if it was invested 75 percent in stocks and 25 percent bonds. If you withdraw only 4 percent of the total with the 75–25 percent

Table 22.1   How Many Years Does It Take to Spend $100,000?

Monthly Withdrawal	Rate of Return						
	3%	4%	5%	6%	7%	8%	9%
$400	20	21	23	24	27	30	35
$600	14	14	15	16	17	18	19
$800	10	11	11	12	12	13	13
$1,000	9	9	9	9	10	10	10
$1,200	7	7	8	8	8	8	8
$1,400	6	6	7	7	7	7	7

allocation you have a 98 percent success rate of having the lump sum last 30 years. Those with enough of a nest egg saved during their accumulation stage can decumulate to best advantage with this 75–25 percent allocation.[1]

This appears to be a risky allocation, but what makes it work is the number of years being used as the time frame. No matter what measure we use stocks have done better in the long run. The Center for Research in Security Prices (CRSP), School of Business, University of Chicago, tracking stock indexes for total return from 1992 to 2002, found that the average growth was:

- S&P 500 (large company stocks)—12.7 percent
- Bonds (long-term)—11 percent
- Bonds (short-term)—7.27 percent

Ibbotson Associates has tabulated that for 76 years from 1926 to 2001, the stock market as measured by the Standard and Poor's 500 Index (the average performance of 500 of our largest companies) went up 54 times or 71 percent of the time and down 22 times or 29 percent of the time. When parsed out in blocks of time the market showed a gain of 90 percent for five-year periods, 90 percent of the time for 10-year periods, and 100 percent of the time for 15-year periods.

So why have you lost so much money in the bear market of the late 1990s and in the past few years? The answer lies in the way the stock market performs in the short term as compared with the long term.

Everlasting Wealth

A New Law for Trustees   Just to show you that stock market investing is more prudent than all income investing, a recent law has made it mandatory that trustees allocate a greater portion of trust assets to the stock market than previously considered prudent. Without market gains, trust funds were underperforming the expectation of beneficiaries in the long run.

Here are the risk numbers, short-term:

- In the worst year of U.S. stocks, the inflation adjusted return was 38.6 percent. In the best year, that return was 66.6 percent, a huge variation.
- In the past 76 years, stocks have produced positive results in 53 years and negative results in 23. Combining these two figures, the likelihood of losing money in any given year is one in four. The chances of that loss being over 10 percent are one in nine.

Here are the time-adjusted risk factors for the same 73-year period:

- Of the 64 overlapping 10-year periods (like 1927 to 1937, 1928 to 1938 and so on), stocks gained in all but two periods.
- For the 59 overlapping 15-year periods, stocks gained *every time!*
- The worst 20-year period (1929 to1948), showed an 84 percent gain!

No wonder investors become ever more leery of stock investing. The number one question I get from my senior readers and listeners is, "Am I too old to buy stocks?" The answer is you must participate in the stock market if you have no other assets that meet inflation. In the world of financial planning there are many names for an aversion to volatility. We call it *conservative, risk averse,* or *guarantee seeking.* We call investments that cater to that feeling *inflation sensitive, income generating, insured,* or *guaranteed.* And indeed these are very important. But if you don't want to go broke at 102 with assets in a securities portfolio, you must have some stocks.

But if you don't want to spend down using a self-created program, and manage your money through decades of changing markets, there is one product that shifts the risk of your long life from your shoulders to that of an insurance or annuity company. It is the long forgotten *immediate annuity.*

Will the Real Annuity Please Stand Up?

I have a pet peeve. There are too many products out there called annuities and it's too confusing. In my view, only one type of product should be called an annuity. That is the little known, and less understood immediate annuity. Nothing else, not the so-called variable annuity, the deferred annuities, the fixed annuity, or the fixed indexed annuity. The latter ones are tax-advantaged ways to participate in the stock market or beat the low interest rates of bonds and CDs. They all can make a powerful difference in your bottom line, and you will read about all of them in the following pages. But they are not annuities.

Only the immediate annuity is a unique longevity product because only it provides lifelong income, with cash flow that lasts as long as you do, and beyond, if you so choose. An annuity lets you convert all or part of your retirement savings into a stream of lifetime income, giving you a form of security that traditional investments can't.

I call immediate annuities *voluntary annuities*. We take a lump sum of money from any source and convert it to a lifelong income stream. Tony Webb, economist and annuity researcher, calls them *longevity insurance*.

Until recently, no one paid much attention to immediate annuities. Who would be dumb enough to take a lump sum of their hard-earned money and transfer it without recourse to an insurance or annuity company, in exchange for a contractual obligation on its part to return a periodic check (every month, quarter, year) for as long as they might live? Who indeed? How about someone who believes in their own longevity and is concerned that they might not have the income to sustain themselves. Today, this is more and more of us. And the immediate annuity has become a viable product and a smart strategy for some.

When should you annuitize, if ever? The variables of your life make the difference in the optimum age to annuitize, and whether to annuitize at all. For example, a single person with no care about leaving a legacy has a free field to annuitze without consideration that the annuity contract ends at death. In 2002, Milevsky and Young did a determination as to the age at which an immediate annuity brings optimal results. For singles, with little or no compulsory annuities (no pension), using immediate annuities linked to an inflation index (ones that give you more income according to an index formula), their surprising finding was that age 64 for women and 71 for men was the optimal age.

Irena Dushi and Anthony Webb in their wonderfully revealing report, *Annuitization: Keeping Your Options Open*, done for the International Longevity Center—USA (May 2003),[2] conclude that "depending on one's state of health and how much of one's money is already annuitized through employer pensions and Social Security, it can be beneficial and usually does little harm for a couple to postpone the annuitization decision until their late seventies or early eighties."

But there is more to annuities than numbers. For some seniors the hope that they will be able to leave a legacy makes them shun annuitization, even if they must skimp to live well. Others will not spend principal even if they have large sums. This rainy day syndrome may not make them officially broke but they live so poorly that they might as well be. This psychological barrier to spending principal is hard to overcome. But the issue of leaving a legacy is easier to deal with than you think.

Immediate Annuities and Legacy Planning

An immediate annuity can be distributed throughout your lifetime, or for at least a minimum of 10 years. These *term certain* arrangements allow you to designate a beneficiary who will receive your distribution should you die in less than 10 years after the annuity takes effect. Or you can opt for a refund of a lump sum to your heirs if you die within a certain period of time after commencement of benefits. You can also buy an annuity based on joint lives so that you and a spouse or sibling can collect until you both go. Finally, you can arrange for a balloon payment to the heir if you die within a specific period of time. Each

Personal Note

I have two children ages 11 and 21 (but you know that by now). Apart from our life insurance, my husband and I have purchased a second-to-die policy that pays off when both of us are gone. These policies give the lowest premium for the death benefit, and also build up cash value. If we decide to annuitize later in life, we have the freedom to do so because a life insurance trust that owns the policy will pay the death benefit tax-free to the children (hopefully very old adults by then) no matter what we do with our principal. It feels good to have the freedom to spend our principle and still have a nice legacy intact.

special arrangement gets you back less each month. For that reason, many people plan to annuitize between ages 75 and 80, but buy an insurance policy earlier in life to cover their desire to leave a legacy.

Annuity Ladders

Another practical way to decide when to purchase an immediate annuity is to convert small amounts of your assets to an annuity at five-year intervals starting at age 65 or 70. In this way heirs have an inheritance should you pass on before complete annuitization. And if interest rates rise or other investments become more robust, you may have new sources of income and avoid the immediate annuity contract for the next interval.

Immediate Annuity Indicators

If you have the following factors in your life, then an immediate annuity is for you.

1. Little compulsory (pension) income.
2. Low risk tolerance.
3. At least age 65 (older is better).

Women get a better deal from annuities bought in their qualified plans than do men (unisex rates). Because women live longer, they don't get as good an annuity deal as men. They are transferring a bigger risk. So any way that a woman can get unisex rates to apply is a good thing. Immediate annuity rates of return are calculated on a unisex basis (gender neutral), if bought in 401(k) plans where annuitization is available (in England, partial annuitization of a 401(k)-type plan is now mandatory, because of the government's concern that boomers will outlive their money). Once we take the money and roll it over into an IRA, or buy a deferred annuity, the rates are gender specific and women don't get as good a deal.

What about Buying Power and Functional Inflation?

To keep up with inflation you can consider the indexed immediate annuity. Since 1952 when TIAA-Cref came out with an immediate annuity indexed to the stock market, it has been possible to both annuitize and receive a basic income and still see growth in the monthly check if the market does well. Like most of these indexed products, there is also a cap beyond which the growth cannot go no matter how bullish the market.

How Secure Is Your Annuity Company?

The insurance company pools the risk of longevity across large groups. As we enjoy longer life expectancy as a nation, actuarial tables are bound to reflect this and annuity risk becomes greater on the shoulders of companies. As usual, this means careful attention to the ratings of a company to be sure they have the financial strength to keep paying. See Appendix D for a sample of ratings and rating websites.

What is, in a way, comforting to realize is that companies take as few chances as they can. For example, in figuring the payouts on immediate annuities they figure in the fact that some people have secret information about themselves. For example, people who know that they are ill will not buy an immediate annuity. As a result, the pool of immediate annuitants are usually healthy seniors. The life expectancy tables used to calculate the risk are different from those used to calculate the risks of life insurance.

The Charitable Annuity

Charitable annuities also may fit the bill for you particularly if you have appreciated assets on which you must pay tax when you sell.

Everlasting Wealth

An immediate annuity is a product like any other. As with any product ask: What does it cost? What are its features? How does it fit my needs? Is there a better choice? Who is selling it? What happens if it breaks (what coverage do you have if the company gets into trouble)? What is the cost, commission, or markup? What are yearly expenses if any?

Like an immediate annuity, the charitable annuity is an *irrevocable* transfer of cash or securities, but this time to a charity, not an insurance company. In exchange for the transfer you get a fixed income stream for life or for the life of yourself and another. Payments may be made annually, semiannually, or quarterly.

For example, at age 77 a gift of $25,000 will give you $1,850 each year for life. You also get a federal income tax deduction of $10,963, which you can take in one year or spread out over five years, since the deductible portion is limited each year to 50 percent of your adjusted gross income. In addition, some of the income you receive each year $1,265.40 is tax-free through 2013, then $970 thereafter. This compares favorably with investing the $25,000 at the historic rate of 5.6 percent, which would give you income of $1,400 before taxes, each year. These figures are approved by the American Council on Gift Annuities (ACGA) for January 1, 2003, with an assumed IRS discount rate of 4.2 percent. This points to the wisdom of buying any annuity when rates are strong; you lock in a lifetime of the higher rate assumptions.

Added to all this is that if you transfer an appreciated asset to the charity and they sell it for you, there is no capital gains tax. All the proceeds are invested to increase your life long income stream.

Many brokers, insurance professionals, and financial planners work with charities to help you create a relationship with a planned giving department through insurance and annuities. I hold a lot of seminars on philanthropy and longevity, and I am amazed how many are attended by insurance professionals who want to bring philanthropy into your life and their own. If you work with a professional ask about the charitable support services of their company. Many frontline financial pros (those that work with the consumer directly) are not familiar with charitable giving. But they almost all have home office support from what the trade calls *the advanced markets*. That' s code for rich people. Well, we're rich too, at least in spirit. So if charity and annuities are a priority for you they will get the information you need.

And if you do have substantial amounts to give to charity, the best way is through a trust that lasts for your life and even that of a loved one. These are called charitable remainder trusts (CRTs). For example, $250,000 in appreciated securities will get you a $113,940 income tax deduction that can be taken over five years and a yearly income stream that varies with interest rates. I've written a book on

Interview: Lorri Grief

Lorri Grief, director of Managed Gifts and Planned Giving for the Crohn's and Colitis Foundation (www.ccsa.org), gives us the rundown on charitable annuities as follows: "A charitable gift annuity is a simple contract between you and a charity. In exchange for your irrevocable gift of cash, securities, or other assets, the charity agrees to pay one or two annuitants you name a fixed sum each year for life. The older your designated annuitants are at the time of the gift, the greater the fixed income the charity can agree to pay. In most cases, part of each payment is tax-free, increasing each payment's after-tax value." Lorri gives the following example, taken from PG Calc Incorporated of Cambridge, Massachusetts. "If you are 75 years old and transfer $100,000 in cash to a charity, the income stream is $6,800 annually for as long as you live." I asked how this stacks up to immediate annuities through a private insurance company. "Part of the benefits is the tax differences. For my example they include a federal income tax deduction of approximately $31,512. Your deduction may vary modestly depending on the timing of your gift." Lori adds, "Deductions for this and other gifts of cash and nonappreciated property will be limited to 50 percent of your adjusted gross income. You may take unused deductions of this kind over the next five years, subject to the same 50 percent limitation. You'll also get fixed payments in quarterly installments totaling $6,800 each year for life. In addition, $4,630.80 of each year's payments will be tax-free for the first 14.8 years." And of course, she smiles when she reminds us, "You will provide generous support to the charity and leave a legacy of generosity."

giving of all types titled *Gifting to People You Love*, (Newmarket Press), that includes charities.

Bonds and Certificates of Deposit

What ever happened to the idea of simply buying bonds or certificates of deposit (CDs) at varying maturity dates and living off that income? Bravo, if you have enough to do that. Many of my subscribers do. If you are among the fortunate, here are a few tips to help you stay that way.

Bonds

Bonds are obligations of the government or a corporation to which you have *lent* your money. They are often used after retirement to generate income because they are thought to be safe. This is not necessarily so. It is true, that if you buy a bond you will receive back the face value of the bond at maturity (the date which your loan must be paid back to you). But that does not mean you can't lose money if you sell before that date. Three factors will determine this:

1. *The Price You Paid.* If you bought the bond at a premium, that is you paid more than the face value, you will lose principal if interest rates go up after you buy. Your prize premium bond may only be worth its face value.

2. *Interest Rate Fluctuations.* Even if you did not pay a premium, if interest rates have risen between the time you bought and the time you have to sell before maturity, the price of the bond will be less than the price paid. Of course it can be worth more if interest rates have fallen. But this is the essence of bond volatility.

3. *The Issuer.* The financial condition of the issuer can be a factor. If the issuer, for whatever reason, cannot pay the face value at maturity, that is, it defaults, the bondholder will have lost most if not the entire principal invested. These caveats are given mainly to make sure that you are not too cavalier about buying bonds. As with any investment, knowledge is power.

Shop for Bonds

Unlike stocks, bonds can vary in price depending on the seller's closeness in the bond chain to the issuer. The more middlemen, the more you will pay. More important, different brokers have different bond inventory. I urge you to seek out a bond specialist when purchasing bonds, rather than a general broker.

Up until a few years ago, the bond market was like a restricted club. Its workings and the access to its information were available only to insiders. As a result, it was almost impossible to determine what bonds were available, what the prices were, and how much a bond you owned was worth on any given day. When was the last time you called your broker and asked to buy a specific bond? Never, right? That is because investors had little access to any information that would tell them for which bonds to ask. Rather, the broker would only tell the investor what bonds were available.

Moreover, the markup, the price charged by the broker for the transaction, is built into the price being quoted. This too varies from broker to broker and bond to bond, with the investors totally in the dark about how much was actually being paid. However, thanks to some new technologies and some informative websites, much of this secret information is now available. Bond seekers and holders can now have access to availability and market information directly. The best of these sites include www.investinginbonds.com, www.direct-notes.com, and www.bondresources.com.

Indexed Treasuries

The U.S. government understands the pain of inflation and has created an indexed bond. You can buy them direct from the Treasury. I am proud to have been chosen for the Greater New York Volunteer Committee of the U.S. Treasury, to help get out the word about the solid return and convenience of indexed treasury bonds. To learn more check out www.savingsbonds.gov and www.treasurydirect.gov.

I Remember Munis

Corporate bond interest is taxable. Treasury bond interest is taxable by the state in which you live. But municipal bonds, bonds issued by the state or municipality in which you live, are neither federally nor state taxable.

Fixed Rate Annuities

Here we go. These are not annuities. Fixed rate annuities are investment products bought from an insurance company that pay you a fixed interest rate for a period of time, usually better than a bank or certificate of deposit. The interest is reinvested tax-deferred until you withdraw the funds. These products offer an up-front rate, which varies in a year or more according to changes in interest rates. These are not securities and are backed by the quality of the company, not by the Securities Investor Protection Corporation (SIPC), a government regulated insurer, or the Federal Deposit Insurance Corporation (FDIC), as it is with bank CDs. Many banks sell fixed annuities and depositors are confused and assume that they too are FDIC-insured like their bank accounts.

Fixed annuities are useful and popular products for wealth accumulation because of their tax deferral and their usually superior rates. They are also long-term products because the company usually penalizes you should you take the money out before a set amount of typically three to seven years.

Lately, two types of fixed annuities have gained popularity because of the need to deal with inflation. The first is the indexed annuity, which raises interest rates as the Consumer Price Index (CPI) rises, according to a formula. The other is the equity-indexed fixed annuity, which offers returns keyed to a stock index like the Standard and Poor's 500. The equity-indexed fixed rate annuity has a cap beyond which it will not go in a great market. But it also has a floor beyond which it cannot fall in a terrible market.

What's my take on these products? I think they can be excellent accumulation products for people who want to have some of the market growth with none of the major downsides. But many of them lock you in for many years, up to nine, charging a penalty if you withdraw the money sooner. For that length of lock-in you may as well buy and hold an indexed mutual fund and have more liquidity. And if the market soars, there is no cap. But if you have a horror of volatility and shop for an equity-indexed fixed annuity with one of the shorter term holding periods (some charge no withdrawal penalty after as little as three years), it can work wonders for your portfolio and your peace of mind.

If you are in the decumulation phase and need to use income, stay away from any fixed annuity. Their purpose is constant tax-free reinvestment not immediate income.

Chapter TWENTY-THREE

Social Security and Your Pension

Will They Carry You Through Longevity?

It was Bismarck that created the notion of Social Security in the 1800s in order to forestall a revolution. At that time he picked age 65 as the cutoff, because he never expected many 19th century Germans to make it to that age. Historians, take heart. I know I am simplifying, but our own system took its cue from the Bismarck innovation, and chose age 65 in the 1940s, when the average American would spend three years in retirement. Bryn T. Douds, vice president and actuary at New York Life, tells us this: "When Social Security was set to start at age 65 there were very few years that we would live after retirement. By the same standards, to the extent that we can retire at age 65, we should consider ourselves lucky. Perhaps there should be a resetting of expectations."[1]

Although Social Security is nearly a senior citizen itself, James W. Green, public affairs specialist at the Social Security Administration, uses a quiz to prove to us how little we really know about longevity's best friend. Take the James W. Green Quiz found in Appendix F and see how well you do.[2]

Can We Rely on Social Security?

First, the good news. I don't anticipate the disappearance of Social Security altogether anytime soon. It may, however, eventually wind up as a non- or semicompulsory annuity program, managed by each recipient under government regulation (modeled on the highly successful Chilean system). If that happens, we better hope that the spirit of Warren Buffet has blessed us, and we are capable of making good investment choices. Now the bad news. Social Security was never meant to carry all of your retirement costs; on the contrary, it is merely a lifelong base on which to build. Because of the low dependency ratio (few current workers paying in per retiree taking out) the continuance of Social Security is probably predicated on taxing those who have earned income after retirement, by decreasing their Social Security benefits and increasing the age of eligibility. Already benefits are taxed for those earning over a set amount per year and taking early retirement. And, the age of eligibility has increased so that now the age of eligibility goes according to the following menu.

Year You Were Born	Normal Retirement Age
1937 or earlier	65
1938	65 plus 2 months
1939	65 plus 4 months
1940	65 plus 6 months
1941	65 plus 8 months
1942	65 plus 10 months
1943 to 1954	66
1955	66 plus 2 months
1956	66 plus 4 months
1957	66 plus 6 months
1958	66 plus 8 months
1959	66 plus 10 months
1960 or later	67

But even with these band-aids how will Social Security survive? If dependency ratios decrease as expected, the crucial date is 2018 (when I will be 70 years old and should have been collecting for about five years. How old will you be?). At that time, the trust fund that holds the surplus paid in over the years will kick in to cover distributions. The trust fund is really just an IOU from the federal government, which I trust has enough to pay its debt. I also expect that bond floats will be necessary and the dollar may have to be devalued to make U.S. bonds attractive to foreign buyers. Don't expect to do a lot of shopping in Europe in 2018.

But it doesn't end there. By 2042, even if the fund is healthy, the principal will begin to erode. (I will be 94 years old. How old will you be?) Although we all must operate as if Social Security will be there for us, we can make some crisis preparation if we stay aware of these crucial dates.

When Should You Start Taking Social Security?

No matter when we were born, all of us can start to take Social Security early, at age 62. Should you? My guess is no, but it's just a guess. If you really believe that Social Security will disappear, take it out early. Wouldn't you want to get your money out of the bank that may be failing? But my plan is to wait, because I ultimately believe in the system and because I do not want the reduced benefits. The discount is 20 percent, rising as the normal retirement age changes. Those whose normal retirement age is 65 and 8 months sacrifice 23.33 percent by taking Social Security early. In the age of longevity, what you would do with 44 months of extra benefits must be compared with the decades of reduced monthly income. If you need them for early cash flow at age 62, that's that. But if you don't, why reduce your lifelong cushion? What if you are ill or have poor longevity genetics? If you are married, I would still wait to the normal retirement age, because that will give your spouse a better benefit when you are gone, unless he or she has a richer Social Security benefit than you do.

By contrast, I'm not a great fan of taking late benefits. If you take late benefits you get a 6.5 percent increase each year. I could give you a headbreaking analysis like the ones I got from my actuary friends. But boil it down to this, the perk should be 8 percent increase a year for waiting until 70, and it's less. So there is no advantage to doing it. Now, visit www.socialsecurity.gov and figure out the permutations as they apply to you.

What Happens When You Work
and Simultaneously Take Early Social Security?

If you take early Social Security benefits at age 62 and work while collecting, you will be docked $1 for every two you earn, from a job or your own business, over $11,520 annually. Many of today's recipients work just up to the threshold earnings that trigger the tax. Ini-

Personal note

In the early 1990s I was host of a show on FNN, Financial New Television Network, called *IRS Tax Beat*. It was sponsored by the IRS and Excedrin (not kidding). I learned that enforcement rules go in cycles, depending on the efficiency and yield of enforcement. I expect the IRS to be pretty strict in enforcing the early retirement tax on earned income from a business you may start after retirement. Keep good records.

tially, you state how much you expect to earn, but the figure is reconciled with your tax return, which is sent to Social Security by the IRS. You may get a refund or you may be charged a penalty-free additional amount if you miscalculated.

For cash flow planning, please realize that the tax is estimated and withheld until it is paid, not deducted as a pro rata reduction from each check. So, for several months you may not get a check, and then get a partial check, until all of the withheld amounts equal the tax. Then your entire monthly benefit is paid for the remainder of the calendar year. *If you wait until your normal retirement age, there is no withholding.* And if you do take early benefits but lose some because of taxes on earned income, your monthly benefits are increased slightly, because you lost some of the early benefits.

So when will you take Social Security? You decide.

The Defined Benefit Plan

The defined benefit plan is called that because you can calculate your benefit so long as you know your years of service and salary (your investment acumen is irrelevant). Most pensions base your monthly stipend on your average salary in the last five years of work. It is a dinosaur from the gold-watch-after-40-years era, but it sure looks wonderful next to a decimated 401(k) plan. It is the ultimate longevity job-related benefit because it is a compulsory annuity that you can never outlive. And the pension is not entirely dead, even for my young readers.

Everlasting Wealth

Taking a Lump Sum and Protecting Your Spouse   About one in four of you will be asked to make a quick and significant choice just before retirement. That is whether to take your maximum monthly benefit or a reduced amount that continues after your death for the life of your spouse. Some companies also offer a pop up. If your beneficiary, in this case the spouse, dies early, you will get some extra dollars that pop up in your monthly check. This is an encouragement to use the pension for a joint life, without concern that your beneficiary will predecease you and your continued payments will be less than full pension.

Of course, your decision, if you are married has a lot to do with longevity and the figures that your company gives you. The calculators found at www.wealth102.com. should help you out.

Along the way, another choice has become fashionable. It is called *pension maximization*. You do take the maximum pension allowed, but you also buy an insurance policy for your spouse to inherit with the difference in the cash flow from your maximum pension to cover the premium. Insurance agents and brokers are skilled at figuring out whether your age, health, and the numbers make sense. They will also help make sure that the death benefit is tax-free both in income and estate tax for your spouse.

Pension Safety

In the days after Enron no one can be smug. Here are some possibilities that can kill your security:

Underfunding. If your pension is underfunded it will say so in the summary annual report of your company. When that happens, the government may require more dollars to be placed in the pension trust. The company usually has five years to comply.

Voluntary Termination. Even a healthy pension can be terminated voluntarily. In that case, you get what's coming to you with no increases. It may be time to say goodbye to the job.

Everlasting Wealth

Two Smart Pension Moves

1. You will have 90 days to make many elections with regard to retirement benefits. Get the numbers early and take three months to plan your decision.

2. If you want pension maximization and insurance to cover your spouse, buy a whole life policy early and cut down on the premiums. You'll pay for a few years extra, but you will also have extra coverage and cash value, which you can borrow out if necessary. Don't wait for the 90-day period to consider maximization. Take your first run through at age 50 to 55 depending on when you intend to retire.

Conversion to a Cash Balance Account. As you recall from the chapter on work (Chapter 2), this type of pension grows evenly throughout one's work life, with no reward for seniority. Those already with decades on the job may lose benefits in this transition. The federal government placed a moratorium on conversion in 1999, but it's been lifted. There are lawsuits pending, but the outcomes are in favor of allowing the program to stand.

Involuntary Termination. The Pension Benefits Guarantee Corporation (PBGC) guarantees even a failed plan, but only up to $44,000 a year for those age 65 and up to $34,700 for those age 62. The irrevocable loss to the company career person banking on a full pension cannot be calculated in dollars and cents. Let us hope they were working at what they loved, and not just for the pension.

Chapter TWENTY-FOUR

Leapfrog Annuities

How Professional Longevity Planners Think

About now you may be thinking about getting professional help to be sure that you don't go broke at 102. If so, you might ask any financial planner or insurance professional whom you interview what the age of their average client is and how much experience they have in financial gerontology. Yes, there is such a thing as a financial gerontologist, but the certification is just beginning to catch on. It was initiated in 2003 by the American Institute of Financial Gerontology with the top names on aging and finance (many like Dr. Moody, interviewed in this book) on the faculty. To learn more visit www.aifg.org. There are also certifications for senior advisors, which have been around for about 12 years. But for the most part, longevity is new territory for people in my field.

The training I give concentrates specifically on the way baby boomers, seniors, and the end-of-alphabet generations, X and Y, make decisions based on longevity. When I introduce my curriculum I find that it still seems novel to many planners. But there is a significant difference between retirement and longevity planning.

First, longevity planning starts at any age. It usually involves real estate and mortgage decisions as well as pension decisions. It calls for an earlier purchase of insurance that is permanent and always either level in premium or with a vanishing premium to take the burden of costs off in older age.

It also involves dreams implemented by real plans like incorporation or use of the real estate IRA to buy retirement homes early. And it always takes long-term healthcare into consideration, for two generations at a time. Longevity planning also focuses on family integration and group wealthbuilding, bringing siblings and even close friends together to make real estate deals, business deals, and relocation decisions for co-retirements. Friendship is the ultimate amenity of longevity. Longevity planning includes some form of charitable giving no matter how small. And finally, longevity planning often includes rehirement after early retirement or even after being excessed.

There are also a few products that help with risk management that have become the centerpiece of longevity planning. They are the long-term care insurance policies bought at a comparatively young age, 40s and 50s, the immediate annuity bought well after retirement, and the second-to-die insurance bought by couples that want a reduced way to leave a legacy. Longevity planning also prizes certain features that are not as essential for growth planning. They are:

- Stability and guarantees where available
- Long-term performance history
- Tiffany stamp insurance reserves and great ratings for claims paid by companies
- Conversion features (what is the ease and tax consequences of converting assets into life long income streams?)

There are some products that are tailor-made for converting growth assets into lifelong immediate annuities. They are variable annuities and death benefit proceeds of life insurance policies. These conversions features are called *settlement options*. You have the option to convert the sum in a variable annuity or the death benefit into an immediate annuity.

Please read this carefully—just because these products have conversion features *does not* make them good investments. They may be just right for you, or they may be all wrong. In fact, the variable annuity (not an annuity, just called an annuity) is usually disliked by television and radio gurus because they can be accompanied by high fees and they can lock you in with withdrawal penalties. I'm pretty sure that as I promote this book on the media the variable annuity will be confused with the real immediate annuity, especially because they are often used as a combined strategy. Let's take a look.

Here comes my pet peeve again. Variable annuities are *not* annuities; they are a way of participating in the stock market without paying taxes on gains as you take and reinvest profits. The gains are tax-deferred, and unlike the fixed annuity (also not an annuity), they are securities with SIPC insurance if the annuity company fails. Your choices will look much like 401(k)-style choices, several mutual funds from which to choose. When you finally do make withdrawals, you will pay ordinary income not capital gains on the cash flow. Variable annuities are commonly used to accumulate wealth. But they have one important feature for the decumulator who wants to leave a legacy. If you don't need the money to live on, but still want to keep a portion of your dollars in the market in the event that there is buying power erosion, the variable annuity guarantees that your heirs will never get less than the highest balance you ever achieved:

1. When you made the investment.
2. At death.
3. On any given yearly anniversary date (provided you select this feature when you buy.)

Take a look at the example given by planner Ken Greenblatt in in the next section.

Be aware, too, that variable annuities allow you to sweep your profits into interest-bearing accounts called *separate accounts* with no tax consequences. Fees for variable annuities used to be very high and many commentators still shun them. But today commissions range from 0.8 to 1.6 percent of the assets per year, much less than money under management, and comparing favorably to that of load mutual fund of 0.1 to 1.25 percent considering the insurance protection for heirs. However, these numbers are higher than for no-load mutual funds, specifically index funds.

Variable annuities are also sometimes called *deferred annuities and lifetime gifts*, when bought as part of a charitable giving plan. When they are bought for the purpose of eventually converting them into an immediate annuity, I call them *leapfrog annuities* because they lie dormant for years then jump up to help you when the time comes when you need lifelong income so your money lasts as least as long as you do.

There are as many ways to structure and time leapfrogs as there are people who need them. Here is my partial list. See if any of them apply to you or to your family.

1. Allow funds to grow tax-deferred in a variable annuity and then convert the proceeds into a lifetime income stream to add to your Social Security.

2. Retire early, but contribute a lump sum to a variable annuity with plans to convert it to an immediate annuity if needed, at a pre-planned age, to supplement your reduced pension.

3. Contribute an unexpected windfall or inheritance to a variable annuity to grow for your life and then distribute income for the life of a child, starting when they reach age 30, whether you are alive.

4. If you are uninsurable, create a long-term healthcare nest egg to be used only if you need assistance. If not, the annuity can be distributed to heirs.

5. If you can no longer take a deduction for the contribution to your IRA, set up a deferred annuity instead for tax deferral. If you have no heirs, set it up as a charitable gift annuity and get an immediate tax deduction.

6. If you are over age 70½ and can no longer make contributions to other plans, you can still build tax-advantaged income for your long future with a deferred annuity. Any source of funds can be used, not just earned income. There is no limitation on the amount of the contribution.

Real Life Advice from Real Life Experts

Here's what happened when I asked planners to write about a case with longevity issues where their plan worked out well for the clients.

Problem to Solve: Make Sure the Wife Has Enough If the Husband Takes a Single Life Pension and Dies, from Kenneth Greenblatt CFP, Time Capital and Bradley Spitz JD, MetLife Investment Specialist

This is a case from Ken and Brad—specialists in retirement, estate planning, and individual money management. The husband, age 67, was a retiring schoolteacher with a guaranteed pension income of

$54,000 per year (single life income) as well as Social Security income of $20,000 per year. The wife, age 63, had no pension of her own from any previous employment. Her Social Security income was $10,000 per year. The couple had no mortgage. And she had amassed $200,000 in stocks, bonds, mutual funds, and bank CDs. The husband also had a 403(b) of $400,000, and the wife an IRA of $50,000.

Living expenses, including travel, gifts, income taxes, and insurance premiums for all insurances including health insurance and long-term care insurance were $60,000.

KEN AND BRAD'S OBSERVATIONS

1. The total of their guaranteed incomes exceeds their cost of living while they are both alive.

2. If the wife dies first, the surviving husband will still have guaranteed income that exceeds his estimated living expenses.

3. If the husband predeceases wife, she will have guaranteed income of only her deceased husband's Social Security ($20,000 per year) and will have estimated living expenses of $50,000, leaving her with a shortage of $30,000 per year.

- Distributions from the qualified and nonqualified investment portfolio at an annualized rate of 4.62 percent would generate the $30,000 needed to cover the projected shortfall without dipping into principal. This simplified observation does not take into account many factors including the effect of inflation on the cost of living and the additional income taxes that may be due on the money distributed from the investment portfolio. These factors can be accounted for in a financial forecast prepared by a financial planner as part of a financial plan.

- The investment principal must be preserved for the benefit of the wife.

Some of the actions needed:

1. Develop and implement an investment strategy based on an asset allocation taking into account the need for growth of the portfolio to provide increasing income to maintain their future standard of living in an inflationary environment as well as the need to protect the principal for the wife. This can be done by:

- Cash reserve (1 year living expenses)—$50,000
- Fifty percent fixed income investments (bonds, CDs, and fixed annuities)—$300,000
- Fifty percent equity investments (large-, mid-, and small-cap domestic equities as well as some exposure to Foreign equity markets)—$300,000

2. Rollover of the husband's 403(b) into a variable annuity also registered as a 403(b) so as to preserve the favorable distribution rules (deferral to age 75 of minimum distributions on 403(b) account values from 12/31/1986 on), and invested therein in equities and fixed accounts in order to implement the asset allocation of the above investment strategy.

Outcome: The husband passed away first leaving the surviving spouse with the cash flow deficit already identified. The variable annuity account grew to a high prior anniversary value in 2000 of $700,000. At the husband's death in 2002, the variable annuity account value had dropped to $550,000. Due to the death benefit feature of the variable annuity, the highest prior anniversary value of $700,000 was paid to the surviving spouse. The $700,000 from the variable annuity was rolled over tax-free by the surviving wife into her own IRA. The surviving wife now has more than enough investment principal, including all qualified and nonqualified accounts, to meet her income needs now and in the future.

This variable annuity death benefit guaranteed a payout to the beneficiary of the greater of any of the following values:

1. Total deposits made into the account less an adjustment for withdrawals taken.

2. Highest value on any contract anniversary date less an adjustment for withdrawals taken plus additional deposits made since that highest anniversary date.

3. The account value at the date of claim.

The guaranteed death benefit features of the annuity empowered these clients to implement the asset allocation strategy and invest 50 percent of their investment portfolio in equities for growth.

Problem: A Serious Potential of Running out of Money Because of Long Life, from Lee Rosenberg, CFP, Founder of ARS Financial and author of *Retirement: Ready or Not*.

A single male client planned to retire at age 65 and needed to supplement a low Social Security income through the use of his $150,000 of accumulated assets. He had no debts and no other income.

Step 1

Lee's solution is to convert $50,000 to an immediate indexed annuity to generate monthly income that could rise if the CPI rose; he added a 10-year certain so that an early death would result in continued payments to the client's son. The additional income was $4,200 per year (interest rates were much higher then, but are now locked in for life). Thereafter, $100,000 was allocated to a deferred fixed annuity at 4 percent return having a value after 10 years of $148,000.

Step 2

At age 75, the client should increase his monthly income by exchanging an additional $50,000 from the deferred annuity to a second immediate annuity paying $4,836 per year at age 75.

The total combined payment is $9,036.

The balance of $98,000 remains in a deferred annuity at 4 percent, with a balance in ten years of $145,000.

Step 3

Today, client, age 85, wants to increase income again. He exchanges another $50,000 to a third immediate annuity bringing the total payments to $15,360. The balance of the deferred annuity to be available either as a death benefit or as an additional source of income via another immediate annuity, if the client dies before age 95.

Problem: Early Planning Reveals That Client Cannot Save Fast Enough to Make Their Retirement Goal, from Paul Gomperz, CLU, ChFC, Founder of Voluntary Benefits Corporation of America and Chairman since 1994 of the Columbia University Alumni Federations' Insurance Committee. (Paul calls his client "David." He knew nothing of Finding David—honest.)

David is a manager for a services firm currently earning $100,000. David's wife, Judy, works part time and earns an additional $20,000 per year. David plans to work until the age of 68, at which point he can begin drawing full Social Security income. He assumes that his salary will increase at an average of 5 percent per year so that by the time he retires he will be earning about $300,000. David is conscious of a healthy lifestyle and feels he should prepare himself financially to live to at least 100. He also feels that he and his wife will want to travel quite a bit after he retires, so he is not looking for his income to decrease after retirement. If anything, he wants his available income after retirement to continue increasing, although at a rate lower than 5 percent per year.

David's retirement plan is basically his 401(k). He had started slowly and, as his salary went up, increased his contributions until he reached the maximum level a few years ago. He plans to continue making the maximum contributions that he can. His account had reached a value of $160,000 in 2000 but since then has decreased in value to about $100,000. David has a long-term faith in the U.S. economy and feels that his future will best be served if he remains invested in a diversified portfolio of equity-based mutual funds. He is prepared to estimate the future average growth of his investments at 10 percent. At that rate, David expects his 401(k) account to be worth $2.3 million at age 68.

He has calculated that his initial income at 68, leaving room for annual increases of 2½ percent, will be $166,000. He believes Social Security will not go away and that at age 68 his initial retirement income will be in the area of $30,000 to $35,000 also subject to cost of living increases. As such, to meet his postretirement income goals, David needs to create another $110,000 of annual income starting at age 68. He realizes that he is calculating these projections using taxable dollars and so, using an estimated 35 percent tax bracket, he can create the same effect if he can create $72,000 of nontaxable income.

Since David is maximizing his 401(k) contribution, the additional accumulations would have to be done in a taxable environment. He used the same 10 percent investment growth assumption considered for his 401(k) but factored in a 28 percent tax bracket (a blend between the ordinary rate applied to short-term gains and dividends and the lower rate used for long-term capital gains). To achieve his goal of creating $110,000 per year of income that would run from age 68 to age 100, he would have to invest $27,350 per year, which is more than he can afford.

Paul explained the tax benefits of variable life insurance. For $14,530 per year, he could create a policy that would pay him $72,046 per year on a totally nontaxable basis beginning at age 68 and designed to continue to age 100. In addition, the life insurance policy would provide an immediate life insurance benefit of $738,000, which is something he hadn't even considered, but which would go a long way toward providing for the security of his wife and children just in case he died early. For that matter, at age 90, after the policy had already paid out almost $1.6 million in income to him, the death benefit would still be $685,000. Remember that life insurance death benefits are free of income tax.

Note: David is currently paying $5,000 per year for a combination of universal life and term insurance that provides less than $738,000 in coverage. In addition, the term insurance will begin to either go away or increase in cost in his late 50s. By replacing his existing coverage—David assumes he will pass the physical—his net cost for creating the additional retirement income will be under $10,000 per year, a cost he feels he can afford.

Problem: Client Needs to Maximize a Defined Benefit Pension, from Michael Mathias, CLU, CFP, Founder and Chairman of Interstate Financial and founder of the White Plains, New York chapter of the Institute of Certified Financial Planners.

Mr. & Mrs. Sam Dennis became clients in 1992 when Sam was forced to retire from a major corporation located in Northern New Jersey. He was 60 years old at the time earning $60,000 a year and his wife who was a public service employee was earning $25,000. He was quite scared, confused, and angry and concerned about his future after 30-plus years with the company. Even though he was not able to secure another good paying position, he did choose to do volunteer work. His wife continued to work until she retired with a small pension and Social Security. Michael recommended a lump sum rollover into several mutual funds rather than a monthly pension, which he still has intact after 11 years, and living a good life, vacations, spending time with children and grandchildren, while still being financially generous. The lump sum gives the client control of the pension, being able to invest and spend as they see fit and will leave a substantial legacy to their loved ones. They have been able to live in the same home, which has appreciated a great deal, while purchasing a $1 million second-to-die life insurance policy that is owned by an irrevocable trust as well as adequate long-term care (LTC) insurance. They have not only taken good care of themselves, but also their children and grandchildren.

Although Sam decided not to annuitize his pension, Michael did have a fall back scenario for him. In that case we would recommend that he take full pension benefits, which are usually 20 percent more than joint benefits. The difference would have been $10,000 a year. For $10,600 he could have bought a $500,000 life insurance policy to be left tax-free to his wife upon his death and the termination of his pension. However, Sam believes in the stock market and he wants to remain a participant. This shows two good plans that both work well. The difference was client temperament.

The Money Challenge Think and Do List

Make an honest assessment of how you want to live and the extent that your spending does not bring you joy.

Make new spending habits—you can do it just the way you approach dieting. It takes time, but change is possible.

Start by eliminating one big expense for a big impact. Then tackle little expenses. Get a better phone plan, get a lower-rate credit card, and calk windows to save fuel costs, and buy in bulk if you eat in bulk. Use www.dealnerd.com as your personal discount shopper. Check out their service on www.wealth102.com.

Use the formulas and methods in this section to determine if you have enough money for your long life.

If not, revisit the work chapters, and consider additional income or longer work years.

Look at real estate ownership as a cash flow alternative. You may have to choose between property you can rent and property you can live in. Compromise and make money.

Visit with the planned giving office of a favorite charity and with a financial planner to discuss annuities that last as long as you do.

Decide on when you will take Social Security by visiting www.socsec.gov and meeting with a planner.

Visit www.wealth102.com to get a head start on a financial forecast before you meet with a professional.

RESOLVED: I WILL NOT GO BROKE AT 102!

Epilogue

I don't want to finish this book. I have so much more to tell you. Every time I convince myself that it's only me holding on to the intimacy I find in writing, something else comes out in the press that you really, really have to know about.

Today is June 16, 2003, exactly one year to the day that I opened my "tomorrow box" and started travel writing. I timed the writing of the epilogue that way. I'm in Marco Beach, Florida, with my daughter Rose gathering information for two articles on traveling with kids, discovering the richness of the Everglades and the wonder of the manatee (the original mermaids of the sea).

This morning, in Everglades City, our driver was about to bring us to an alligator encounter, when he mentioned that housing in this corner of old Florida now costs $185,000 for a simple cottage. "Most people buy it now, because they plan to live here at retirement. But at first they stay only a couple of weeks a year. This was the last place you'd think would become an upscale haven. Some years ago the entire town was arrested for selling pot. Well," he chuckles, "times have changed."

Indeed.

A few miles away on Marco Island, land that was $20 an acre is going for $2.4 million. Our guide's friend just paid $10,000 for a quarter of an acre in Port Charlotte, but it's still under water. "Retirement village," our guide tells us knowingly, "they will use landfill to make another retirement village."

I contrasted this with the interviews I had done with long-time natives of Naples, Florida (there are few longtime natives of Marco Island, which is new as a shiny penny, but in Naples, there are some). Their stories were remarkably the same. Most came from the Midwest, some were farmers, others businessmen. They bought small places and maintained two homes seasonally while they were young, often paying no more than two or three thousand dollars for the house and land. Eventually, one or the other spouse got tired of owning two homes and they moved. Many ran their old businesses long distance out of Florida. Years later, they retired. There was no such thing as a gated community or an assisted living facility. They did not live on a golf course; they lived on the Gulf Coast. Their goal was not retirement living, just living.

It seems that today, no matter how old we are, retirement is the elephant in the room. Everyone knows that it is there but no one dares mention it. We may or may not be directly planning for it, but our inner voice brings it up all the time. Whether we are organized or disorganized about it, the new longevity is making us plan.

For two weeks I have been buying newspapers and magazines at random. My conceit was to make a point to you. I wanted to go through the magazines and make a list of all the articles that related to longevity and prove that the topic is everywhere and influencing most everything. But then I kept traveling and losing all the papers. Now that I'm finally writing the epilogue, all I have is today's *Wall Street Journal* which the concierge gave me and *Business Monday* from the *Naples Daily News*. Well, to prove my point it doesn't get any better than that.

On the front page of the Naples paper is an Associated Press article by Joyce Rosenberg.[1] She tells us that the IRS is sending letters to small-business owners urging them to open up retirement accounts like the new 401 uni-ks and also "putting more information about retirement plans on its website at www.irs.gov." Publication 560 is on a link, so no one need scrounge around for information when they set up their plans. The government wants to get the word out that small-business owners need to take care of their futures.

The front page of the *Wall Street Journal*, does not disappoint either. The above the fold headline reads, "With Medical Costs Climbing, Workers Are Asked to Pay More."[2] The article begins this way, "Audrey Sims can't afford to get all three of her prescription drugs filled each month. So she alternates, sometimes skipping her thyroid medication, at other times forgoing her acid-reflux pills or her hormone treatment." Ms. Sims, columnist Barbara Martinez tells us, is not a poverty level senior, but a 46-year-old government employee without prescription drug benefits. Medication would cost her a tenth of her salary, and she has a 12-year-old daughter to support. Martinez cautions, "overall spending on healthcare by employers continues to climb as aging Americans use more medical services."[3] I know my family keeps telling me to leave out the statistics, but I am like a lemming, suicidal to prove the point. Here it is: Out-of-pocket healthcare rose 26 percent since 1995 (Bureau of Labor Statistics). Workers' average monthly contribution to premiums tripled since 1988, and co-pay for prescription drugs jumped 62 percent since 2000.

Healthcare became a widespread job benefit only in the 1960s, and now many employers find it unsustainable. General Electric, Lockheed, and Hershey have encountered labor strikes over the issue of cutbacks. What was an entitlement may not be very soon. According to the Washington Business Group on Health, a consortium of 200 major employers, 80 percent of their members plan to raise co-pays. As for the chronic diseases of longevity, Rand is completing a study of 90,000 people. Its findings so far are that the doubling of co-pays results in a 10 to 12 percent reduction in use of mitigating drugs.

Just this morning the news reported that the cost of living went down again. Tell that to a diabetic.

So where does my story stop? At the villages near Ocala, Florida, where a common amenity is elephants and giraffes? At the wedding of my 38-year-old hairdresser, who is the youngest of her friends to get married? At my 86-year-old mother's $100 order for Omega-3 fish oil capsules? At my own list of to-dos, as soon as the manuscript is delivered, next Monday?

Get a colonoscopy

Check my thyroid

Go to the dentist

Visit Utah to see a possible retirement home

Get rid of more stuff so I can sell my house

Find a smaller house suitable until Rose graduates from high school

Set up more travel assignments so I can follow my dream

Plan something for my 31st anniversary in August (probably Chinese food and a movie)

Nag Stuart to get his prostate checked

Work toward a new radio show on longevity and/or a television show on universal design and downscaling and retirement living

Above all,

To do what I can to not go broke at 102! And to believe in longevity.

Well, it's settled. I cannot let go of this book. So here's the solution. E-mail. Please e-mail me with your questions and comments, solutions, issues and ideas, and I'll answer all I can and post them on www.wealth102.com. Remember, friendship is the new amenity.

Simpler, Richer, Wiser:
How www.wealth102.com Can Help You

Imagine a center devoted to everything you need for your longevity: all the diverse and seemingly unrelated information, services, and resources that you need to meet the challenge of living a longer, simpler, richer, and even wiser life. That's what www.wealth102.com is. At our website we bring under one roof, so to speak, the best resources for each of the major longevity categories: work, money, housing, fulfillment, education, travel, and family matters. And we add more categories and resources as we discover them.

For example, we'll help you incorporate if you plan to "hire yourself." We'll bring you articles and contacts for relocating to almost anywhere in the country. We'll help you buy real estate in your IRA. We'll refer you to the best websites from the government, private and not-for-profit sectors that relate to longevity.

We'll hold online informational forums to hear about your needs and also your solutions. Everything—from universal designs and decorating for longevity to the latest philanthropy programs to enrich your life—is part of the scope of www.wealth102.com.

You'll be able to follow me on my speaking trail, ask questions by e-mail, and tune in to Internet conferences. In this way, we can network with each other and longevity professionals for years to come. And I expect that there will be many of them.

Here are just a few of the ways that www.wealth102.com can make your life and the lives of those you love simpler, richer, and wiser:

- Learn the latest avenues to education for retooling and pretooling for retirement.
- Discover the most innovative companies in hiring the experienced worker.
- Contact new housing communities that strike your fancy.
- Incorporate a new or home business with one phone call or on the Web.
- Learn how to buy real estate in your IRA.
- Calculate mortgage financing costs and contact national financing companies.
- Read articles by top elder law attorneys, geriatric care managers, and insurance professionals.
- Contact these professionals when you need them.
- Use online calculators to help make daily financial as well as long-term decisions.

Appendix A

Find Your Ideal Place to Live

- *50 Fabulous Places to Raise Your Family* by Lee Rosenberg, et al. (paperback)
- *The Great Towns of America: A Guide to the 100 Best Getaways for a Vacation or Lifetime* by David Vokac (paperback)
- *Retirement Places Rated* by David Savageau (paperback)
- *The 100 Best Small Art Towns in America: Where to Discover Creative Communities, Fresh Air, and Affordable Living* by John Villani (paperback)
- *Choose a College Town for Retirement: Retirement Discoveries for Every Budget* (Choose Retirement Series) by Joseph M. Lubow (paperback)

Appendix B

Understanding
Conservatorship Proceedings

As an elder law attorney, one goal of mine is always to avoid a conservatorship proceeding. They are, at best, expensive for the family, when truly warranted. *Conservatorship proceedings* are state court adjudications that appoint a conservator (manager) of your money, and therefore, de facto, the guardian of your lifestyle and well-being. For the independent American, the thought is chilling. But, even the appointment of a caring and loving conservator, like an adult child, will cause the family the stress of a legal proceeding and a cost that varies from $3,500 to tens of thousands of dollars.

To become a conservator, one must first petition the court for the post even if they already take care of the individual. Next, comes a depressing battle to prove the parent incompetent. That means doctors reports and testimony. It also means payment for those reports, directly to the physician and the attorney handling the matter. Others in interest, like other siblings or potential heirs, must be notified of the conservatorship proceeding. They can intervene to stop the proceedings based on a claim of actual capacity, and ask that the parent be kept in charge of the finances. Most of the time they admit incapacity and fight to have themselves named conservator.

Even if things go smoothly, the conservator must be judged by a guardian ad litem appointed by the court. The guardian ad litem is paid, usually several thousand dollars. The judge makes their appointment. In the past, horrendous favors of patronage were perpetrated. Today, the judicial act has been cleaned up. Still, it is costly. The guardian will require that a lifestyle plan be submitted. Their task is to protect the incapacitated person, and to be sure that their surroundings, healthcare, and more will be taken care of and the money won't be wasted. This sounds good, but do you really want two strangers (judge and guardian) with very little knowledge of the family deciding what is right for all of you?

It has been my experience that the worst situations crop up when a family business is involved. The conservatorship plan cannot deflect funds to support such a business through a rough time, even if "Pop would have wanted it that way." What Pop wants is not the issue. What's good for Pop objectively is the issue.

And finally, if the plan is approved, the conservator remains under the watchful eye of the court, it is a fiduciary to all heirs and cannot invest assets except in certain conservative investment grade securities. This doesn't always make sense for all families all the time.

Fortunately, some firms, including many accounting firms, will act as a back office for the conservator making sure bills are paid, taxes are filed, and accountings are rendered to the courts and interested parties. More fees. Still, even with good bookkeeping, in these litigious days, the job of conservator can be treacherous.

Appendix C

Living Wills, Healthcare Proxies, and Powers of Attorneys

Living Wills and Healthcare Proxies

A living will is neither a will, nor does it have anything to do with living. It's just a euphemism to make the idea more palatable. It's really a declaration of the level of life support devices you want used in the case of a terminal illness. In most cases, the patient cannot respond coherently or at all when the time comes. Their written wishes take the place of their present expression.

So, what do you want for yourself? No one ever promised you an easy question. All I can do is show you how to keep control of your medical care.

Three Choices for Living Wills

1. *The Healthcare Proxy.* You delegate the decision to another person. This is essential for those in nontraditional relationships, but not good if you have no close loved ones.
2. *The Living Will.* If you don't want the plug pulled say so; most forms favor termination of support.
3. *The Healthcare Power of Attorney.* Same as the proxy except you can add specific wishes and give powers if circumstances are different than foreseen.

Power of Attorney

If you cannot act on your own behalf for *any* reason, including an extended vacation, an illness, or temporary or permanent physical or mental incompetence, the Power of Attorney (POA) gives another person, preselected by you, the right to act on your behalf (see page 267). Your Attorney in Fact has all the legal rights to transfer money, pay bills, buy and sell investments, fix a house, and even gift away money, as you would have. This is called a *general power of attorney*.

Most of the time a loved one and a successor if they cannot serve are named as your Attorney in Fact. Your financial life goes on as you would have wanted it to be in the hands of a trusted relative, friend, or professional. You can fire them at any time just by destroying the POA, or by making a new one.

I caution you not to have too many old ones floating around; they cause confusion. Indeed, the peace of mind you get is that no confusion will be caused by your mental or physical absence from the scene.

You can also limit their powers. Sign a limited POA solely giving the right to make investment decisions over a very specific amount or account. For complicated or large money matters, it can make sense to appoint joint Attorneys in Fact to act in concert. Of course, if they disagree, the situation can be less than peaceful, so you can designate any kind of tiebreaker or allow one to act on their own in specific matters.

Most of the time even friction between your Attorneys in Fact is better than going to court. Conservatorship proceedings not only cost lawyers fees, but also can bring uncaring relatives out of the woodwork or result in patronisim, judges appointing attorneys or other professionals to handle your money with little supervision and at great cost.

Powers of Attorney come in three varieties: regular, durable, and springing. The regular POA expires if you become incompetent. This is when you want a limited use because you are away. The durable power remains in effect if you become incompetent. The springing power only comes into effect when you are incompetent and need proof from a doctor that you are in that state.

Living Wills

While the POA deals with a surrogate for your money, the living will appoints a surrogate for your health decisions. It allows a designee to decide what type of medical treatment you will have if you can not decide for yourself. Different states have different rules. But, the U.S. Supreme Court has made them all binding.

In some states, you may simply give over a Healthcare Proxy to one you trust and let them make the decision when the time comes. In other states, you may make a formal statement, sometimes called a *living will*, stating that you do not want extraordinary measures taken to keep you alive (i.e., intravenous tube feeding when you are medically brain dead). But pulling the plug is not the only way to go. You may request cryonic freezing, like Tom Cruise in the movie *Vanilla Sky*. If you do so, you must arrange for that in advance with an appropriate institution and designate an insurance policy to pay for the procedure. As we learn more about life extension, your living will options will expand. Today the majority of the wishes are to forestall the money and grief expended by family members when you can be kept alive, but not sensate, by artificial means. In the future who knows where science will take us?

Here are just some of the many ways that the POA comes in handy:

1. To handle money when you are on vacation.
2. To close real estate or business deals.
3. To fund a trust or give away a gift if you become incompetent to save estate taxes or get a child to college.
4. To pay bills, pay doctors, and generally take financial care of you without an expensive court procedure.

General Durable Power of Attorney

On this   day of   , 200 , I, YOUR NAME, residing at YOUR ADDRESS ("Principal") appoint my spouse, SPOUSE'S NAME, presently residing at SPOUSE'S ADDRESS, as my Attorney in Fact. In the event that said NAME OF SPOUSE shall be unable or unwilling to serve as my Attorney in Fact, then I appoint my NAME SUCCESSOR TRUSTEE presently residing at ADDRESS OF SUCCESSOR TRUSTEE as my Successor Attorney in Fact. The following shall apply to said appointments:

Article I

My Attorney in Fact's Powers

This Power of Attorney shall apply and authorize my Attorney in Fact to act in any lawful way with respect to all of the following powers except for a power that I have crossed out.

Real property transactions

Tangible personal property transactions

Stock and bond transactions

Commodity and option transactions

Banking, credit card, and other financial institution transactions

Business operating transactions

Insurance and annuity transactions

Estate, trust, and other beneficiary transactions

Claims and litigation

Personal and family maintenance

Benefits from Social Security, Medicare, Medicaid, or other governmental programs or civil or military service

Retirement plan transactions

Tax matters

If no power listed above is crossed out, this document shall be construed and interpreted as a general power of attorney and my attorney in fact shall have the power and authority to perform or undertake any action I could perform or undertake if I were personally present.

Article II

Durability

This power of attorney shall not terminate on my disability, and my Attorney in Fact shall continue to be able to exercise any power or authority I have given to my Attorney in Fact, notwithstanding my subsequent disability, incompetence, or incapacity.

Article III

Revocation of Power

This power may be revoked by me at any time, by a written instrument. However, all persons shall recognize my Attorney in Fact's authority to manage my affairs and transact my business as my Attorney in Fact, until actual receipt of a written notice of revocation. No person shall be liable to me or my estate in any way for any losses resulting from his or her good faith recognition of my Attorney in Fact's authority prior to having received a written notice of revocation.

Article IV

Certified Copy

Any person may rely fully, completely, and equally on the original of this power of attorney or on a certified copy of this power of attorney. My Attorney in Fact may create a certified copy of this power of attorney by executing a facsimile of the affidavit in Appendix of this instrument, and attaching it to a copy of this power of attorney. Such certified copy shall conclusively constitute proof on which any person may rely that this power of attorney is, on the date such affidavit is executed, in full force and effect in all respects, that my Attorney in Fact has no reason to believe that this power of attorney has been revoked, that my Attorney in Fact has in any way been deprived of the authority granted to my Attorney-in-Fact in my behalf, or that I am no longer alive.

Article V

Miscellaneous

A. This power of attorney shall be governed by and construed according to the laws of the state of Your State.

B. Whenever the context of this power of attorney requires, the masculine gender includes the feminine or neuter, and vice versa, and the singular number includes the plural, and vice versa.

_____

YOUR NAME, Principal

Sworn to before me this   day of   200   Notary Public

Appendix D

Insurance Company Rating Services

www.ambest.com, www.ambest.com/ratings

www.insure.com/ratings

www.standardandpoors.com/RatingsActions/RatingsLists/

www3.ambest.com/ratings/Advanced.asp

insurance.about.com/cs/companyratings

www.weissratings.com

Appendix E

Additional Resources

Mutual fund café, www.mfcafe.com

Mutual fund investor's center, Mutual Fund Education Alliance, www.mfea.com

Investor Education Network, www.investoreducation.org

Securities Industry Association, www.sia.com

AARP, www.aarp.org/confacts/housing/ccrc.html

American Association of Homes and Services for the Aged, www.aahsa.org/publicccrc.htm

www.Benefitscheckup.com

Lawyers National Senior Citizen Center, www.nsclc.com; www.elderweb.com

The Assisted Living Federation of America, www.alfa.org

The National Center for Assisted Living, www.ncal.org

Consumer Consortium on Assisted Living, www.ccal.org

National Academy of Elder Law Attorneys, www.naela.org

American Bar Association, Elder Law Committee, www.abanet.org /elderly

AAA National Association of Area Agencies, www.N4A.org; to find nursing homes, Nursing Home Ombudsman Program, www.aoa.gov

"Medicare and You," a publication of the U.S. government sent each year, www.medicare.gov

Center for Medicare Information, 2519 Connecticut Avenue, NW Washington DC, 20008-1520

National Association of Home Care Providers, www.nahc.org

Consumer's Union, articles on healthcare at www.consumersunion.org/pub/care___health.html.

Appendix F

Test Your Social Security Knowledge

Circle the correct answer(s). Note that more than one answer may be correct.

1. At what age can a person receive Social Security benefits?
   a. 10
   b. 50
   c. 60
   d. 62
   e. 65

2. How much is the average Social Security retirement benefit?
   a. About $875
   b. About $1,200
   c. About $1,550
   d. About $2,000

3. How many years, on average, of earnings are used to calculate a person's Social Security retirement benefit?
   a. 3
   b. 5
   c. 10
   d. 20
   e. 35
   f. 40

4. Based on any worker's record, Social Security may be able to pay simultaneous benefits to which of the following? (circle all that apply)
   a. Worker
   b. Worker's spouse
   c. Worker's child

    d. Worker's divorced spouse
    e. Worker's other divorced spouse
    f. Worker's parent(s)

5. A 65-year-old employee who is still working is allowed to earn how much in salary without losing any Social Security benefits?
    a. $11,800
    b. $25,000
    c. $30,000
    d. $50,000
    e. $84,900

Answers:

1. All answers are correct.

Minor children can receive benefits if a parent is deceased or receiving Social Security disability or retirement benefits. Disabled adults can receive benefits at any age. Widows and widowers can collect benefits as early as age 60 (or 50 if disabled), and workers can collect retirement benefits as early as age 62.

2. a.

The average Social Security retirement benefit is about $875. The maximum benefit payable to an individual who is 65 in 2002 is $1,660 per month.

3. e.

When calculating a retirement benefit, a worker's earnings are indexed for inflation, then the highest 35 years are averaged and a formula is applied to that 35-year average. If the worker has fewer than 35 years of earnings, zeroes are added to make up the total. If a worker has more than 35 years of earnings, the highest years are used.

4. There are two correct multiple answers: either a, b, c, d, and e *or* b, c, d, e, and f.

Parent's benefits are payable only to the surviving parent(s) of a deceased worker, so if the worker is alive and receiving benefits, benefits cannot be paid to the parent(s). If the worker is deceased, the parent(s) may qualify for benefits. Everyone else on the list (spouse, child, divorced spouse, and the other divorced spouse) may potentially (and simultaneously) receive benefits whether the worker is alive or deceased.

5. All answers are correct.

Based on the Freedom to Work Act, which President Clinton signed into law in April 2000, workers are now eligible to receive all of their Social Security retirement benefits upon reaching full retirement age (which is currently 65), whether they continue to work and regardless of how much they earn.

For workers born in 1938 and later, the full retirement age will no longer be 65, but will begin to increase gradually—to 65 and 2 months for those born in 1938, and 65 and 4 months for those born in 1939 and so on. This gradual increase will continue until full retirement age eventually increases to age 67 for those who were born in 1960 and later.

Notes

INTRODUCTION   What's Going on Here? How Longevity Is Affecting Our Life Choices

1. *Another Country: Navigating the Emotional Terrain of Our Elders*, Mary Bray Pipher (Reed Business Information, 1999).
2. *In Memory Yet Green*, Isaac Asimov (Doubleday, 1979).
3. See discussion of the former and still enduring idea that age is a disease, *Successful Aging*, John W. Rowe, M.D. and Robert L. Kahn, Ph.D. (Dell, 1998).
4. Dell Webb and the Baby Boomer Report, Annual Opinion Survey, 2003, Results Summary, ©Pulte Homes, Inc.
5. Starting in 1984, the John D. and Catherine T. MacArthur Foundation began an extensive study of more than 1,000 high-functioning elders over an eight-year period to discern what made them age so successfully, both physically and mentally. Their findings are published in Rowe and Kahn, *Successful Aging*. The importance of staying relevant to the family and community is found on page 46 of the work.

CHAPTER ONE   The Longevity Revolution

1. "65+ in the United States" is a 1996 joint report of the U.S. Department of Commerce, Economics and Statistics Administration, the Bureau of the Census, the U.S. Department of Health and Human Services, the National Institute on Aging, and the National Institutes of Health. It covers longevity and health, economics, geography, social, and other characteristics of Americans over the age of 65.
2. *Retire Early and Live the Life You Want Now*, John F. Wasik (Henry Holt, 1999).

3. Ibid., Preface, x.
4. "The Baltimore Longitudinal Study on Aging," National Institute on Aging, Gerontology Research Center (1958 to date), available at http://blswww.grc.nia.hih.gov.
5. "Whatever It Is, I'm against It," by Bert Kelmir and Harry Ruby, from the movie *Horsefeathers*, sung by Groucho as his character Professor Quincy Adams.
6. Human Life Table Database, September 1, 2003, www.demogr.mpg.de/.
7. *The Swedish Adoption/Twin Study of Aging (SATSA)*. (Center for Developmental Health and Geriatrics, Pennsylvania State University, 1986).
8. "Calling All Elders: The Vital Importance of Role Modeling," Dr. Lyn Mac Beath, "Spiritual Elderly Newsletter," Winter 2002, Boulder, CO: Spiritual Eldering Institute).
9. "Highlights of Women's Earning in 2001," U.S. Department of Labor, Bureau of Labor Statistics, May 2002 (Report 960); Arias E. United States life tables, 2000. National Vital Statistics reports, vol. 51, no. 3 (Hyattsville, Maryland: Center for Health Statistics, 2002).
10. U.S. Department of Labor, Bureau of Labor Statistics, Tables of Employment and Earnings, Annual Average Data, Table 37. (Can be downloaded as www.bls.gov/cps/cpsaat37.pdf.)
11. MetLife Mature Market Study.
12. *Scientific American*, Samuel H. Preston, University of Pennsylvania Study, (1984).
13. *Born to Pay: The New Politics of Aging in America*, Philip Longman (Houghton Mifflin, 1987).
14. *Longevity Revolution: As Boomers Become Elders*, Theodore Rozak (Publishers Group West, 2001).
15. *The Yogi Book*, Yogi Berra (Workman Press, 1998), p. 118.

PART ONE   Longevity and Work

1. http://users.rcn.com/brill/freudarc.html, August 15, 2003.
2. *Do What You Love, the Money Will Follow: Discovering Your Right Livelihood*, Marsha Sinetar (Dell, 1989).
3. *Workforce 2001, Report of the New York State Taskforce on Older Workers* (December 1992).
4. *Prime Time: How Baby Boomers Will Revolutionize Retirement*, Marc Freedman (Public Affairs, 1999), p. 39.
5. "Relevance After 60," Weiner, Edrich, Brown White Paper (March 2002).
6. The Harris Workforce Taskforce Study (1990), conducted for the U.S. Department of Health and Human Resources.
7. Ibid.

CHAPTER TWO   The Aging Worker Paradox

1. "Older Workers and the Dependency Ratio," General Accounting Office of the U.S., GAO-02-85.

2. *Demography and Destiny: Winning the War for Talent: Managing the Workforce of the Future* (Watson and Wyatt Worldwide, 1999), p. 2.
3. "The proportion of all Americans who are elderly will be the same as the proportion in Florida today. . . . America, in effect, will become a Nation of Floridas." From the *Atlantic Monthly*, as cited in Watson & Wyatt Worldwide, ibid.
4. *Tips for Successfully Managing Your 401(k)*, Ted Benna (Benna Publishing, 2001).
5. "Living to 100 and Beyond, Implications of Longer Life Spans," Anna Rappaport and Alan Parikh, William Mercer, Inc., for the January 2002 Symposium Sponsored by the Society of Actuaries.

CHAPTER THREE   Recent Innovative and Progressive Workplace Solutions

1. Older Worker Study, General Accounting Office of the United States, GAO-02-85.
2. *Eaton v. Onan Corporation*, 117 Fed. Supp. 2d 812 (S.D. Ind. 2000).

CHAPTER FOUR   Making Rehirement a Reality

1. AARP, www.aarp.org/money; a premiere site to visit for articles on all the challenges of longevity.
2. *Inc. Yourself: How to Profit By Setting Up Your Own Corporation*, Judith Mc-Quown (Career Press, 2002).
3. See www.wealth102.com for more details on incorporation.

CHAPTER FIVE   Dream Fulfillment and Compromise— They Are Both Okay

1. *How Good Guys Grow Rich: Proven Strategies to Achieve Financial Success and Lifelong Satisfaction*, Milton Gralla and Adriane G. Berg (Dearborn Financial Publishing, 1995).
2. *In Memory Yet Green*, Issac Asimov (Doubleday 1979).
3. "Retirement: Avoiding a Panic Attack," *Business Week*, July 29, 2002, available at www.businessweek.com/magazine/content/02 30/b3793601.htm.

CHAPTER SIX   Securing Your Retirement with An End Run Job

1. "Incentives for Early Retirement in Private Pension and Health Insurance Plans," Urban Institute (Policy Brief, March 1, 1999).
2. From *Tips for Successfully Managing Your 401(k)*, Ted Benna (Benna Publications, 2001), monograph "Making Twenty Years of Savings Last Thirty Years," p. 28.
3. Ibid.

PART TWO   Longevity and Your Home

CHAPTER SEVEN   Aging in Place

1. "Fixing to Stay: A National Survey on Home Modification Issues," Ada-Helen Bayer and Leon Harper (AARP, 2000). http://research.aarp.org/: home_mod_l.html.
2. U.S. Bureau of the Census, Current Population Reports, Special Studies, pp. 23ff. "65+ in the United States."
3. "Older Home Owners and Renters in Six U.S. Cities," Drs. Kottai Gnanasekaran, Kenneth Knapp, and Irena Dushi (International Longevity Center, 2001), www.ilcusa.org.

CHAPTER TEN   Affordable Lifestyle Dreams for Sale

1. *Rich Dad Poor Dad* is the original in the series by Robert T. Kiyosaki (Warner Books, 2000), that started a spate of related books, seminars, and other informational materials, all with the thrust that you can generate lifelong cash flow separate from your job income and be financially independent forever.

CHAPTER ELEVEN   The Real Estate IRA—How to Buy Real Estate Now, and Avoid the Baby Boom Rush

1. The taxes you will pay on income from property owned in your IRA that has been mortgaged are called taxes on unrelated debt financed income (UDFI), and may be higher in rate than on ordinary income.

PART THREE   Longevity and Family

1. *The Making of a Counter Culture: Reflections on the Technocratic Society and Its Youthful Opposition*, Theodore Roszak (University of California Press, 1995).
2. *America the Wise: The Longevity Revolution and the True Wealth of Nations*, Theodore Roszak (Houghton Mifflin, 1998).

CHAPTER THIRTEEN   Whose House (and Money) Is It Anyway?

1. *Matter of Carolla*, FH (Fair Hearing) 3565848H.

CHAPTER FIFTEEN   The New Family Financial Dialogue

1. *77 Truths About Marketing to the 50+ Consumer*, Kurt Medina and John Micliaccio (Maturity Mark Services Co. and Medina Associates, 1999), p. 48.
2. *Why Survive? Being Old in America*, Dr. Robert N. Butler, (John Hopkins University Press, 2003).

3. *Gifting to People You Love: The Complete Family Guide to Making Gifts, Bequests and Investments for Children*, Adriane G. Berg (Newmarket Press, 1996).

PART FOUR   Longevity and Health

1. "Longevity, Determination and Aging," Dr. Leonard Hayflick, Ph.D., a paper presented at the Living to 100 and Beyond: Survival at Advanced Ages, Society of Actuaries, Lake Buena Vista, Florida, January 2002.
2. Ibid.

CHAPTER SIXTEEN   Wealth is Health-Life for Sale

1. National Long Term Care Survey, Duke Center for Demographic Studies, D. Kenneth, G. Manton, Principal Investigator (Studies 1989, 1994, 1999, and slated for 2004), www.cds.duke.edu.
2. See also ICPSR, Inter University Consortium for Political and Social Research (1989, 1994, 1999).
3. "Longevity and Medicare Expenditures," James Lubitz, M.P.H., James Beebe, B.A., and Colin Baker, M.P.P., *New England Journal of Medicine* 332:999–1003, April 13, 1995.
4. Ibid.

CHAPTER EIGHTEEN   Medicare and Medicaid

1. Office of Inspector General of the Department of Health and Human Services, "Medicaid Estate Recoveries," OAI-0986-00078, ii, June 1998.

CHAPTER TWENTY   Long-Term Care Policies—Choice Not Chance

1. The Merrill Lynch Retirement Index, Douglass Bernheim (1996).
2. National Committee to Preserve Social Security and Medicare, Barbara Kennelly, president and CEO, www.ncpssm.org, August 11, 2002.
3. *Health Care Financing for All Americans, Private Market Reform and Public Responsibility* (Health Insurance Association of America, 1991), www.hiaa.org.

PART FIVE   Longevity and Your Money Life

1. "How Much Do External Factors Affect Wellbeing? A Way to Use 'Happiness Economics' to Decide," Andrew J. Oswald, Department of Economics, University of Warwick, United Kingdom, August 2002.
2. "How to Lead a Rich Life," Polly LaBarre, *Fast Company*, March 2003.
3. *The Millionaire Next Door: The Surprising Secrets of America's Wealthy*, Thomas J. Stanley and William D. Danko (Pocket Books, 1998).
4. *The Influentials: One American in Ten Tells the Other Nine How to Vote, Where to Eat, and What to Buy*, Ed Keller and Jon Berry (Free Press, 2002).

CHAPTER TWENTY-ONE   Living the Handcrafted Life

1. "Necessity," *Finian's Rainbow*, music by Burton Lane, lyrics by E.Y. Harburg and Fred Saidy.
2. *The Pursuit of Loneliness: American Culture at the Breaking Point* Philip Elliot Slater (Beacon Press, 1976).
3. "Skidmore Scope," Jesse Bank and Catherine Anderson-Hanley, Fall 2002, available at www.skidmore.edu/scope/fall 2002/oncampus/dance.html.
4. AARP Public Policy Institute, Analysis of CPI Data for the Bureau of Labor Statistics (February 1, 2001).
5. "Who's Ready to Retire?" www.aon.com, August 11, 2003.
6. www.bls.gov/cpi/home.htm.

CHAPTER TWENTY-TWO   Preserving Your Future If You Do Not Have Enough

1. "Retirement Savings: Choosing a Withdrawal Rate That Is Sustainable," Philip Cooley, Carl Hubbard, and Daniel Walz, *Investors Journal*, Vol. XX, No. 2, February 1998, available at www.aaii.com/promo/mstar/feature.shtml.
2. "Annuitization: Keeping Your Options Open," Prepared for the Fifth Annual Joint Conference of the Retirement Research Consortium, "Securing Retirement Income for Tomorrow's Retirees," Irena Dushi and Anthony Webb, International Longevity Center—USA (May 2003), p. 3.

CHAPTER TWENTY-THREE   Social Security and Your Pension: Will They Carry You Through Longevity

1. Interview with Bryn T. Douds, May 2003.
2. This quiz was prepared by James W. Green in his capacity as public affairs liaison between the Social Security Administration and the public. He uses the quizzes at his seminars and did so at a joint seminar we gave at the New York Financial Expo, Sheraton New York, September 2002.

EPILOGUE

1. "Business Monday," Joyce Rosenberg, *Naples Daily News* (July 16, 2003), p. 1.
2. "With Medical Costs Climbing, Workers Are Asked to Pay More," Barbara Martinez, *Wall Street Journal* (July 16, 2003), p. 1.
3. Ibid.

Index